Legislative Drafting
Step-by-Step

Legislative Drafting
Step-by-Step

Arthur J. Rynearson

INTERNATIONAL LAW INSTITUTE
Washington, D.C.

CAROLINA ACADEMIC PRESS
Durham, North Carolina

Library of Congress Cataloging-in-Publication Data

Rynearson, Arthur J.
  Legislative drafting step-by-step / Arthur J. Rynearson.
      pages cm
  Includes bibliographical references and index.
  ISBN 978-1-61163-380-1 (alk. paper)
  1. Bill drafting--United States. I. Title.

  KF4950.R98 2013
  328.73'0773--dc23

                          2013000071

Co-Published by:

INTERNATIONAL LAW INSTITUTE
1055 Thomas Jefferson Street, NW
Washington, D.C. 20007
Telephone (202) 247-6006
www.ili.org

CAROLINA ACADEMIC PRESS
700 Kent Street
Durham, North Carolina 27701
Telephone (919) 489-7486
Fax (919) 493-5668
www.cap-press.com

2022 Printing
Printed in the United States of America

This book is dedicated to the professional legislative drafters of Congress, who toil anonymously for the rule of law.

Contents

Appendices

A Note about the Author

Arthur J. Rynearson is the former Deputy Legislative Counsel of the United States Senate. For more than a quarter of a century, Mr. Rynearson drafted legislation in the nonpartisan Legislative Counsel's Office of the Senate. He has drafted thousands of bills, resolutions, and amendments at every stage of the legislative process, including the preparation of committee reported bills and conference reports. Mr. Rynearson has taught legislative drafting as adjunct professor of law at the Washington College of Law at American University, Washington, D.C., and as faculty of the International Law Institute of Washington, D.C. A graduate of Cornell University Law School and Hamilton College, Arthur is a member of the District of Columbia Bar.

Foreword: The Five Steps of Legislative Drafting & Other Matters

The Story Behind This Manual

For more than a quarter of a century, I was privileged to serve with a small group of Capitol Hill lawyers who drafted most of the bills, resolutions, and amendments that came before the United States Senate and its committees. We drafted legislation at every stage of the legislative process up to the enactment of law. So, in a very real sense, I "wrote the law".

The Senators and their staffs were my clients, especially the staffs. They made the policy and were the true authors of every legislative measure I drafted. I was simply their instrument, their legislative ghostwriter. Working daily with these policymakers gave me a front row seat on history, for which I will always be grateful.

My job, like most, had its challenges. My clients brought me legislative proposals from every political and policy angle imaginable, sometimes reflecting strong partisanship, all of which I handled without favoritism. Their requests came to me in various forms, by telephone or e-mail or as memoranda or even as rough draft legislation.

What most of my Senate staff clients had in common—perhaps the only thing they had in common—was that they did not know what I would do with their work. In fact, many did not know what type of work I did. Some thought I was a type of printer. Others believed I was a legislative guru who could solve the unsolvable policy dilemma. A few did not even know what they were asking me to do. Mainly, they were just following orders from the Senators to engage my services.

The confusion about legislative drafting is understandable. At heart it comes from the mystery that surrounds the field. There is a dearth of concise, user-friendly guides about legislative drafting, and congressional staff training in legislation has been notoriously spotty or nonexistent. Many assume that legislative drafting is an art—perhaps a dark art—that springs from the political exigencies of the moment and cannot be learned. Each draft appears to be a uniquely political creation. Others believe that legislative drafting is so technical that its practice is unknowable to the layman. It may only be learned after years of working directly with a drafting technician.

So, then, what is legislative drafting: an art or a science?

What Is Professional Legislative Drafting?

Professional legislative drafting is a way of writing legislation in a systematic, almost scientific manner that may be applied to all legislation regardless of content. To do this, the drafter applies techniques that ensure that the legislative policy is captured precisely and that the legislation is legally and technically sufficient.

The techniques employed by this form of writing were first applied to Federal legislation in the early 1900s on a trial basis,[1] and Congress was so impressed by the results that it established a nonpartisan, in-House service, the Legislative Drafting Service, to continue this work. The current Senate and House Legislative Counsel offices are the direct descendants of the long-defunct Legislative Drafting Service. They are the only offices in Congress that are exclusively dedicated to drafting legislation, and they draft the bulk of Congress' legislative work product.

I served in the Senate Legislative Counsel's Office and learned my skill at drafting from other more senior attorneys, who in turn had learned from their predecessors. There were no manuals to read, and I learned from doing.

This manual is my way of helping the next generation of drafters. In this manual I have crystallized five key steps that I took in preparing each piece of draft legislation, and I believe that understanding these steps offers the drafter the best chance to save many hours of trial and error.

What Are the Five Key Steps?

The following are the five key steps that I have identified and that this manual teaches for drafting legislation:

(1) **Legalize.** — Achieving the intended legal effect.

(2) **Formalize.** — Choosing the right legislative vehicle.

---

1. The reference is to the demonstration project on legislative drafting conducted by Middleton Beaman in the House of Representatives during the period 1916–1918. Recognition must also be accorded to Gouverneur Morris, who, as a member of the Committee of Style and Arrangement of the Constitutional Convention of 1787, skillfully produced the polished final draft of the Constitution, making Morris the first Federal draftsman.

(3) **Integrate.** — Relating new law to existing law.

(4) **Organize.** — Organizing the legislative text.

(5) **Clarify.** — Achieving clarity of expression.

It makes sense to do these steps in the order in which they are listed, and that order is replicated in the organization of this manual. Occasionally, however, the drafter may find it more convenient to take a step out of order, and that is entirely all right. So the five steps may simply be viewed as a checklist to be completed sometime during the drafting process.

What do these five steps have in common? The answer is that they all involve establishing relationships.

Achieving the intended legal effect and relating new law to existing law both involve establishing relationships of law, including the relation between the branches of Government, between the Federal Government and the States, and between citizens and their Government, and the relationship between new law and old law.

Choosing the right vehicle and organizing it properly both involve establishing relationships of form: the relationship of the vehicle to the lawmaking process, on the one hand, and the relationship of each legislative provision to the whole vehicle, on the other.

Finally, clarity of expression is largely a matter of choosing the right word within the context of the whole legislation. We may say that this is the relationship of one word to another.

Legislative drafting is the process of establishing all these relationships in a written document with respect to a specific legislative policy. The drafting rules set forth in this manual are designed to show exactly how this may be done.

What Makes a Good Legislative Drafter?

To be an effective legislative drafter requires more than good analysis and a knowledge of drafting rules. There is more to drafting than what this manual can teach. It requires a certain temperament, which may be developed over time as more and more drafting is done.

What constitutes the "right stuff" for a legislative drafter? It depends in part on how we answer the earlier question of whether legislative drafting is an art or a science.

When a drafter establishes the proper relationships of law, form, and words with respect to a specific legislative policy, which we may treat as a blueprint, the drafter acts both as an artist and a scientist. As a scientist, the drafter knows that choosing a particular relationship of law, form, or words will produce a predictable legal, procedural, or interpretive result. Great care must be taken with drafting. The Devil truly is in the details.

As an artist, however, the drafter must exercise judgment in applying the correct relationships to any given legislative blueprint, using what the drafter knows about the legislative intent of the political actors involved. The "presentation" of a bill may have a political impact. There is room for creativity in drafting.

Combining both creativity and system, then, perhaps it is better said that the drafter is more of an engineer than a pure artist or pure scientist. The drafter is constantly striving to build into legislation the correct relationships, proportions, and perspectives much as an engineer does in building a house, knowing that although there may be more than one way to build that house there are many ways that are unsound and to be avoided. This legislative engineering is truly what it means to be a professional legislative drafter. As the former Senate Legislative Counsel Frederick Lee once famously said, for an attorney to be most effective in the Legislative Counsel's office, the attorney "has to have an analytical, constructive mind rather than the ordinary analytical, destructive mind that the practicing lawyer must have".[2]

While a manual cannot teach temperament, I fervently hope that this step-by-step approach to drafting, when repeatedly applied, will help develop in the user the constructive, engineering mindset of the legislative drafter.

The Purpose of This Manual

The purpose of this manual, then, is to provide a five-step framework for analysis, together with easy-to-use rules, to guide the beginner or intermediate drafter in converting a legislative proposal into an actual piece of legislation. The manual seeks to untangle the web of confusion and technical detail that surrounds legislative drafting and to present drafting in a simplified, easy-to-understand way. In so doing, the author hopes to show legislative drafting to be a fun, intellectually engaging endeavor and not an intimidating prospect to be dreaded. In short, this manual seeks to demystify legislative drafting.

This manual is designed to assist legislators, their staffs, and all who participate in the legislative process to better understand the basics of legislative drafting so that their work product may be fully worthy of the people they serve. To this end, the manual may be treated as a source of supplementary information for working with legislative drafting offices or as an introduction to legislative drafting.

One caveat should be kept in mind, however. This manual teaches the *craft* of legislative drafting. Just as learning the rules of any craft will not, by itself, make you a master craftsperson, so, too, learning the rules of legislative drafting, through a manual or otherwise, will not make you a master legislative drafter. Good drafters draft—a lot. So learning the rules and techniques of legislative drafting is not the end of the

---

2. Hearings on the Legislative Establishment Appropriation Bill, 1929, at p. 125.

road but the beginning of the drafter's journey—an important beginning. Together with a drafter's temperament, a person armed with the knowledge described in this manual will be ready to face the exciting challenges of writing the law.

A Note on Methodology

Many examples of draft language in this manual are displayed in italics. This is done to highlight the language in this book only and not to instruct the reader to use italics. Most real-world legislative drafting is done in Roman type.

Application to Other Legal Systems

One final note: The analysis, rules, and techniques taught in this manual may be applied to any democratic legal system, not just to that of the United States.

At a basic level, legislative drafters worldwide face many of the same technical challenges. Among these are difficult choices involving law, form, and words, choices that are carefully weighed and discussed in this manual.

More fundamental, however, is the problem of how to write the law so that it may reflect certain universal, democratic values that transcend any particular legal system.

Behind each step in legislative drafting lie important rule-of-law values that are promoted by that step. These values are, or ought to be, the goals of legislative drafters everywhere.

As you read through this manual, can you identify the democratic, rule-of-law values furthered by the rules and techniques taught in each chapter? Make a list and check it at the end.

A clear understanding of your goals is always the best guide.

Arthur J. Rynearson, Esq.
Arlington, Virginia

Legislative Drafting
Step-by-Step

Chapter One

How to Achieve the Intended Legal Effect

"It is not every act, legislative in form, that is law. Law is something more than mere will exerted as an act of power."[1]

Step One: "Legalize!"

The first and most important step in transforming any proposal for public policy into draft legislation is to "legalize"[2] it. This is shorthand for saying that the drafter's first concern must always be to capture the intended legal effect of the legislator. Failure to "legalize" makes legislation nothing more than a political treatise, inoperative as law.

In Search of the Elusive Legal Effect

A dirty little secret of legislative drafters is that they do not spend most of their time drafting! Until the intended legal effect is determined, drafting is a waste of time. Determining legal intent may be a lengthy process as legislators and their staffs see things from a political perspective and often are slow to recognize what is deficient about the current law that requires fixing. They tend to see only the real world shortcomings of public policy and not the legal impediment causing the broken policy.

It, therefore, falls on the drafter, through hours of meetings and seemingly endless exchanges of e-mail and memoranda with the legislative client, to identify the precise deficiency in the law before beginning to draft. Sometimes the intended legal effect is a mystery even to the legislative staffer who first brings the idea to the drafter, and outside legal experts and lobbyists must then be consulted. Only when the elusive legal "problem" is identified may the writing begin. This chapter begins where the first step in drafting must begin: establishing legal relationships.

---

1. *Hurtado v. California*, 110 U.S. 516, 535–536 (1884) (Matthews, J., writing for the Court).

2. "Legalizing" is not to be confused with drafting legalese, which the author adamantly opposes. *See* Chapter Five for the reasons why.

Part I: Establishing Legal Relationships

What Do Laws Do, Really?

At the outset we should ask, "What do laws do, legally speaking?" Setting aside the public policies expressed in law, we see that each law establishes legal relationships and that these relationships fall into certain recurring, easily recognizable categories. Among these are legal duties and delegations ("authorizations") conferred upon government officials and rights and responsibilities conferred upon private citizens. Some laws act directly and immediately ("self-executing"), while most require implementation. Some statutory provisions are nothing more than a set of instructions for navigating the statute itself, but these too have legal significance. Other provisions are not legally binding at all.

What these varied legal relationships have in common is that they all are achieved by the manipulation of the grammar of a sentence through the choice of subjects and verbs. Let us see how this is done.

Subpart A: Choosing the Subject of a Sentence

Seven Rules

Let us begin at the beginning — of a sentence, that is. The grammatical subject of a legislative sentence carries a legal significance that is important and that is easily overlooked. Achieving the intended legal effect requires making the legally best choice of a subject for each sentence. This may be done using the following rules:

Rule No. 1: Never Mention "The Government"!

Avoid naming as the subject of a sentence the "United States", the "Government", the "Federal Government", the "executive branch of Government", or any other political subdivision. These expressions are simply too broad to allow for any accountability.

Rule No. 2: Name Officials, Not Bureaucracies

In General. — Most legislative language involves implementation by the executive branch of Government. In these provisions, a Federal official, not a unit of the bureaucracy, should be the subject. The reason for this is simple: a bureaucracy cannot be held accountable but an official can. So, for example, write "the Secretary of State shall submit a report", not "the Department of State shall submit a report".

Exception. — It is wrong, however, to make a single Federal official the subject of a sentence where the official is the head of a governmental body consisting of several officials having an equal vote, and the body is acting as a group. Such bodies include commissions, committees, task forces, and courts. However, where the matter is purely administrative, such as calling a meeting or issuing a travel voucher, there may be a need for a single official to take charge, and the proper subject should be the chairman or director.

Rule No. 3: Name Statutory Officials

Not all Government officials make suitable subjects of sentences. To carry out a statutory duty or delegation, an officer of the Government whose position is established *by statute*, not *by regulation*, should be selected. Any position created by regulation may also be abolished by regulation, leaving any statutory reference to the position meaningless.

Rule No. 4: Name Agency Heads

In General.—The most appropriate Federal official to name as the subject of a sentence is almost always the official who is the head of the department or agency having jurisdiction over the subject matter. Drafters refer to this official as the "agency head".

Avoid Naming Subordinates.—A common drafting mistake is to name a Federal official who is a subordinate of the agency head. For example, Under Secretaries of State and Assistant Secretaries of State are frequently named, wrongly, in rough drafts. Why is this wrong? The reason is that these officials serve at the pleasure of the President and the Secretary of State, who are the "principal officers". A principal officer may ensure that any duty imposed on a subordinate is not carried out simply by firing the subordinate.

Agencies Must Have Statutory Status.—It is important, however, that the agency head selected be the head of a department or agency established *by statute*. If the agency is merely the creature of an Executive order, directive, or other regulation issued by the President or a department head, any duty or responsibility imposed *by statute* on the agency head may be evaded just by revoking the *regulation* creating the agency.

Agencies Must Have Legal Personality.—It is also important that the agency have "legal personality", that is, one that can sue or be sued. The head of an agency with legal personality will always have power to hire and fire and have power over a budget. To determine if a governmental body has legal personality, examine its statutory charter. The mere administrative designation of a subunit of a department as an "agency" is not enough.

Administrative Delegations Are Unnecessary to State.—Because an agency head may further delegate any duty, it is unnecessary to insert "or designee" or "or delegatee" after a reference to the agency head. Authority to make such a delegation may be found either in the agency's charter Act or by application of principal-agency law. Those added words tend to be inserted by novice drafters bent on demonstrating (incorrectly) their legal prowess. The only effect is to clutter up the law and interfere with readability.

Any Prohibition on Administrative Delegation Must Be Stated. — If Congress wishes to prohibit an agency head from further delegating a statutory duty or delegation, the prohibition must be expressly stated.

Example:

> (4) *Nondelegation.* — *The Attorney General may delegate the authority provided under paragraph (3) only to the Deputy Attorney General. The Deputy Attorney General may not delegate such authority.*[3]

Rule No. 5: Avoid Naming the President, Usually

In General. — A failure to identify the proper statutory agency head as the subject of a sentence sometimes results, wrongly, in placing all duties, responsibilities, or exhortations on the President. Although the chief executive, the President is ordinarily not the proper subject of any sentence that deals with a matter internal to a Federal department or agency, such as any personnel or other administrative matter or any matter vested by statute in the agency head. So, for example, legislation should address the Secretary of State, not the President, regarding the administration of the Foreign Service personnel system.

The President is the appropriate subject where the legislation addresses a constitutional power exclusive to the President or a legal authority previously vested by statute[4] in the President or where Congress chooses to have the President implement a policy concerning more than one department or agency of the United States.

Cases of Concurrent Authority. — Where both the President and the department head have concurrent authority, the drafter has to make a difficult decision based on the subject matter being expressed.

The choice between the President and the Secretary of State may illustrate the proper analysis. Where a foreign policy matter is at issue, either official may plausibly be named. A rough rule of thumb is that, where the matter involves national security or another foreign policy matter vital to the United States, especially one that implicates more than one department or agency of the United States, name the President. Where the matter involves diplomatic communication at a level below head of state, that is, at the ministerial level or lower, name the Secretary of State.

This may test the drafter's judgment. A clever drafter may opt to acknowledge the President's authority but require that it be exercised through a specific agency head.

---

3. Section 236A(a)(4) of the Immigration and Nationality Act (8 U.S.C. 1226a).

4. *See, e.g.,* the Foreign Assistance Act of 1961 (22 U.S.C. 2151 et seq.), which vests its authorities in the President.

Example:

The President, *acting through the Secretary of State and the Secretary of Defense*, shall submit to Congress a report that ...

Rule No. 6: Name Congress, the Statute, or the Action Itself in Certain Circumstances

In General.—Where legislation is intended to address a matter directly and not through a Government official, the subject of the sentence will be one of the following: Congress (or a House of Congress), a statutory provision, money, a position or office, or a governmental body.

Examples:

- *The Senate condemns the Government of North Korea ...*
- *This section does not apply to ...*
- *There is authorized to be appropriated $_____ ...*
- *There is established the Commission on International Religious Freedom.*
- *Section ___ of _____ Act is amended by _____.*

Rule No. 7: Treat Multiple Subjects Specially

Where two or more agencies of Government are intended to have equal responsibility over the matter being legislated, the President or the agency heads "acting jointly" are the proper subjects of the sentence. Where one agency is to take the lead, but the input of another agency is desired, the head of the lead agency acts "in consultation with" or "in coordination with" the head of the secondary agency. Consider the following examples and the different legal effects of their phrasing:

Examples:

- *The Secretary of State and the Secretary of Defense, acting jointly, shall submit to Congress a report that ...*
- *In consultation with the Secretary of Defense, the Secretary of State shall submit to Congress a report that ...*

Subpart B: Choosing the Mood and Tense of Verbs

Introduction

The mood and tense of verbs used in legislation should vary with whether the legislative provision is intended to be binding or nonbinding and, if binding, what precise legal effect is desired. Consistency in the use of verbs to achieve the same legal effect is important to ensure the desired judicial interpretation. (*See also* Figure 1-1.)

Binding Verbs

Mandatory or Directory Language

Use of "Shall".—Where the legal effect intended is to impose a duty or requirement on an official or other person, mandatory or directory language, which uses the helping verb "shall", is required. "Shall" expresses the imperative mood of the verb "to be" in the third person and is used immediately preceding the principal verb of the sentence.

Use of "Must" Not Favored.—Some drafters choose to use "must" instead of "shall" in condition precedents such as in the phrase "to be eligible to hold the position of _____, a person *must* be _____". While an argument can be made for this,[5]

Figure 1-1

Legislative Language: Verbs					
Description	Legal Effect	Mood	Verb	Example	Do Not Use
Binding Language					
Mandatory	Duty	Imperative	shall	The President shall do X	will, must, directed, obligated
Authorizing	Delegation/ Responsibility	Permissive	may is authorized	The President may do X	can, empowered has the authority
Entitlement	Right	Indicative	is entitled/ shall	A person is entitled to X A person shall receive X	may
Self-executing	Requirement	Indicative	is/are	There is established X	shall
"Housekeeping"	Internal Rule	Indicative	present tense verbs	The term "X" means Y	shall
Nonbinding Language					
Hortatory	None	Hortatory	should	The President should do X	urged, requested, encouraged
Preambular, Findings	None, Interpretive	Indicative	present tense verbs	Congress finds X	binding verbs

---

5. *See, e.g.,* Reed Dickerson, *The Fundamentals of Legal Drafting* (1986), § 9.4 at 214.

this strikes the author as too fine a distinction and is not universally followed by professional legislative drafters. Furthermore, "must" sounds overly emphatic to serve as a complete substitute for "shall". There is no reason why "shall" may not encompass both duties and qualifications. The United States Constitution and more than 200 years of Federal statutes are replete with this use of "shall".

Alternatives to "Shall" to Avoid. — Avoid using "will" to express mandatory language because "will", when used in the third person, is only a helping verb in a prospective, predictive sense.[6] Also, avoid using "is authorized and directed", "is directed", or "is obligated" as a substitute for "shall" because such usage is either overly emphatic or wordy, as the case may be.

Exception for "Will". — The helping verb "will" does retain a limited usage in legislative provisions setting forth conditions that require the use of the future tense. In foreign affairs legislation, for example, these conditions are frequently attached to mandatory language requiring the President to certify to Congress future cooperation by a foreign government.

> **Example:** *The President shall submit a certification to Congress that the Government of North Korea will comply with international safeguards on nuclear weapons-grade materials.*

In the example, the only legal duty in the statute is the one established between the President and Congress. The part of the sentence dealing with compliance by North Korea is merely a prediction or assurance that the President would give.

Use as a Prohibition. — The negative form of "shall", also known as a "prohibition", is either "shall not" or "may not", which for most purposes may be used interchangeably. Technically, "may not" is the stronger prohibition, since "shall not" negates only the duty not the authority,[7] but in most sentences this distinction makes no practical difference, and Members of Congress tend to prefer the "shall not" form, mistakenly believing it to be the stronger of the two.

In the rare situation where the prohibition applies to more officials than may be easily named in a sentence, it is acceptable to omit the officials and negate the duty using "shall not". Alternatively, the duty being prohibited may be described, and the sentence ended with "is prohibited".

False Imperatives. — Special care needs to be given to avoiding the use of "shall" in a phrase where the legal effect intended is "may" — in other words, a delegation. Examples of these "false imperatives" are the phrases "shall have the right to", "shall have the power to", "shall be empowered to", "shall to the extent possible", and "shall to the maximum extent practicable". These phrases look like directives but are actu-

---

6. For an example of an incorrect use of "will" in statute, *see* section 286(q)(4) of the Immigration and Nationality Act (8 U.S.C. 1356(q)(4)), which contains the following: "The Attorney General will prepare and submit annually to the Congress statements of financial condition of the Land Border Immigration Fee Account…".

7. *See* Reed Dickerson, *The Fundamentals of Legal Drafting* (1986), §9.4 at 215.

ally permissive! Using a false imperative may be politically attractive because it is a way to make the legislation sound tough, but it is misleading and confusing and, therefore, bad drafting.

Advantages. — When used correctly, there are several advantages to mandatory language. The language creates a duty or requirement that may serve as a rule of decision for enforcement in a court of law. Also, because the language does not allow for the exercise of discretion, the use of mandatory language enables Congress to assert its primacy and to maintain control over the directed official or agency. There is no doubt that the official or agency is accountable to Congress for the action (or forbearance) that Congress directs.

Disadvantages. — A disadvantage is that Congress assumes primary responsibility for the directive. As a practical matter, this means that Congress must have the ability to formulate a rule in sufficient detail and clarity for the directive to be effective. With a complex policy matter, or with a policy that is evolving or uncertain, or that requires information not currently available, this may be impossible. As a political matter, using mandatory language means that if the policy that is being directed fails after being faithfully carried out, Congress will be answerable to the people — perhaps more so than the President.

Another disadvantage is that a directive requires compliance, which may be difficult to enforce (such as an immigration law violation), politically undesirable, or constitutionally questionable.

Special Problem of "Backdoor Spending". — The use of mandatory language must be qualified if the language might be construed to permit the entering of contracts or the incurrence of debt that would amount to a circumvention of the appropriations lawmaking process — in other words, where no appropriations are provided for. Budgetary law requires that the legislation must state that each contracting or debt-incurring provision "is to be effective for any fiscal year only to such extent or in such amounts as are provided in appropriations Acts".[8] A shorthand way of expressing this is "subject to the availability of appropriations".

Example:

(_) *Subject to the availability of appropriations, the Secretary of Homeland Security shall enter into contracts with nonprofit agencies having expertise in the delivery of immigration-related legal services to children in order to carry out this Act.*

Authorizing or Delegatory Language

Use of "May". — Whenever Congress seeks to delegate authority to the executive branch or the judiciary, the appropriate helping verb for that delegation is "may",

---

8. Section 401(a) of the Congressional Budget and Impoundment Act of 1974 (2 U.S.C. 651). The requirement is enforceable in each House of Congress by a point of order, which of course is waivable.

which is the permissive mood of the verb "to be", and is used immediately preceding the principal verb of the sentence.

Limited Use of "Is Authorized To". — The phrase "is authorized to" is an acceptable alternative to "may" in the limited circumstances (1) where the delegatee of the authority is indefinite, as in the phrase "there is authorized to be appropriated", or (2) where the drafter seeks to emphasize the fact of the delegation of authority, especially where the executive branch contests the constitutional power of Congress to make the delegation.[9] Where there is no such dispute, the better choice is "may".

Accompanied by Standards. — Generally, authorizing language is accompanied by a legal standard in order to constrain the discretion of the executive branch official receiving the delegation. A standard may be expressed in broad, general terms. All that is required is that the delegation "sufficiently marks the field within which the Administrator is to act so that it may be known whether he has kept within it in compliance with the legislative will".[10]

"Factors" or "Guidelines" Language. — After setting forth a broad standard, it is useful to list the factors or guidelines, if any, that an official may "consider" or "take into account" in applying the standard.

Example:

(a) Authority. — The President may sell any defense article to any foreign country whenever the President determines that it is vital to the national security to do so.

(b) Factors for Consideration. — In making the determination under subsection (a), the President shall consider the following factors:

(1) Whether the country will use the article solely for defensive purposes.

(2) Whether the country will agree not to retransfer the article to any other country without the consent of the United States.

Alternatives to Avoid. — Do not use "can", "enabled", "empowered", or "is conferred the authority" as an alternative for "may" or "is authorized to". "Can" and "enabled" are wrong because they relate to capability, which is not legally relevant, and do not convey permission. "Empowered" and "is conferred the authority" are wrong because they are too flowery and wordy, respectively.

Use as a Prohibition. — The negative form of "may", of course, is "may not". In the rare situation where the prohibition applies to more officials than may be easily named in a sentence, it is acceptable to omit naming the officials and simply negate the authority, using "may not". Alternatively, the authority being prohibited may be described, and the sentence ended with "is prohibited".

---

9. This second situation is frequently encountered in writing foreign affairs legislation.

10. *Yakus v. United States*, 321 U.S. 414, 425 (1944).

Advantages. — Authorizing language has all the advantages that come with decentralized policymaking. The authorized official will have discretion whether or not to carry out the delegated act and, if the official does act, the discretion to choose the means of carrying out the act. This relieves Congress of the burden of arriving at a detailed policy and permits Congress to shift the responsibility for implementing the policy to the official to whom the authority is being delegated.

Decentralized lawmaking may promote harmony between Congress and the President, who, craving flexibility, typically seeks discretionary authority.

Disadvantages. — The primary disadvantage to authorizing language is simply that Congress loses control. The executive branch may choose not to act or may act in a way that Congress never intended. In short, the discretion conferred may be unused or abused.

Decentralized policymaking enables both Congress and the President to point the finger of blame at each other for a failed policy, which makes it difficult to hold either accountable.

Entitlement Language

Use of "Shall" or "Is Entitled". — Entitlement language establishes a legal right that is best expressed using either "shall" or "is entitled to".

> **Example:** *A member of the Board shall be paid compensation at the daily equivalent of the annual rate of basic pay in effect for a position at level IV of the Executive Schedule under section 5315 of title 5, United States Code.*

Although the use of "shall" occurs both in mandatory and entitlement language, entitlement language is ascertained by examining the sentence as a whole to determine whether or not an individual or a State is the recipient of a Government benefit enforceable in a court of law, a much less common use of "shall".

Alternatives to Avoid. — In writing entitlement language, the same verbs should be avoided that are sometimes wrongly used for mandatory language, such as false imperatives. "May" especially should be avoided since the concept of entitlement does not allow any notion of discretion.

Use as a Prohibition. — An entitlement may be prohibited by using "shall not", "may not", or "is not entitled to".

Formulas and Allotments. — When entitlement language calls for Federal payments to be made based on a computation,[11] a formula is required. In the case of Federal benefits divided among the States, the formula is referred to as an "allotment" or "apportionment" and calls for stating a fraction, always written in the present tense, indicative mood.

> **Example:** *From funds appropriated for the National Highway System for a fiscal year, the Secretary of Transportation shall allot to each State an amount that*

---

11. *See also* this Part: Housekeeping Language, *infra.*

bears the same proportion to the total amount appropriated for that fiscal year
as the population of that State bears to the total population of all the States.

Advantage. — The principal advantage of an entitlement is to establish a Government benefit that may be enforced by legal proceedings in a court of law.

Disadvantage. — The principal disadvantage of an entitlement is that it denies the Government discretionary budget authority. It is a claim on the United States Treasury that must be satisfied without regard to the fiscal health of the Government.

Self-Executing Language

Use of the Indicative Mood. — Whenever language is intended to operate directly, without implementation, the drafter should employ verbs in the present tense, indicative mood. Verbs in the indicative mood that are commonly found in legislation include "is" and "are". Resist the temptation to insert "hereby" after "is" or "are", as this clutters the sentence unnecessarily.

Common Uses. — This type of direct operating language is found where the Constitution vests Congress with full power to execute a law by a simple declaratory statement. So, for example, if Congress wishes to appropriate funds, establish Government offices, declare war, or amend a prior Act, Congress need only say so.

Examples:

- *There is appropriated ...*
- *There is authorized to be appropriated ...*
- *There is established the Department of Homeland Security ...*
- *A state of war exists between the United States and ...*
- *Section __ of _____ Act is amended ...*

Alternatives to Avoid. — The drafter should also resist the temptation to insert the mandatory helping verb "shall" in self-executing language. The use of the verb "shall" adds unnecessary verbiage and may imply, incorrectly, that the language requires implementation by some unnamed official, which would directly contradict the purpose of this language.

Advantage. — The use of self-executing language means that the full legal effect of the language occurs upon the effective date of the language, which is usually the date of enactment. No implementation of the language is required and, thus, there is no need to seek accountability from an official to carry out the will of Congress.

Disadvantage. — Self-executing language is usable only in the circumstances where an act by an official is not required.

"Housekeeping" Language

Use of the Indicative Mood. — Whenever the drafter needs to state a rule of internal operation for a legislative measure or statute, what may be referred to as "housekeeping" language, the drafter should write this language in the present tense, indicative mood, using verbs such as "is", "are", "means", "includes", and "applies".

Examples:

- *The purposes of this Act are....* ("Purposes" section).

- *In this Act, the term "Secretary" means the Secretary of State.* (Definition).

- *This Act takes effect 30 days after its date of enactment.* (Effective date).

These kinds of provisions are instructions for the statute's use—a type of built-in user manual. They enable the reader to navigate the statute with ease.

Computations.—A computation is another example of "housekeeping" language. Where legislation requires a number to be calculated, the calculation must be expressed verbally,[12] not mathematically. Like a definition, a computation determines a "meaning", which can later be plugged into mandatory, authorizing, or entitlement language.

Example:[13] *(c)(1)(A) The worldwide level of family-sponsored immigrants for a fiscal year is equal to—*

(i) 480,000, minus

(ii) the number of immigrants in the previous fiscal year, plus

(iii) the number (if any) that is the difference between the worldwide level established for the previous fiscal year and the number of visas issued during that fiscal year.

Alternatives to Avoid.—The drafter should resist the temptation to insert the mandatory helping verb "shall" in "housekeeping" language. As with self-executing language, the use of "shall" adds unnecessary verbiage and may infer, incorrectly, that the language requires implementation by an unspecified official, an inference that directly contradicts the purpose of this language.

Advantage.—"Housekeeping" language is the way a drafter sets rules for the scope, application, interpretation, and duration of a legislative measure or statute and, therefore, is an important means of ensuring that the legislative intent will be achieved and that unintended consequences will be avoided.[14]

Disadvantages.—There are no disadvantages to using "housekeeping" language. The language is, however, sometimes wrongly characterized as being a mere declaratory statement and, thus, nonbinding.

---

12. While the *calculation* is expressed verbally, any *number* that is part of the calculation is best written in Arabic numerals and not spelled out. Spelled out numbers are extraordinarily difficult to read. This rule applies to the use of numerals in any legislative provision except for numerals less than ten, which may be spelled out in the discretion of the drafter.

13. The example is a simplified, and thus distorted, rewrite of section 201(c)(1)(A) of the Immigration and Nationality Act (8 U.S.C. 1151).

14. *See also* Chapter Five, Part IV, *infra*.

Nonbinding Verbs

Congressional Findings; Preambular Language

Use of the Indicative Mood.—Wherever Congress as a whole, or the Senate or House of Representatives acting singly, wishes to express a finding of fact, the drafter should express the statement using a verb in the indicative mood. Bills and statutes are replete with "findings" sections that begin with "Congress finds that" or "Congress makes the following findings:". In a resolution, congressional findings appear in the preamble as "Whereas" clauses.

Examples:

- *Congress finds that the sky is blue.*

- *Whereas the sky is blue; and*

  Whereas the grass is green;

Verbs to Avoid.—Findings and preambles are written to convey background information supporting the legislation or statute and, therefore, carry no legal effect except occasionally as a source of legislative intent. Such language does not call upon any official to take action and, consequently, the helping verbs "shall", "may", and "should" are not appropriate.

Limited Use of the Past Tense.—While the past tense is used in findings or preambular language when making an historical statement, generally, findings and preambles are written in the present tense.

Advantage.—The use of findings and preambles are useful politically as a means to set forth the strongest case for passage of a legislative measure.

Disadvantages.—Used excessively, nonbinding findings and preambles run the risk of overshadowing the substantive provisions of the legislation and may consume an enormous amount of the drafter's time ensuring the accuracy of the facts and statistics, which are sometimes in flux. It is never a good thing for the opening act to outshine the main performance!

Hortatory Language

Use of "Should".—Wherever the legal effect is intended to be hortatory, that is, an exhortation to action, which is always nonbinding, then the proper helping verb is "should". In Federal legislation, such sentences typically begin "It is the sense of Congress that", "it is the sense of the Senate that", or "it is the sense of the House of Representatives that", whichever is appropriate. The addition of the "sense" language is nothing more than a custom or practice, technically unnecessary, but the addition does have the advantage of highlighting the nonbinding nature of the language so that "should" sentences are not confused with "shall" sentences.

Example: *It is the sense of Congress that the President should undertake negotiations with the Government of North Korea.*

Alternatives to Avoid.—The drafter should resist the temptation to use more emphatic alternatives to "should" such as "is urged to", "is encouraged to", or "is requested to". This amounts to Congress saying "we really, really mean this". Not only is this a wordy, inefficient use of language but also runs the risk of both distracting and confusing the reader into believing that different meanings are intended for what is essentially the same nonbinding legal effect.

Advantage.—Hortatory language has the advantage that, since it is nonbinding, it may be used to express any legislative policy. For that reason, hortatory sentences are also known as "statements of policy". In addition, the use of hortatory language enables Congress to avoid violating the separation of powers doctrine and the Federalist principle underlying the Federal-State allocation of powers.[15]

In the foreign affairs field, for example, hortatory language is particularly useful because its use avoids a direct confrontation between Congress and the executive branch, thereby avoiding any embarrassment of the President in the President's dealings with foreign countries.

Disadvantage.—The nonbinding nature of hortatory language is also its disadvantage. Because hortatory language imposes no legal duties or responsibilities, hortatory language is incapable of holding any person accountable under the law. Consequently, hortatory language is unenforceable. The more detailed the hortatory language the greater the likelihood that some aspects of the policy being expressed will be ignored.

Verbs to Avoid

Subjunctives.—In the 18th and 19th centuries, legislative language frequently contained verbs expressed in the subjunctive mood, especially in resolutions. The subjunctive verb form was used to express uncertainty or contingency, as in the following example: "*Resolved,* That the Senate *advise and consent* to the ratification of the XYZ Treaty.". Using language in this way, however, violates the modern principle of interpretation that statutory language is to be read as of the date of its application. In other words, language should be written as if it is currently being applied. If that is done, there is no uncertainty to be expressed. The Senate "advises and consents" to the ratification of the XYZ Treaty; there is no "maybe" about it!

Declaratory Verbs.—Avoid writing general declaratory statements in legislation. Drafting legislation is not the same thing as writing a novel. Narrative-type language has no legal content but may be misinterpreted as establishing a legal relationship. The only exception to this admonition is where the subject of the sentence is "Con-

---

15. *See also* Part III of this Chapter, *infra.*

gress", the "Senate", or the "House of Representatives". In that case, the sentence may properly use a declaratory verb such as "finds", "states", or "condemns". What explains the difference? It is inappropriate for the Government as a whole to make unattributed, God-like assertions in statute about the state of the world, but certainly Congress or a House of Congress has a right to express its findings or sentiments. This comes down to a matter of form, but the distinction is strictly maintained in legislative writing.

Verbs Reaffirming Existing Law. — Verbs that "reaffirm", "reassert", or "restate" existing law, without directly amending the law, are ticking time bombs. No purpose is served by restating what is already law, and much is risked in the attempt. It is more likely than not that the drafter will misstate the existing law and in doing so lay the foundation for interpretive challenges to the existing law. Even an accurate restatement of law runs the risk that a jurist, applying basic canons of statutory construction, will conclude that Congress must be articulating a new rule.

Part II: Enforcing the Law

When Is an Enforcement Provision Necessary?

Mandatory Language. — Using mandatory language always raises the question of whether or not to write an accompanying enforcement provision. This is so because a legal duty is being established, and the drafter needs to determine what, if anything, will be the consequence of a violation of that duty. The seriousness of the violation must be weighed, and a violation of a reporting requirement or any other technical or ministerial duty is not usually enforced.

Authorizing Language. — The exercise of an authorization being discretionary, there is no point in drafting a statutory penalty for a failure to act to carry out authorizing language, although Congress may take political sanctions such as the withholding of unrelated funds or holding up Presidential nominations. In the case of acts that amount to abuses of discretion, or arbitrary or capricious exercises of discretion, the courts will set aside the acts through judicial review[16] under the so-called "Administrative Procedure Act",[17] and ordinarily no special statutory treatment is required.

However, where the executive branch decides to act within the scope of the law, authorizing language serves as the legal basis for the issuance of regulations to implement that action. To underscore the need for these regulations, the statute may provide for the regulations explicitly by stating that "the [authorized official] shall

---

16. 5 U.S.C. §706(2)(A) (2012).

17. A misnomer for the provisions found at 5 U.S.C. §551 et seq. *See*, Chapter Three, Part IV, *infra*.

prescribe such regulations as may be necessary to carry out this [provision of law]". Or, the statute may remain silent, relying entirely on an official's pre-existing authority to issue regulations.

Either way, Congress may provide in advance, by a special enforcement provision in the statute, specific criminal or civil penalties for the violation of any regulation that the official may issue. Alternatively, there may be no need for a new enactment of penalties where existing statutory penalties are applicable to enforce the new regulations.

Hortatory Language. — In the case of hortatory language, an accompanying enforcement provision is never appropriate since nothing is being mandated, and no authority is being conferred. There is nothing to enforce! Presumably, when Congress urges an official to act, the official has previously been authorized to take that action and is already fully empowered to enforce the action.

Menu of Enforcement Options

To enforce a legislative provision, the principal mechanisms available to Congress are the following:

(1) A criminal penalty.

(2) A civil penalty.

(3) A funding "cut-off".

(4) An "earmark".

(*See* Figure 1–2 for a comparison of model language on enforcement provisions.)

Let us explore each option and the consequences of doing nothing.

Enforcement Options

Criminal Penalties

In General. — The preferred means to enforce a prohibition directed against a private person, as opposed to a public official or governmental body, is to attach criminal penalties. Criminal penalties may also be applied to the wrongdoing of public officials that amounts to more than bad judgment or a violation of policy.

Whenever a criminal penalty is desired, the penalty must be provided by statute and may not be increased by administrative regulation.[18] A criminal penalty should

---

18. "[I]t is for Congress to prescribe the penalties for the laws which it writes. It would transcend both the judicial and administrative function to make additions to those which Congress has placed behind a statute". *L.P. Steuart & Bro. v. Bowles*, 322 U.S. 398, 404 (1944).

be drafted as an amendment to title 18, United States Code, which is conclusive evidence of the criminal laws of the United States.[19]

Each criminal penalty provision may be subdivided into three parts, as follows:

- The Offense.
- The Penalty.
- The Effective Date (or Application).

Although the "boilerplate" language traditionally used for these components violates basic rules of good drafting, the language may be too well entrenched in Anglo-American statutes to change. Let us examine the peculiarities of each component in the discussion that follows. *See* Figure 1-2 on the next page.

The Offense.—

Illegality Required.—Historically, criminal penalty provisions began with "it *shall* be unlawful for any person to [do X]". Strictly speaking, the helping verb "shall" is unnecessary here, and this should instead be phrased as "it *is* unlawful for any person" because the sentence is self-executing and requires no implementation. Probably the reason "it is unlawful" has not been used more often is that the phrase sounds like a reaffirmation of existing law, something to avoid in drafting legislation. However, any confusion is easily resolved by the proximity of the follow-up phrase stipulating the maximum punishment that may be imposed. So there really is no barrier to using the better phrase "it is unlawful". Alternatively, the illegality may be left unstated by simply beginning the sentence with "Whoever".

Criminal Intent Required.—To constitute a criminal offense, criminal intent (or *mens rea*) must be present. This element is expressly stated by inserting before a description of the proscribed conduct the phrase "knowingly and willfully" (or "knowingly and intentionally"). The phrase "knowingly and willfully" has attained such a boilerplate status that a drafter may easily forget that it does not cover situations of intentional ignorance, ostrich-like, "head-in-the-sand" situations. To cover those situations, "knowingly" must be defined.

Example:

(_) Knowingly Defined. __

(1) In general. __ For purposes of this section, the term "knowingly" means the state of mind of a person with respect to conduct, a circumstance, or a result in which —

(A) the person is aware that the person is engaging in the conduct, that the circumstance exists, or that the result is substantially certain to occur; or

(B) the person has a firm belief that the circumstance exists or that the result is substantially certain to occur.

---

19. *See* Chapter Three, Part IV, *infra*.

Figure 1-2

Enforcement Provision	Model Language
(1) Ultra Vires Proscription	It is unlawful to hire an undocumented alien.
(2) Civil Penalty	(1) It is unlawful to hire an undocumented alien. (2) Any person who, after notice and opportunity to be heard, is determined by a preponderance of the evidence to have violated paragraph (1) shall be subject to a civil penalty of $_____ for each violation.
(3) Criminal Penalty	(1) It is unlawful knowingly and willfully to hire an undocumented alien. (2) Any person who violates paragraph (1) shall be punishable by a fine in accordance with title 18 of the United States Code, or imprisonment for not more than _____ years, or both.
(4) Funding Prohibition	No funds available to [_____ Agency] may be made available to any person who hires an undocumented alien. [OR] None of the funds authorized to be appropriated by this Act may be available to any person who hires an undocumented alien.
(5) Earmark	Of the amount appropriated under _____, not less that $_____ shall be available only for the prosecution of persons hiring undocumented aliens.

(2) Knowledge of the existence of a particular circumstance. __ If knowledge of the existence of a particular circumstance is required for an offense, that knowledge is established if a person is aware of a high probability of the existence of the circumstance, unless the person actually believes that the circumstance does not exist.

Proscribed Conduct.—The conduct that is being proscribed must be described in a way that avoids vagueness in order to comply with the Due Process Clause of the Constitution.[20]

---

20. *See also* Chapter Five, Part I.

The Penalty. — The maximum punishment is best phrased as follows: *shall be punishable by a fine in accordance with title 18 of the United States Code,*[21] *or imprisoned for not more than [X] years, or both.* Notice that "shall be punishable" is a false imperative. The concept being expressed is actually that the criminal "may" be punished. Nevertheless, this phrase is so deeply rooted in criminal law, that to rephrase it now would only raise questions about prior provisions involving criminal penalties.

The Effective Date (or Application). — To avoid any interpretation that conduct is made criminal unconstitutionally *ex post facto,*[22] the drafter should state that the criminal provision "applies to offenses occurring on or after the date of enactment of this Act".

Civil Penalties

In General. — A second enforcement option, which may stand alone or be used together with criminal penalties, is to make a violation of the law subject to a civil penalty, which is almost always a monetary amount, and may also include a cease and desist order or other injunction. Civil penalties differ from criminal penalties in that they do not require a finding of criminal intent, and the lack of criminal intent means that the offender may not be punished by a fixed term of imprisonment, although civil contempt may result in an imprisonment that terminates upon compliance.

Proscribed Conduct. — As in the case of a criminal penalty, the statute must contain a prohibition, the violation of which will trigger the penalty.

Determinations of Violations. — Before a civil penalty may be imposed, the statute must require an agency head to determine, based on a "preponderance of the evidence", that a violation of the prohibition has occurred and to issue an order requiring cessation of the violation and payment of the monetary amount. The agency head typically delegates this duty to an administrative law judge. Basic due process considerations of fundamental fairness require that this determination be made only after affording the prospective offender notice of the upcoming determination and an opportunity to be heard, and the statute should expressly so provide.

Monetary Fines and Cease and Desist Orders. — The statute must also state the dollar amount that may be imposed on that person and may even provide that repeat violations may be subject to higher amounts. These repeat violations are sometimes referred to as "pattern or practice" violations.

Example:

SEC. . CIVIL PENALTIES.

　　(a) Duty. — *It is unlawful for any person to violate [provision X].*

---

21. The lack of specificity in stating fines is attributable to the establishment by regulation of the United States Sentencing Guidelines under chapter 227 of title 18, United States Code.
22. U.S. Const., art. I, §9, cl. 3.

(b) Hearing. — *Before imposing an order described in subsection (c) against a person for a violation of subsection (a), the [agency head] shall provide the person with notice and, upon request, a hearing with respect to the violation.*

(c) Cease and Desist Order with Civil Money Penalty. — *With respect to a violation of subsection (a) determined by a preponderance of the evidence, the order under this section shall require the person to cease and desist from such violation and to pay a civil penalty in an amount of not less than $____ and not more than $____ for each violation of subsection (a) that occurred.*

Injunctions. — A statute may also provide a procedure for obtaining a court-ordered injunction as a civil enforcement mechanism.

Example:

(_) Injunctive Relief. __ When it appears to the [agency head] that a person [or entity] is engaged, or about to engage, in any act or practice constituting a violation of _____ [provision of law], the [agency head] may bring a civil action in an appropriate district court of the United States to enjoin that act or practice, and upon a proper showing, a permanent injunction or a temporary restraining order shall be granted without bond.

The drafter may choose to add language providing for the administration of oaths, the subpoenaing of witnesses and documents, and the enforcement of subpoenas.[23]

Funding "Cut-Offs"

In General. — A third enforcement option is to prohibit or restrict the availability of funds for a purpose, program, project, or activity of Government. Legislative staffers refer to these provisions as "funding cut-offs" but this phrase is too colloquial and, consequently, not used by drafters. Instead, funding cut-offs are usually styled in statutes as "prohibitions" or "restrictions" on the use of funds.

A funding cut-off is a powerful instrument because, when a program's funds are cut off, the salary or other compensation for officials of Government carrying out the program is cut off as well. *See* Figure 1-2 for "authorization" Acts examples.

Prohibitions and Restrictions Compared. — The distinction between a funding prohibition and a funding restriction is simple. A prohibition is an unconditional directive that funds are not to be available.

Example (Appropriations Act):

None of the funds appropriated or otherwise made available by this Act may be available for North Korea.

A restriction is a prohibition that contains a condition. Restrictions are easy to identify because they contain a word of contingency such as "unless", "until", or "if".

---

23. *See also* Chapter Four, Part I(A): Administrative Provisions, *infra*.

Example (Authorization Act):

> *None of the funds made available under this Act may be available for North Korea until North Korea accepts international nuclear safeguards for its nuclear facilities.*

Effective in Separation of Powers and Federalism Disputes. — Funding prohibitions and restrictions are highly effective means of enforcement wherever public monies are involved. This is especially the case where Congress seeks to enforce its will over the executive branch or against the States. So, writing funding prohibitions and restrictions into law is a handy trump card for Congress to play to surmount its separation of powers disputes with the executive branch, or its Federalism disputes with the States, but only if the Constitution permits Congress to act. Where the Constitution grants an exclusive, plenary power to the President, Congress is disabled from enacting any funding prohibition or restriction or otherwise legislating to curb presidential power.[24] Where the Constitution reserves a power to the States, Congress may not enact a restriction on the availability of Federal funds that coerces State action.[25]

Earmarks

In General. — Another enforcement mechanism is the "earmark". An earmark (known to drafters as a "minimum allocation") is a fencing or set aside of funds to be available only for a specific purpose. The purpose may be any program, project, or activity, or any person, organization, government, or country that is eligible to receive public funds. If the funds are not used for the purpose specified, they are not available for other purposes although the overall account from which the funds are drawn may be authorized for those other purposes. In short, earmarked funds may not be reprogrammed.

Function. — An earmark is a useful legislative tool by which Congress prioritizes Government spending. By restricting the discretion of the executive branch, it acts as a strong inducement for implementation of a law the way Congress desires.

It is also true that earmarks may be used for wasteful, "pork-barrel" spending,[26] sometimes the product of *quid pro quo* corruption. However, efforts to prevent Congress from prioritizing spending are doomed to fail since Congress may circumvent any ban on earmarks by creating, and appropriating to, multiple accounts within the Treasury instead of earmarking a single account. The corruption lies not in the legislative device but in the use which is made of it.

---

24. *See also* Part III of this Chapter.

25. *Id.*

26. The classic example was the attempt in 2005 to earmark a Federal highway bill to set aside funds for construction of a bridge, estimated to cost $398,000,000, between the town of Ketchikan, Alaska, and the Island of Gravina, population 50, which contained a regional airport. Critics of the earmark dubbed the bridge the "Bridge to Nowhere".

Examples:

- *Of the amount appropriated under [cited provision], not less than $___ shall be available only for ___.*

- [**Alternative:**] *Of the amount appropriated under [cited provision], $___ shall be available for ___.*

Ultra Vires Violations

The drafter may choose not to include any explicit enforcement provision. This may be prudent where to enforce the statute would arguably violate the Constitution, especially the separation of powers doctrine. On the other hand, to omit an enforcement provision may be merely convenient; Congress may wish to avoid confrontation with the executive branch over less important legal duties and responsibilities. So, for example, it is rare to find an enforcement provision attached to a reporting requirement.

The absence of an enforcement provision does not mean, however, that no violation of law has occurred when the legal duty or responsibility is violated. Rather, the offending act is considered to be *ultra vires*. *Ultra vires* violations do have political consequences. They may subject the executive branch to demands for accountability at a congressional hearing, a rejection of the President's nominees for high office, a funding "cut off" on an unrelated appropriation, or enactment of another statutory sanction. In the extreme, noncompliance by the Executive with a statute might even constitute an impeachable offense under the Constitution.

Judicial Enforcement

In General. — Aside from setting penalties for violations of a statute, Congress may include in a statute provisions that affect judicial review of the statute or of civil actions under the statute, but only if the provisions do not violate the "case or controversy" requirement under the Constitution.[27] Typical provisions relate to jurisdiction, causes of action, justiciability, expedited appeals, and preclusion of review.

Jurisdiction. — Congress may by statute establish the inferior courts of the Federal judiciary[28] and determine their jurisdiction within the Federal judicial power set forth in Article III of the Constitution.

Example:

The district courts shall have original jurisdiction of any civil action involving the right of any person, in whole or in part of Indian blood or descent, to any allotment of land under any Act or treaty.[29]

---

27. U.S. Const., art. III, §2. The requirement limits the extent of the Federal judicial power.
28. U.S. Const., art. I, §8, cl. 9.
29. 28 U.S.C. §1353 (2012).

Establishing jurisdiction may involve removing sovereign immunity.

Example:

A foreign state shall not be immune from the jurisdiction of courts of the United States or of the States in any case ...[30]

Causes of Action.—It is not enough that a statute opens the Federal courts to specified parties. There must also be a cause of action provided by statute.

Example:

(a) Liability.—An individual who, under actual or apparent authority, or color of law, of any foreign nation—

(1) subjects an individual to torture shall, in a civil action, be liable for damages to that individual; or

(2) subjects an individual to extrajudicial killing shall, in a civil action, be liable for damages to the individual's legal representative, or to any person who may be a claimant in an action for wrongful death.[31]

Justiciability.—Federal courts may decline to decide cases on the merits, citing a lack of standing or ripeness, mootness, or a political question, in short, for lack of justiciability. Efforts to remove these legal obstacles in advance through statutory language are perilous where the nonjusticiability is rooted in the constitutional requirement of a "case or controversy".

Example:

Any Member of Congress or any individual adversely affected by [this Act] may bring an action, in the United States District Court for the District of Columbia, for declaratory judgment and injunctive relief on the ground that any provision of this part violates the Constitution.[32]

Expedited Appeals.—Less questionable, perhaps, are statutory provisions that attempt to expedite judicial review.

Example:

(a) Appeal to the Supreme Court.—Notwithstanding any other provision of law, any order of the United States District Court ... shall be reviewable by appeal directly to the Supreme Court of the United States. Any such appeal shall be taken by a notice of appeal filed within 10 calendar days after the order is en-

---

30. 28 U.S.C. § 1605A (2012) (relating to the terrorism exception to the jurisdictional immunity of a foreign state).

31. Section 2(a) of the Torture Victim Protection Act of 1991 (28 U.S.C. § 1350 note), enacted to implement United States obligations under certain international agreements.

32. Section 3(a)(1) of the Line Item Veto Act (2 U.S.C. § 692(a)(1)) could not provide standing to a Member of Congress who suffered an "institutional injury", not sufficiently concrete and particularized to meet the case or controversy standard of Article III. *Raines v. Byrd*, 521 U.S. 811 (1997).

tered. The jurisdictional statement shall be filed within 30 calendar days after the order is entered. No stay of an order issued … shall be issued by a single Justice of the Supreme Court.

(b) Expedited Consideration. — It shall be the duty of the District Court for the District of Columbia and the Supreme Court of the United States to advance on the docket and to expedite to the greatest possible extent the disposition of any matter brought under _____.

Preclusion of Review. — From time-to-time drafters are called upon to prohibit judicial review of a matter. Questions of violations of the Due Process Clause or habeas corpus inevitably arise.

Example:

(2) Matters not subject to judicial review. —

(A) Review relating to section 235(b)(1) [of the Immigration and Nationality Act]. — Notwithstanding any other provision of law, no court shall have jurisdiction to review —

(i) … any other cause or claim arising from or relating to the implementation or operation of an order of removal …[33]

Part III: Respecting the Constitution

Introduction

The legislative drafter is tempted to ignore the Constitution. After all, the demands on the drafter's time are many, and the Congressional power to legislate under the Constitution is broad. The enumerated legislative powers of Article I, section 8, are supplemented at the end by the residual Necessary and Proper Clause,[34] which the Supreme Court has construed generously, as follows:

> Let the end be legitimate, let it be within the scope of the constitution, and all means which are appropriate, which are plainly adapted to that end, which are not prohibited, but consist with the letter and spirit of the Constitution, are constitutional.[35]

This is undoubtedly a Federal legislative drafter's favorite Supreme Court utterance since it supports much of what the drafter does.

---

33. Section 242(a)(2)(A)(i) of the Immigration and Nationality Act (8 U.S.C. 1252(a)(2)(A)(i)); relating to judicial review of orders of removal).

34. "To make all Laws which shall be necessary and proper for carrying into Execution the foregoing Powers, and all other Powers vested by this Constitution in the Government of the United States, or in any Department or Officer thereof". U.S. Const., art. I, § 8, cl. 18.

35. *McCullough v. Maryland*, 17 U.S. 316, 420 (1819).

As if this were not enough, Congress has both the Spending Clause[36] and the Appropriations Clause,[37] collectively known as the "Power of the Purse", to justify almost any kind of legislation involving public moneys.

Also noteworthy among the enumerated powers are the Commerce Clause,[38] often cited in support of an array of Federal legislation regulating the economy, including matters traditionally thought to be internal to the States,[39] and the Tax Power,[40] which even supports Federal statutory penalties not originally intended as taxation.[41]

All of which bolsters the national legislative power to the point that the drafter, otherwise immersed in technical detail, might easily overlook Constitutional constraints on the subject matter being drafted. This would be a mistake — a big mistake. The prospect of spending months — sometimes years — enacting a bill only to have the Court invalidate one or more of its provisions should give the bill's sponsors and drafters great pause. While the legislative counsels of Congress are obliged to salute and draft any provision directed by the Members of Congress, I found that when I pointed out that a legislative proposal was most likely to be constitutionally infirm, my legislative staff clients would invariably change the proposal to conform to current understandings of Constitutional limits. At no other time would they listen so well to me!

The Big Three

It is implied by the Supremacy Clause of the United States Constitution[42] that all Federal statutes are subject to the prohibitions and restrictions of the Constitution.[43] While a review of constitutional constraints is not the purpose of this manual, the legislative drafter should always keep in mind the Big Three: The Due Process Clause[44] (fundamental fairness), the Equal Protection Clause[45] (nondiscrimination, with respect to State action, and, as applied through the Due Process Clause, with respect to Federal action), and the First Amendment (freedom of

---

36. "Congress shall have Power … to pay the Debts and provide for the … general Welfare of the United States". U.S. Const., art. I, §8, cl. 1.

37. U.S. Const., art. I, §9, cl. 7.

38. U.S. Const., art. I, §8, cl.3.

39. *But see, e.g.*, *National Federation of Independent Business v. Sebelius*, 567 U.S. ___ (2012), and *United States v. Lopez*, 514 U.S. 549 (1995), for the proposition that the power to legislate under the Commerce Clause is not unlimited. In *Sebelius*, the Court found that the power to regulate commerce did not include power to mandate the private purchase of health insurance.

40. U.S. Const., Art I, §8, cl. 1.

41. *National Federation of Independent Business v. Sebelius*, 567 U.S. ___ (2012).

42. U.S. Const., art. VI, cl. 2.

43. *Marbury v. Madison*, 5 U.S. 137, 180 (1803).

44. U.S. Const., amend. V, cl. 3. Amend. XIV, §1, applies the Due Process Clause to the States.

45. U.S. Const., amend. XIV, §1.

speech, press, assembly, right to petition government, free exercise of religion and prohibition on governmental establishment of religion). The judicial doctrines around these provisions are complex, and the drafting language required will vary with the circumstances.

In general, Federal courts will find a statute to be fair, reasonable, or nondiscriminatory if the classifications created by the statute bear a rational relationship to a legitimate governmental interest. This rational basis is ordinarily not difficult to establish since an expansive reading of the Constitution supports a finding of Federal interests in a wide range of circumstances.

Where, on the other hand, a statute has the purpose or effect of creating a classification based on race or national origin, also known as a "suspect classification", or restricting a fundamental right, the distinction drawn will be found constitutionally infirm, unless it serves a compelling governmental interest. Such compelling interests are hard to find under this judicial strict scrutiny test.[46] In addition, Federal courts require that any statutory restriction of a fundamental right to be valid must be precisely and narrowly tailored to the compelling governmental interest.

In the case of certain statutory categories that do not amount to a suspect class or a restriction of a fundamental right, such as gender or alienage classifications, Federal courts will apply an intermediate level of scrutiny that requires the classification to "serve important governmental objectives" and "be substantially related to achievement of those objectives".[47]

In sum, there is no simple formula for drawing lines in a statute to steer clear of a Big Three problem, and a drafter's best guide is knowledge of how the courts have previously applied the various constitutional tests to the particular subject matter being drafted.

Five Constitutional Traps

There are, however, five Constitutional traps waiting to ensnare the unwitting drafter that are easier to avoid than the Big Three and that are more often encountered, too. In most cases, the trap may be averted simply by changing a helping verb. These traps are the following:

Trap No. 1: Legislative "Encroachments"

Trap.—It is a violation of the separation of powers doctrine for a statute to invade the "core" functions of either the executive or judicial branch. This doctrine is not explicitly stated in the Constitution but is implied from its structure and certain pro-

---

46. *But see Korematsu v. United States*, 323 U.S. 214 (1944), which found military necessity as justifying a classification based on national origin, in a decision that first applied the suspect classification analysis. The Court wrongly applied the analysis, however, in the author's view.

47. *Craig v. Boren*, 429 U.S. 190, 197 (1976).

visions.[48] This trap is most frequently encountered where Congress attempts to regulate a power exclusive to the President—for example, the conduct of diplomacy.

Direct Avoidance.—Avoid the use of mandatory or authorizing verbs with respect to powers exclusively vested by the Constitution in the President or the Federal judiciary. The same expression may be easily made, but with nonbinding effect, by substituting "should" for "shall", "may", or "is authorized to".

Indirect Avoidance.—There is, however, a twilight zone where it is unclear whether or not a power is exclusively vested in the President or the judiciary, or where a power is conferred concurrently on Congress and another branch.[49] For legislation in the twilight zone, Congress may use binding verbs in order to "occupy the field" before the President or the courts act.

Trap No. 2: Violations of the Nondelegation Doctrine

Trap.—Just as Congress may not encroach on the core functions of another branch, so, too, Congress may not relinquish its own core functions. In particular, a statute may not give the Executive lawmaking power.[50] Although the Federal courts have relaxed the application of the doctrine of the nondelegation of lawmaking powers,[51] the doctrine is not dead,[52] for it is rooted in the separation of powers.

Avoidance.—Do not delegate to the Executive powers exclusively reserved to Congress by Article I of the Constitution, and when a delegation of other authority is made, ensure that it is accompanied by a standard,[53] however general, that constitutes an "intelligible principle"[54] by which the exercise of the delegation may be confined.

Trap No. 3: Unconstitutional Legislative Vetoes[55]

Trap.—Whenever legislation delegates authority to the Executive, or prohibits action by the Executive, the drafter is sorely tempted to attach a condition that reserves

---

48. *See, e.g.,* U.S. Const., art. I, sec. 6, cl. 2, relating to the prohibition on any Officer of the United States serving at the same time as a Member of Congress.

49. *Youngstown Sheet & Tube Co. v. Sawyer*, 343 U.S. 579, 586 (1952) (concurring opinion of Justice Robert Jackson).

50. "In the framework of our Constitution, the President's power to see that the laws are faithfully executed refutes the idea that he is to be a lawmaker." *Id.* at 587. Rulemaking, while resembling lawmaking, requires the Executive to remain within the parameters of the statute that is the basis of the rulemaking. *INS v. Chadha*, 462 U.S. 919, 953 (1983) at note 16.

51. "Congress is not confined to that method of executing its policy which involves the least possible delegation of discretion to administrative officers." *Yakus v. United States*, 425–426, *supra* note 10.

52. The Supreme Court invalidated a statute delegating to the President authority to repeal portions of two Acts of Congress in violation of Article I, §7. *Clinton v. City of New York*, 524 U.S. 417 (1998).

53. *See* "Authorizing or Delegatory Language", Part I, *supra*.

54. *J.W. Hampton, Jr. & Co. v. United States*, 276 U.S. 394, 409 (1928).

55. *See* Chapter Two, Part III, *infra,* for a full explanation of this Constitutional trap.

to Congress alone the power to micromanage the exercise of that authority or to relax the prohibition, as the case may be. Do not do this! The Supreme Court has invalidated all such conditions as violations of Article I of the United States Constitution.[56]

Avoidance. — Whenever the operation of any statutory provision is made contingent on future Congressional action having the force of law, the drafter must ensure that the future action is not taken by the mere *passage* of a bill or resolution but by the *enactment* of a bill or joint resolution, thus engaging the full lawmaking process, including the role that the President plays in it.

In addition, any contingency providing for the enactment of future legislation should be accompanied by expedited ("fast track") procedures[57] because, without those procedures, it is pointless to empower a future Congress to enact newer laws. Congress is always free to do that. A later Congress is never bound by an earlier Congress but could very well use fast track procedures to move its legislation.

Trap No. 4: Violations of the Appointments Clause

Trap. — The Appointments Clause[58] sets forth a comprehensive rule for the appointment of all "Officers of the United States". For principal officers, the appointment must be made by the President, "by and with the advice and consent of the Senate" — popularly known as "Senate confirmation".[59] For inferior officers, the appointment must be made by one of the following actors in whose power the appointment is vested by statute: (1) the President, (2) the Courts, or (3) the "head of a department".

The trap is sprung when a drafter unwittingly creates a mixed Congressional-Executive commission and confers upon the commission executive branch-type functions. The commission is constitutionally infirm because the inclusion of Congressional appointees means that the commission is in effect tainted by having a membership not drawn entirely from individuals qualifying under the Appointments Clause rule. Not having a membership composed wholly of Officers of the United States, the commission is barred from exercising "significant authority pursuant to the laws of the United States".[60]

Avoidance. — Whether or not the composition of a "mixed" government commission complies with the Constitution depends on the powers conferred upon it. When drafting a mixed Congressional-Executive commission, the drafter needs to avoid assigning the commission any significant governmental duty such as an enforcement power (including the power to seek judicial relief), determinations of eligibility for

---

56. *INS v. Chadha*, 462 U.S. 919 (1983).

57. *See* Chapter Two, Part IV, *infra,* for a full explanation of expedited procedures.

58. U.S. Const., art. II, §2. cl. 2.

59. Note that the addition of a Senate confirmation requirement to an existing occupied position amounts to an unconstitutional removal of the occupant and, thus, must be made effective prospectively.

60. *Buckley v. Valeo*, 424 U.S. 1, 126 (1976).

Federal funding, or the power to change executive branch regulations.[61] The power of inquiry, including the subpoena power, on the other hand, is an attribute of the power to legislate and therefore may be exercised by the Congressional-Executive commission.[62]

In other words, the commission must be strictly advisory, investigatory, or informative and not "executive". The advisory function may be accomplished by using such verbs as "advise" and "recommend" or by using the hortatory "should". The investigatory or informative function may be drafted using boilerplate investigatory and reporting requirements.

Trap No. 5: Violations of Federalism

Trap.—It is a basic tenet of Federalism that powers not delegated to the Federal Government nor prohibited to the States are reserved to the States and the people.[63] In other words, the Constitution does not confer the police power or any other power of a strictly local nature on the Federal Government and, therefore, those powers are beyond the legislative reach of Congress. Congress may not enact legislation that "instructs" the States with respect to those powers. Provisions that direct governors or other State officials, that require the States to regulate, or that commandeer a State's legislative or administrative apparatus for Federal purposes are especially suspect.

Direct Avoidance.—To avoid this trap, the drafter needs to ensure that no binding verbs are used in legislative provisions addressing the reserved powers of the States. Specifically, the drafter must substitute "should" for "shall", "may", or "authorized to" in any sentence that is aimed at the Governor or other official of a State.

Indirect Avoidance.—Even where Congress may not command a State directly, Congress may enact legislation that strongly induces or encourages State action that Congress favors. This is done by restricting a State's eligibility for Federal funding unless State law adheres to a specified Federal policy. The Supreme Court will be most reluctant to invalidate this sort of withholding of funds provision as it is based on the Spending Clause.[64] The Court does impose a three-part standard—relatively easily satisfied—that the congressional exercise of the Spending Clause be (1) in pursuit of "the general welfare"; (2) expressed unambiguously so that the States may know the consequences of receiving Federal funds; and (3) related to the Federal interest in the particular program or project being funded.[65] These cooperative State-Federal Spending Clause programs are in the nature of a contract that must be voluntarily and knowingly accepted by a State without coercion.[66]

---

61. *Id.* at 138.

62. *Id.* at 138.

63. U.S. Const., amend. X.

64. *See, e.g., South Dakota v. Dole*, 483 U.S. 203, 207 (1987) (upholding the withholding of Federal highway funds to States not adhering to a uniform minimum drinking age).

65. *Id.* at 207.

66. Where a Federal statute threatened to withhold all of a State's Medicaid grants unless the State accepted a new, expanded Medicaid program, Federal pressure had turned into compul-

Test Your "Legalizing" Skills

Drafting Exercise No. 1

"Legalize" the following text:

> The Assistant Secretary of State for International Narcotics and Law En-
> forcement[67] will be empowered to provide counternarcotics assistance
> to West African countries through which illegal drugs are trafficked. In
> addition, other foreign countries ought to provide similar assistance to
> West Africa. A report describing the results of the United States assis-
> tance needs to be sent by the Department of State to Congress periodi-
> cally. If Congress agrees to a concurrent resolution disapproving a report,
> no further aid may be provided. The term "counternarcotics assistance"
> shall mean the donation of equipment for interdiction and the training
> of law enforcement officials.

Check your answer in Appendix C.

---

sion, and the withholding of funds provision was constitutionally invalid as violative of the Federal System. *National Federation of Independent Business* v. *Sebelius*, 567 U.S. ___ (2012).

67. Note that the position of Assistant Secretary of State for International Narcotics and Law
Enforcement is designated by the Secretary of State and not created by statute.

Chapter Two

How to Choose the Right Legislative Vehicle

"Matter without form is chaos; power without form is anarchy. The state, were it to disregard forms, would not be a government, but a mob."[1]

Step Two: "Formalize!"

Having "legalized" a legislative proposal, the drafter is now ready for the second step in drafting: choosing the right legislative vehicle. We might call this step "formalizing" as the drafter will be largely guided by the formalistic requirements of the Constitution, the United States Code, and congressional rules. Legislative vehicles used by Congress are mainly bills and resolutions and amendments to bills and resolutions. Before making our choice of a bill, resolution, or legislative amendment, let us first examine the function, legal basis, and composition of each (Parts I and II) to determine the suitability of the vehicle for carrying the legislative language we chose in Chapter One. Then, if we have chosen a resolution, let us be aware of the special rules and usages that may apply to such a choice (Parts III and IV).

Part I: About Bills and Resolutions

What Is Legislation?

There is much confusion over the use of the words "legislation", "statute", and "law". At the heart of the problem is an ambiguity about "legislation"; there is both a narrow and broad way to define the word.

In a narrow sense, sometimes found in Supreme Court decisions, "legislation" means only those provisions of bills and resolutions that contain mandatory, authorizing, or entitlement language, in other words, that contain legally "binding" text. This usage requires a determination as to whether or not a statutory provision is "legislative" based upon the legal function served by its language.

---

1. *Cochran v. State*, 62 Ga. 731, 732 (1879).

A broader, more inclusive view is that any bill, resolution, or amendment, whether or not containing binding text, is legislation by virtue of being the written product (or the potential written product) of a legislative body. This usage does not distinguish between particular provisions but simply views the role of the whole instrument in the legislative process.

This manual uses "legislation" in the broader sense for two reasons. In actuality, most bills are hybrids, that is, they contain both binding and nonbinding text. To say that part of a bill, which may be signed into law by the President, is "not legislative" is to make a distinction that is confusing and counterintuitive since the entire bill traversed the legislative process. Conversely, to say that a concurrent or simple resolution, which is equally the product of Congress as a bill, is "not legislative" because the resolution is entirely nonbinding is to diminish the Congressional action in passing the measure. Not surprisingly, then, Members of Congress and their staffs favor the broader usage of "legislation" in their common parlance.

"Legislation" and "statute" are also commonly confused. Since "legislation" has meaning only within the confines of the legislative process, it necessarily follows that once legislation is enacted into law the instrument ceases to be "legislation" and becomes a statute. In this manual, "statute" refers to any enactment, whether an Act of Congress or a positive law title of the United States Code.[2]

A common mistake is to speak of a statute as "legislation", for example, by saying that a specific piece of legislation was violated or enforced. This is impossible. Only statutes may be violated or enforced because only in a statute does binding language become legally effective.

The sharp distinction between "legislation" and "statute" is blurred by the word "law". "Law" may be used loosely to refer to a statute as a whole, which may contain both binding and nonbinding language. "Law" may also be used to refer only to the legally binding language of the statute, that is, "a provision of law". The drafter should make absolutely clear in the text surrounding "law" which meaning is intended.

Types of Legislative Vehicles, Generally[3]

There are four principal types of legislative vehicles that are capable of standing on their own and going to final passage in the House or Senate, as follows:

- A bill.

- A joint resolution.

---

2. *See* Chapter Three, Part IV, *infra*, for a description of positive law titles.

3. *See* Appendix A, *infra*, for a detailed description of how legislative vehicles travel through the United States legislative process.

- A concurrent resolution.
- A "simple" resolution.

The use of each of these vehicles is either specifically required or generally authorized by the Constitution.

Each legislative vehicle is divided into four or five constituent parts required by the United States Code and the House and Senate rules. What follows is a detailed description of each type of legislative vehicle and its components.[4] (*See* Figure 2-1.)

A bill or resolution is best found by its numbered Congress, House of origin, and numerical designation at the following online site:

www.congress.gov

Bills

Function.—A bill is one of two legislative vehicles that may be used to make a statute, and it is the one most commonly used for that purpose. A bill may address any subject over which Congress may legislate under the Constitution. By custom, however, bills are not used to legislate on matters that are the distinct province of joint resolutions.

Every bill must contain at least one provision of binding legislative language but may contain nonbinding language as well. Most bills are hybrids—they contain both binding and nonbinding language.

Figure 2-1

Legislative Vehicles					
Legislative Vehicle	Designations		Elements	Legis. Process	Authority (US Const.)
	Senate	House			
Bill	S.	H.R.	Title, Text	Bicameralism + Presentment	Art. I, Sec. 7, Cl. 2
Joint Resolution	S.J. Res.	H.J.Res.	Title, Preamble (?), Text	Bicameralism + Presentment	Art. I, Sec. 7, Cl. 3
Concurrent Resolution	S.Con.Res.	H.Con.Res.	Title, Preamble (?), Text	Bicameralism	Art. 1, Sec. 7, Cl.3; Art. I, Sec. 5, Cl. 2
Simple Resolution	S.Res.	H.Res.	Title, Preamble (?), Text	Unicameralism	Art. I, Sec. 5, Cl. 2

---

4. *See* Appendix B, *infra,* for the legislative forms of the House of Representatives and the Senate.

Legal Basis.—The use of bills as legislation antedates the Constitution, having its origins in the parliaments of Medieval England.[5] However, the use of bills by the Federal Government is not a matter of following English custom but is expressly provided for by Article I, section 7, clause 2 of the Constitution, and the structure of bills is governed by the United States Code and congressional rules.

Composition.—Bills consist of four parts, as follows: (1) The endorsement, (2) the long title, (3) the enacting clause, and (4) the text.

The Endorsement.—The endorsement is the information provided at the beginning of a bill that sets forth its parliamentary status. An endorsement always specifies the House of Congress of origin, the sequential number of introduction of the bill, the numbered Congress and session of Congress, and the name of the Member of Congress ("sponsor") introducing the bill. The House of origin is always indicated both by a designation that precedes the bill number and by express reference to "**In the Senate of the United States**" or "**In the House of Representatives**", as the case may be. The designation of a bill originating in the Senate is "**S.**" and in the House of Representatives is "**H.R.**".

In addition, if a bill is referred to, or reported by, a committee of Congress, the endorsement provides all information pertinent to the referral or reporting, including, in the case of a reported bill, the name of the Member of Congress reporting the bill, the bill's numerical designation, the number assigned to the bill on the legislative calendar, and the number of the accompanying committee report discussing the bill.

As a bill advances through each stage of the legislative process, the bill is reprinted, and each reprint updates the information conveyed by the endorsement.[6] If a House of Congress receives a bill passed by the other House, the receiving House will label the bill as "**An Act**" but will omit the information in the endorsement that relates to introduction, referral, or reporting of the legislation in the first House. As the "Act" travels through the second House, its endorsement will of course add any referral or reporting information as the second House acts on the measure.

The Long Title.—The long title (also known as the "official title") appears immediately below "**A BILL**" and states the purpose of the bill, if enacted. Do not confuse the long title, as many Members of Congress do, with the first paragraph of the bill, which appears after the enacting clause. The long title of a bill should always begin with "To [do X]". In most bills, there is no single purpose that may be expressed so the catchall phrase ", and for other purposes" is added at the end.

In the early Congresses, the long title was the only title available for use as a legal citation of a statute. Under this approach, a statute would be cited, as follows: *An Act*

---

5. The word "bill" is traceable to the Medieval Latin word "bulla" referring to a seal affixed to a document, or the document itself such as a Papal bull. The English changed "bulla" first to "billa" then to "bill". In 1362, William Langland's *Piers Plowman* refers to it as "bylle".

6. *See* Appendix B(3) for examples of how the front page of a bill changes during the lawmaking process.

entitled "An Act to establish the Judicial Courts of the United States", approved by the President on September 24, 1789.[7]

The role of the long title as a citation aid has been supplanted by the modern practice of including a "short title" in the first section of the text. The long title remains valuable, however. The long title is an important element of transparency in a legislative measure and is the official way to record the legislation in legislative journals and calendars. The short title, in contrast, provides merely a popular name for the legislation, which may not convey its actual purpose.

The Enacting Clause.—The United States Code requires that every bill have an enacting clause that reads as follows: "*Be it enacted by the Senate and House of Representatives of the United States of America in Congress assembled,*"[8] The phrasing remains exactly as stated, without regard to the House of origin, and is always printed in italic. The enacting clause appears after the long title, usually separated by a space of one or two lines. There is never any language between the long title and the enacting clause since bills never take preambular language.

A mistake occasionally made with enacting clauses is to include two or more enacting clauses within a bill. This is specifically prohibited by the United States Code.[9]

The Text.—All language appearing after the enacting clause through the end of the bill is the text. Traditionally, the text always began with "That", which reflected the drafter's desire to complete the sentence begun by the enacting clause. This resulted in the oddity that the first designated section of the text, usually begun by the second sentence of the text, would be "Sec. 2.". The first sentence would simply be considered an undesignated first section.

The modern practice has been to omit "That" and instead begin the text with "**SECTION 1.**" on the first full line below the enacting clause. This makes the organization of the text more transparent and understandable but leaves the enacting clause dangling as a sentence fragment.

The text of a bill may consist of binding language, nonbinding language, or both binding and nonbinding language. However, since all enacted bills are the supreme law of the United States,[10] it would be overkill to enact a bill without any binding provision.

References within the text of a bill to the entire vehicle are always made to "this Act" and not to "this bill". This may seem anomalous since the bill has not yet been enacted, but it has the great advantage of saving the Enrolling Clerk's time and effort in converting "bill" references to "Act" references in the event the bill is enrolled for presentation to the President.

---

7. The statute cited established all the Federal courts below the Supreme Court, arguably the most important enactment of Congress.
8. 1 U.S.C. § 101 (2012).
9. 1 U.S.C. § 103 (2012).
10. U.S. Const., art. VI, cl. 2 (also known as the "Supremacy Clause").

Joint Resolutions

Function. — A joint resolution is a second type of legislative vehicle that may be used to make a statute. A joint resolution may address any subject over which Congress may legislate under the Constitution, but its use is limited by custom to certain circumstances of an extraordinary or emergency nature, including the following:

- To propose an amendment to the Constitution.

- To declare, authorize, terminate, or regulate war or the use of force.

- To terminate treaties.

- To continue appropriations into the next fiscal year, on a temporary basis, when annual appropriations Acts have not been enacted ("continuing resolutions").

- To designate particular days, weeks, months, and years for commemoration ("commemorative resolutions").

- To make technical corrections in previously enacted statutes.[11]

- To approve or disapprove proposed executive branch actions under expedited procedures ("fast track" resolutions).

Every joint resolution, like a bill, should contain at least one provision of binding legislative language but may contain nonbinding language as well.

Legal Basis. — Although the Constitution does not specifically refer to joint resolutions, the Constitution does allow Congress to create a class of resolutions that are subject to the same legislative process as bills and, if enacted, would have the same legal effect as bills, namely, as statutes of the United States.[12] This process is, of course, the lawmaking process of bicameral passage and presentation to the President[13] (also known as "presentment").

The Framers of the Constitution created this legal redundancy — always a bad drafting idea — between bills and joint resolutions out of a concern that the President's veto could be circumvented by the mere denomination of a legislative vehicle as something other than a "Bill".[14]

Like bills, the structure of joint resolutions is governed by the United States Code and congressional rules.

Composition. — Joint resolutions consist of four required parts and one optional part. As in bills, the required parts are as follows: (1) The endorsement, (2) the

---

11. The technical corrections function is also performed by bills.

12. U.S. Const., art. I, § 7, cl. 3.

13. The only exception to the requirement of presentation of a joint resolution to the President is where the joint resolution is proposing an amendment to the U.S. Constitution. In that case, the Supreme Court has held that the supermajority required by the Constitution for passage of the proposed constitutional amendment makes the veto of the President moot since Congress has the votes to override any veto. *See Hollingsworth v. Virginia*, 3 U.S. 378 (1798).

14. 2 M. Farrand, *The Records of the Federal Convention of 1787,* at 301–302.

long title, (3) the resolving clause, and (4) the text. The optional part is a preamble.

Endorsement. — The endorsement of a joint resolution contains the same type of information as is found in the endorsement of bills, except that the designation of a joint resolution originating in the Senate is "**S.J.Res.**" and in the House of Representatives is "**H.J.Res.**". Another technical difference from bills is that joint resolutions are referred to as "submitted", not "introduced".

Long Title.[15] — The long title (also known as the "official title") serves the same function as it does in bills. The long title of a joint resolution appears immediately below "**JOINT RESOLUTION**" on the form. By custom, however, the long title of a joint resolution often begins with a present participle form of a verb (i.e., a verb with an "ing" ending) and not with "To".

Preamble. — Between the long title and the resolving clause, the drafter may insert a preamble.[16] A preamble is a series of clauses reciting the background facts or findings that support the need for the legislation. These clauses tend to address the question of the motivation behind the legislation, not the purpose of the legislation. For that reason, Federal courts rarely find preambles useful in determining legislative intent. Accordingly, preambles are best kept short.

The practice of Congress is to apply a uniform style and punctuation to preambles. Each clause should begin with "Whereas" and end with a semicolon, except that the next to the last whereas clause should end with "; and" and the last whereas clause should end with ": Now, therefore, be it", which is always left dangling on the line above the resolving clause.

Example:[17]

Whereas on September 11, 2001, acts of treacherous violence were committed against the United States;

Whereas those acts continue to pose a threat to the national security of the United States; and

Whereas the President has authority under the Constitution to take action to deter and prevent acts of international terrorism against the United States: Now, therefore, be it

The Resolving Clause. — The United States Code requires that every joint resolution have a resolving clause that reads as follows: *"Resolved by the Senate and House of Representatives of the United States of America in Congress assembled,"*.[18] The text remains

---

15. *See also* "Bills: Long Title", *supra*.

16. The inclusion of preambles in statutes may be traced to Henry VIII of England, who first used them in the Parliament of 1529–34 as devices to justify the English Reformation. *See* Warren M. Billings, *A Little Parliament* (2004) at 192.

17. The example is a revised and abridged version of the preamble to Senate Joint Resolution 23 of the One Hundred Seventh Congress, as passed the Senate on September 14, 2001.

18. 1 U.S.C. § 102 (2012).

exactly as stated, without regard to the House of origin, and is always printed in italic. The resolving clause appears after the long title, usually separated by a space of one or two lines.

A mistake occasionally made with resolving clauses is to repeat the clause within a joint resolution. This is specifically prohibited by the United States Code.[19]

The Text.—All language appearing after the resolving clause through the end of the joint resolution is the text. For the same reasons as discussed for bills, the text of a joint resolution begins with "**SECTION 1.**".

The text of a joint resolution may consist of binding language, nonbinding language, or both binding and nonbinding language. However, since all enacted joint resolutions are the supreme law of the United States,[20] a joint resolution should contain at least one binding provision.

References within the text of a joint resolution to the entire vehicle are always made to "this joint resolution" and not to "this Act", as is the case with bills. This is anomalous as both joint resolutions and bills are *enacted* into law. Perhaps the explanation is that joint resolutions are authorized by a different constitutional provision than are bills. In any event, all enacted joint resolutions are statutes and in effect Acts of Congress. In doing cross-references to statutes, however, some drafters choose to use the collective phrase "Acts of Congress and joint resolutions". Where there is doubt, the better course is to define "Act of Congress" to include enacted joint resolutions. In this manual, the term "Act of Congress" includes enacted joint resolutions.

Concurrent Resolutions

Function.—While a concurrent resolution requires passage by both Houses of Congress, a concurrent resolution is never submitted to the President for approval and, therefore, constitutionally, never becomes a statute. However, this does not mean that a concurrent resolution has no use.

In fact, concurrent resolutions have two possible uses. First, they may be used to convey any nonbinding expression of Congress on any matter. For example, in the foreign affairs field, concurrent resolutions are frequently passed so that Congress may comment on an international event of interest to Congress, such as a violation of human rights in a foreign country, or so that Congress may comment on a foreign policy of the United States.

Secondly, Congress may pass a concurrent resolution to direct a matter that is strictly internal to Congress but of concern to both Houses, such as the operations or organization of Congress, including any of the following:

---

19. 1 U.S.C. § 103 (2012).
20. *Supra* at note 10.

- To establish a joint committee of Congress.
- To establish a budget for the United States Government for a specific fiscal year ("budget resolution").
- To provide for an adjournment of Congress of more than three days ("adjournment resolution").
- To make corrections in the enrollment of any bill or joint resolution ("corrections resolution").

Legal Basis. — Although the Constitution does not specifically refer to concurrent resolutions, the same Constitutional provision[21] that permits the creation of joint resolutions is also read as allowing Congress to create a class of resolutions not presented to the President and, thus, not capable of becoming a statute. This important legal distinction between joint and concurrent resolutions has frustrated generations of Capitol Hill staff, who must memorize the difference between "joint" and "concurrent" and accept the unpleasant reality that, at least with the choice of legislative vehicles, form does matter.

Additional authorization for concurrent resolutions may be derived from Article I, section 5, clause 2 of the Constitution that states that each House of Congress "may determine the Rules of its Proceedings". Presumably this applies to the Houses acting concurrently as well as singly.

Composition. — Concurrent resolutions, like joint resolutions, consist of four required parts and one optional part. The required parts are as follows: (1) The endorsement, (2) the long title, (3) the resolving clause, and (4) the text. The optional part is a preamble.

Endorsement. — The endorsement of a concurrent resolution contains the same type of information as is found in the endorsement of bills, except that the designation of a concurrent resolution originating in the Senate is "**S.Con.Res.**" and in the House of Representatives is "**H.Con.Res.**". Another technical difference from bills is that concurrent resolutions are referred to as "submitted", not "introduced".

Long Title.[22] — The long title (also known as the "official title") serves the same function as it does in bills and appears immediately below "**CONCURRENT RESOLUTION**" on the form. By custom, however, the long title of a concurrent resolution often begins with the present participle form of a verb (i.e., a verb with an "ing" ending) and not with "To".

Preamble.[23] — Between the long title and the resolving clause, the drafter may insert a preamble. The style and form of preambles are uniform for all resolutions.

---

21. U.S. Const., art. I, §7, cl. 3.
22. *See also* "Bills: Long Title", *supra.*
23. *See also* "Joint Resolutions: Preamble", *supra.*

The Resolving Clause.—Unlike a joint resolution, the wording of the resolving clause of a concurrent resolution varies with the House of origin. In the case of a concurrent resolution originating in the Senate, the resolving clause reads as follows: "*Resolved by the Senate (the House of Representatives concurring),*". In the case of a concurrent resolution originating in the House of Representatives, the resolving clause reads as follows: "*Resolved by the House of Representatives (the Senate concurring),*". The resolving clause appears after the long title, usually separated by a space of one or two lines, and is always printed in italic.

A mistake occasionally made with resolving clauses is to repeat the clause within a concurrent resolution. This is specifically prohibited by the United States Code.[24]

The Text.—All language appearing after the resolving clause through the end of the concurrent resolution is the text. For the same reasons discussed for bills, the text of a concurrent resolution begins with "**SECTION 1.**".

The text of a concurrent resolution consists of nonbinding language when merely expressing a sentiment of Congress or binding language when directing matters internal to Congress, or both. Where nonbinding language is used to urge action by a third party, the text customarily begins with "It is the sense of Congress that".

Since adopted concurrent resolutions are never considered Acts of Congress, references within the text of a concurrent resolution to the entire vehicle are always made to "this concurrent resolution" and not to "this Act", as is the case with bills.

Where a concurrent resolution calls for action by an executive branch official, it is advisable to include a sentence at the end of the text directing the Secretary of the Senate or the Clerk of the House, as the case may be, to transmit a copy of the concurrent resolution to the official so that notice may be taken of Congress' policy.

Example:

SEC. 2. TRANSMITTAL.

The Secretary of the Senate shall transmit a copy of this concurrent resolution to the President.

"Simple" (One-House) Resolutions

Function.—Since a "simple" resolution requires passage by only one House of Congress, a simple resolution is not a bicameral act, is never submitted to the President for approval, and therefore constitutionally may never become a statute. Like a concurrent resolution, however, a simple resolution has its uses.

First, a simple resolution may be used to convey any nonbinding expression of the respective House of Congress on any matter. For example, in the foreign affairs field, simple resolutions are frequently passed so that the Senate or the House of Repre-

---

24. 1 U.S.C. § 103 (2012).

sentatives may comment on an international event of interest, such as a violation of human rights in a foreign country, or so that the Senate or the House may comment on a foreign policy of the United States.

Secondly, a House of Congress may pass a simple resolution to direct a matter that is strictly internal to that House, such as the operations or organization of the House. For example, a simple resolution is the proper legislative vehicle to establish a new committee within a single House of Congress.

Legal Basis.—Although the Constitution does not specifically refer to simple resolutions, authorization for simple resolutions may be derived from Article I, section 5, clause 2 of the Constitution, which states that each House of Congress "may determine the Rules of its Proceedings".

Composition.—Simple resolutions, like joint and concurrent resolutions, consist of four required parts and one optional part. The required parts are as follows: (1) The endorsement, (2) the long title, (3) the resolving clause, and (4) the text. The optional part is a preamble.

Endorsement.—The endorsement of a simple resolution contains the same type of information as is found in the endorsement of bills, except that the designation of a simple resolution originating in the Senate is "**S.Res.**" and in the House of Representatives is "**H.Res.**". As with joint and concurrent resolutions, simple resolutions are referred to as "submitted", not "introduced".

Long Title.[25]—The long title (also known as the "official title") serves the same function as in bills and other resolutions and appears immediately below "**RESOLUTION**" on the form. By custom, however, the long title of a simple resolution often begins with the present participle form of a verb (i.e., a verb with an "ing" ending) and not with "To".

Preamble.[26]—Between the long title and the resolving clause, the drafter may insert a preamble. The style and form of preambles are uniform for all resolutions.

The Resolving Clause.—The resolving clause of a simple resolution is as follows: "*Resolved,*". The text remains exactly as stated without referencing any House of origin and is always printed in italic. The resolving clause appears after the long title, usually separated by a space of one or two lines.

A mistake occasionally made with resolving clauses is to repeat the clause within a simple resolution. This is specifically prohibited by the United States Code.[27]

The Text.—All language appearing after the resolving clause through the end of the simple resolution is the text. For the same reasons discussed for bills, the text of a simple resolution begins with "**SECTION 1.**".

---

25. *See also* "Bills: Long Title", *supra.*
26. *See also* "Joint Resolutions: Preamble", *supra.*
27. 1 U.S.C. § 103 (2012).

The text of a simple resolution consists of nonbinding language when merely expressing a sentiment of one House of Congress or binding language when directing matters internal to the House of Congress originating the resolution, or both. Where nonbinding language is used to urge action by a third party, the text customarily begins with "It is the sense of [the Senate][the House of Representatives] that".

Since adopted simple resolutions are never considered Acts of Congress, references within the text to the entire vehicle are always made to "this resolution" and not to "this Act", as is the case with bills.

As with concurrent resolutions, where a simple resolution addresses an official of the executive branch, a sentence directing transmittal of a copy of the resolution to the official should be included.

Matching Language to Legislative Forms

Form Matters. — Knowledge of the varying procedures under the Constitution applicable to bills and resolutions enables us to choose the appropriate legislative vehicle for any particular legislative language chosen under Chapter One.

Bills and joint resolutions may carry the whole range of binding and nonbinding language. Concurrent and simple resolutions, on the other hand, are more limited. Since concurrent and simple resolutions are never presented to the President for approval, it follows that a concurrent or simple resolution never has the force of law.[28] It also follows, then, that legislative language that establishes a legal duty, responsibility, or right will not be legally effective if written as a provision of a concurrent or simple resolution.

This means that the legislative drafter should avoid writing binding language such as "shall", "may", "is authorized to", or "is entitled to" within a concurrent or simple resolution except in the limited circumstance described below. Unlike other areas of law, in the field of Federal legislative law, form does matter. (*See* Figure 2-2.)

Exception. — Binding language is permitted on a concurrent or simple resolution where the language is limited to binding Congress itself and not any other branch of Government or any private citizen. The use of "shall" or "may" is acceptable, therefore, on those resolutions that make congressional rules, establish congressional committees or offices, or impose duties or authorities on congressional officials.

---

28. *But see* Senate Judiciary Report No. 1335 (1897), finding that Article 1, §7, cl. 3 of the Constitution requires the presentation to the President of any concurrent resolution that would purport to exercise the legislative powers of Congress under Article 1, §1. A stronger demonstration of this congressional intent would seem to be required than the use of "shall" or "may" in the text as Members of Congress occasionally use those words inexactly. Also, if such intent were expressed on the floor, the Senate or House Enrolling Clerk might enroll the concurrent resolution as a joint resolution. Report No. 1335 does acknowledge, however, the "uniform practice of Congress" not to present concurrent resolutions to the President.

Figure 2-2

		Legal Effect		
		Mandatory	Authorizing	Hortatory
Legislation	Bill	Yes	Yes	Yes[a]
	J. Res.	Yes	Yes	Yes[b]
	Con. Res.	No[c]	No[d]	Yes
	Res.	No[e]	No[f]	Yes
	Amdt.	*	*	*

[a] Denotes that these legislative measures should take some language other than hortatory.
[b] *Id.*
[c] May mandate matters internal to Congress.
[d] May authorize matters internal to Congress.
[e] May mandate matters internal to a House of Congress.
[f] May authorize matters internal to a House of Congress.

Part II: Legislative Amendments

Introduction

An alternative to drafting a bill or resolution is to draft a legislative amendment to someone else's bill or resolution. As a legislative strategy, it is ordinarily better to "piggyback" on a bill or resolution already being considered by a House of Congress or one of its committees instead of starting from scratch with the introduction of a bill or resolution since Congress never acts on most introduced legislation.

A legislative amendment[29] is the form that Congress requires to be used to propose a change in the wording of a specific bill or resolution pending on the floor of the Senate or the House of Representatives.[30] For this reason, legislative amendments are most commonly known as "floor amendments", but their usefulness extends beyond the chambers of the Senate and the House of Representatives.

An amendment proposed in a congressional committee markup[31] to a bill or resolution or in a conference committee on a bill or resolution may also use the legisla-

---

29. Sometimes referred to simply as an "amendment", but the term does not answer the question: "Amendment to statute or amendment to pending legislation?" The dual uses for the word "amendment" have prompted the author to create the terms "legislative amendments" and "statutory amendments".

30. *See* Appendix A, *infra,* for a detailed description of how legislative amendments are used in the United States legislative process.

31. *See* Appendix A, *infra.*

tive amendment form or may be made less formally. Accordingly, in a broader sense, a legislative amendment is any amendment that targets any bill or resolution before a House of Congress or a congressional committee.

A legislative amendment may be proposed to the text of a bill or resolution (also known as a "first degree amendment") or to the text of a first degree amendment (also known as a "second degree amendment").[32] Third degree amendments are not permitted under the House and Senate rules and precedents.

It is worth noting that, contrary to the understanding of many Members of Congress, a bill or resolution may not be used to amend another bill or resolution. That function is exclusively reserved for the legislative amendment. If you had a dollar for every time a Senator has risen on the Senate floor to offer "a bill" to another Senator's bill, you'd be rich.

Elements of the Legislative Amendment Form

In General. — The legislative amendment takes the same form whether its target is a bill or a resolution. The form consists of three parts, as follows: (1) The purpose; (2) the endorsement; and (3) the "viz" language. A brief description of each element follows:

"The Purpose". — The legislative clerks of the Senate and the House require that each legislative amendment state the purpose of the amendment at the top of the form. The purpose serves the same function as the long title of a bill or resolution, that is, to provide transparency in recording the document. The purpose always begins with "To" whether or not the amendment is being proposed to a bill or a resolution.

The Endorsement. — The endorsement of a legislative amendment contains the amendment number assigned by the legislative clerk, the calendar number of the bill or resolution, the bill or resolution's House-of-origin designation, number, and long title, and the name of the sponsor of the amendment. If the amendment is an amendment in the second degree, then the endorsement should also identify both amendments, as follows: "Amendment intended to be proposed by [Mr./Ms. _____] to the amendment (no. ____) proposed by [Mr./Ms. _____]". If language at more than one place in the bill or resolution is being amended, the form should be labeled "Amendments".

"Viz" Language, Generally. — Each legislative amendment form contains the acronym "Viz". "Viz" is the acronym for the Latin "videlicet" meaning "that is to say" or, in this context, "namely". The substance of the amendment (or amendments) should begin immediately after this acronym and may be referred to as "viz" language.

---

32. *Id.*

The "viz" language is written as a directive to "strike", "insert", or "strike and insert" a word, phrase, or block of text.[33] The executor of the directive is the Enrolling Clerk, in the case of a "floor" amendment, or committee staff (acting through the Legislative Counsel), in the case of an amendment made in committee, but neither the Clerk nor the staff is specifically addressed by an amendment.

Words and phrases proposed to be amended should be identified within quotation marks, and it is unnecessary to precede the quoted matter with "word" or "phrase". Just the quoted language will suffice. A block of text should not be placed within quotation marks unless the block of text is part of a proposed statutory amendment[34] made by the bill or joint resolution.

Each legislative amendment on the same form is separated from the previous amendment by skipping one line. It is a technical violation of the rules to propose more than one amendment on a legislative amendment form, and a Member of Congress has a right to demand a separate vote on each amendment.[35] Conversely, when no such "severing" is demanded, multiple legislative amendments on the same form may be adopted by a single vote, *en bloc*. Despite their parliamentary risk, *en bloc* amendments are common and an indispensable tool to amending long bills. By listing multiple amendments together, the drafter avoids having to rewrite a large chunk of text.

The legal effect of any language inserted by a legislative amendment must be limited to the legal effects appropriate to the bill or resolution targeted by the amendment.

Types of Legislative Amendments

Perfecting Amendments. — A perfecting amendment is one that proposes to strike less than the entire text of the target legislation or first degree amendment or that proposes only to insert language in the legislation or the amendment.

The target of the perfecting amendment should be identified by page and line numbers of the printed bill or resolution and not by the section number or other designation contained within the text of the bill or resolution as these designations are unreliable — they may have been previously amended without the knowledge of the drafter.

The way a perfecting amendment is drafted depends on the amount of legislative text affected by the amendment. Consider the following three ways in which perfecting amendments to strike are worded:

---

33. The terms "strike", "insert", and "strike and insert" are derived from the Senate and House rules and precedents. Alternative words such as "delete", "omit", "replace", and "substitute" should not be used in Federal legislation.

34. *See* Chapter Three, Part II, *infra.*

35. *See, e.g.,* Rule XV(3) of the Standing Rules of the Senate.

One-Line Amendments.— Most perfecting amendments target a word or phrase appearing on just one line of the legislation.

Examples:

On page ___, line __, strike "_____".

On page ___, line __, insert "____" after "_____".

On page ___, line __, strike "____" and insert "_____".

Multi-Line Amendments.— Where the target language spans fragments of two or more lines on the same page, in order to save verbiage, the amendment is phrased as follows:

On page ___, beginning on line ___, strike "_____" and all that follows through "_____" on line _____.

This saves reciting the entire language to be stricken.

Multi-Page Amendments.— Similarly, where the target language spans fragments of pages, to save reciting the entire language the amendment is phrased as follows:

Beginning on page ___, line ___, strike "_____" and all that follows through "_____" on line _____ of page ____.

Substitute Amendments.— A substitute amendment is one that proposes to strike and insert the entire text of a bill or resolution or the entire text of a first degree amendment to a bill or resolution.

Where the amendment replaces the text of a bill or resolution, the legislative amendment form specifically identifies itself (in the sponsorship line) as an Amendment in the Nature of a Substitute. The "viz language" of an Amendment in the Nature of a Substitute will always read as follows:

Strike all after the [enacting][resolving] clause and insert the following:

Where the substitute amendment is to a first degree amendment, the "viz" language will read as follows:

In lieu of the matter proposed to be inserted by the amendment, insert the following:

Enacting and Resolving Clauses Not Amendable.— An enacting clause or resolving clause may not be amended because the language of the clause is prescribed by law and is an integral part of the form on which it appears.

Long Titles and Preambles Amended Separately.— The rules of the Senate and the House of Representatives make it in order to consider an amendment to a long title or a preamble[36] only after all amendments have been made to the text, and the text has been adopted. Consequently, a legislative amendment to a long title or a preamble should be drafted on a separate form and not made part of a form containing amendments to the text.

---

36. *See, e.g.,* Rule XIV(8) of the Standing Rules of the Senate.

Long titles and preambles are usually amended by substitute amendments, that is, by language stating that the object of the amendment is "amended to read as follows".

Because long titles and preambles are amended separately and enacting clauses and resolving clauses are not amendable at all, it follows that a single legislative amendment may never replace the entire wording of a legislative vehicle.

"Clean Up" Amendments

It is a good practice for the drafter to "clean up" the mess made by a legislative amendment by further amending the bill to redesignate sections, revise cross-references, or make conforming changes, where necessary.

On the other hand, where time is short, or where there is a significant risk that a Member of Congress will demand a separate vote[37] on a "clean up" amendment, the drafter should forgo the "cleanup" and rely instead on the Enrolling Clerk or, in the case of a committee markup, the Legislative Counsel, to handle the matter through the official's discretionary authority.

> **Example ("Clean up" amendments following the insertion of a new section 5 in an 8-section bill):**
>
> *viz: On page 5, between lines 2 and 3, insert the following new section:*
>
> *SEC. 5. WAIVER AUTHORITY.*
>
> *The President may waive the application of section 4 if the President determines that it is vital to the national security interests of the United States to do so.*
>
> *On page 5, line 20, strike "SEC. 5." and insert "SEC. 6.".*
>
> *On page 6, line 3, strike "SEC. 6." and insert "SEC. 7.".*
>
> *On page 6, line 20, strike "SEC. 7." and insert "SEC. 8.".*
>
> *On page 7, line 3, strike "SEC. 8." and insert "SEC. 9.".*

Impact of Budgetary Scoring on Legislative Amendments

Legislative amendments are often drawn to achieve budget neutrality, that is, if an amendment adds funds to a bill, then another accompanying amendment must be proposed to offset that increase with a reduction of funds from another account in the bill. To achieve an equal budgetary impact, however, simply reducing by the same dollar amount as the increase will often not work. This is so because appropriated

---

37. Under the regular order, a Member of Congress is entitled to demand the severance of any legislative amendment.

funds are disbursed at different rates over time, depending primarily on the pay-out schedules of the contracts involved.

Accordingly, to achieve an equal impact on budgetary outlays in the same fiscal year a different dollar amount for a reduction may be necessary to offset an increase. The best way to determine the exact offset required is to consult the budgetary "scoring" of the appropriation made by the Congressional Budget Office (CBO), which estimates the outlays for each fiscal year.

Converting a Bill to a Legislative Amendment

When Congress fails to act on a bill, the sponsor's only recourse is to convert the text into a legislative amendment. This may be done as follows:

- Make the long title the "purpose" of the amendment.
- After "viz:", write: *On page ___, between lines ___ and ___, insert the following:*
- Compress the bill text into a single section, changing sections to subsections, subsections to paragraphs, etc.
- Conform internal cross-references, accordingly, making especially sure to change "this Act" to "this section".
- Insert the modified section after the "viz:" language.

Part III: The Legislative Veto

INS v. Chadha[38]

History of the Legislative Veto. — Beginning in 1932, Congress from time-to-time would enact into law a bill or joint resolution containing a provision the operation of which was contingent on the future passage of a concurrent resolution, simple resolution, or committee resolution approving or disapproving a specific executive branch implementation of the law. In effect, Congress was micromanaging the executive branch's administration of its legal authorities. By 1983, Congress had enacted 295 of these so-called "legislative veto" provisions in 196 different statutes, with the greatest number having been enacted during the 1970s.

Constitutional Law Issue. — While it was unquestionably true that a concurrent, simple, or committee resolution, standing alone, could not make law, it was argued that the passage of such a resolution in execution of a condition in a statute was effective to veto Executive action since the statute had already been duly enacted in

---

38. *INS v. Chadha*, 462 U.S. 919 (1983).

accordance with Constitutional procedures. In its landmark decision in *INS* v. *Chadha*, the Supreme Court reviewed the constitutionality of one of these legislative vetoes.

Facts of the Case.—Chadha was a temporary ("nonimmigrant") alien admitted to the United States who became deportable by overstaying the expiration of his nonimmigrant visa. Section 244(a) of the Immigration and Nationality Act authorized the Attorney General to suspend the deportation of certain aliens in cases of extreme hardship, and the Attorney General did suspend the deportation of Chadha. However, section 244(c)(2) of that Act provided for the veto of any decision by the Attorney General to suspend deportation if a single House of Congress passed a simple resolution expressing its objection to the decision. The House of Representatives did pass such a resolution with respect to Chadha, effectively requiring his deportation, and Chadha challenged the constitutionality of section 244(c)(2) in Federal court.

The Supreme Court held—in a landmark decision that is read more broadly than its narrow ruling—that Chadha was not deportable.

Narrow Holding.—A statute, duly enacted in accordance with Article I of the Constitution, may not constitutionally grant an authority to an executive branch official subject to the condition that one House of Congress may veto the exercise of that authority.

Broad Holding.—Any provision of a statute the legal operation of which is made contingent on congressional action that does not satisfy the bicameralism requirement and does not comply with the Presentment Clauses of Article I of the Constitution is unconstitutional. The broad holding has the effect of invalidating any legislative veto provision, including provisions using vetoes by concurrent resolutions and committee resolutions, as well as by simple resolutions.

Implications of the *Chadha* Decision.—The reasoning of the Court invalidates not only legislative veto provisions but also any legislative triggering mechanism that would in effect make law short of meeting the bicameralism and presentment requirements of the Constitution. In other words, any proposed change in a legal right, duty, or responsibility short of the enactment of a new statute is unconstitutional. Such triggering provisions may sound quite reasonable but are actually unconstitutional, as in the following example: *Unless Congress agrees, the President may not use force against Iran.*

Reasoning of the Court.—The Supreme Court relied primarily on three reasons for its decision in the *Chadha* case, as follows:

> First, the Framers intended that the legislative power be exercised "in accord with a single, finely wrought and exhaustively considered procedure",[39] which includes a bicameral requirement and compliance with the Presentment Clauses.

---

39. *Id.* at 951.

Secondly, the one-House veto exercised in this case was of a "legislative character"[40] because the House of Representatives intended to change the legal status of the alien, and therefore the exercise of the veto was required to comply with the Constitutional procedure for enacting legislation.

Thirdly, where the Framers permitted one House of Congress to "act alone with the unreviewable force of law",[41] they specifically so provided in the Constitution in four unambiguous provisions: impeachments, impeachment trials, confirmation of appointees, and approval of treaties. This infers that bicameralism and Presentment are the general, default rule for the exercise of lawmaking.

Legacy of the *Chadha* Decision

Alteration of Legal Regimes. — The sweeping holding in *Chadha* has had the legal effect of invalidating more statutory provisions than any other judicial invalidation in history, but, for political reasons, most of the provisions have not been repealed — they are merely unenforceable. Each invalidated veto provision is treated as severed from its statute with the remainder of the statute continuing in effect.[42] The result has been to alter significantly the original statutory schemes. If Congress had known of the unconstitutionality of the legislative veto at the time of enactment, Congress might not have delegated the authority to the executive branch or at least not in the same way that Congress chose. In short, the Supreme Court has altered the legal landscape by not invalidating the entirety of the provisions containing the legislative vetoes.

Substitution of Joint Resolutions and Bills in Veto Provisions. — Congress has corrected the constitutional defect in some legislative veto provisions by amending the statutes to substitute the *enactment* of a joint resolution or bill for the *passage* of a concurrent, simple, or committee resolution. These changes only make sense if expedited procedures are available to ensure the timely enactment of the joint resolution or bill, and it should be noted that the changes do not restore the pre-*Chadha* balance of power between the legislative and executive branches, which favored Congress.

Circumvention by Congress. — Congressional committees have been particularly reluctant to surrender their power to veto Executive action. Based on either of the following two types of legislative provisions, congressional committees have maintained an informal, behind-the-scenes legislative veto in limited situations, acquiesced in by the executive branch as a matter of comity, not of legal right:

---

40. *Id.* at 952. The Court is using "legislative" in the narrow sense described in Part I of this Chapter.

41. *Id.* at 955.

42. *See also* Chapter Five, Part IV: Presumptions. Section 240A of the Immigration and Nationality Act (8 U.S.C. 1229b(b)), stripped of the legislative veto, is the current equivalent of the suspension of deportation provision at issue in the *Chadha* case.

(1) **Reprogramming Notifications.** — Backed by the Power of the Purse, with its power to withhold funds from the Executive, the Appropriations Committees of the House and Senate have required the executive branch to notify the Committees in advance of any plans to make changes in the use of funds involving programs already funded by Congress. These "reprogramming notification" requirements are a form of "report and wait" provision, with the "wait" period offering the Committees the chance to object to the proposed reprogramming. By informal agreement with the executive branch, these objections are respected.

Example:

None of the funds appropriated under this Act may be obligated for any activity not justified, or in excess of the amount justified, to Congress for obligation unless the Committee on Appropriations of each House of Congress is notified 15 days in advance of the obligation.

(2) **"Same Procedures As" Reprogramming Notifications.** — So effective have been the procedures applicable to reprogramming notifications in maintaining legislative vetoes by the Appropriations Committees that "authorizing" committees of Congress have sought to piggyback on those procedures with respect to Executive actions that may have nothing to do with the obligation of funds. The authorizing committees have devised legislative language to obtain the same deference by the Executive to committee objections to specific types of proposed Executive actions, and this language now appears with increasing frequency in bills enacted by Congress.

Example:

At least 15 days before the President proposes to _____, the President shall notify the appropriate congressional committees in accordance with the same procedures as are applicable to reprogramming notifications [made to the Appropriations Committees] under section _____ of _____ Act.

Loss of a Useful Legislative Tool. — Last, but not least, the practical result of *INS v. Chadha* has been to deprive Congress of a useful legislative tool, as described by Justice White, the lone dissenting justice in the case, as follows:

Without the legislative veto, Congress is faced with a Hobson's choice: either to refrain from delegating the necessary authority, leaving itself with a hopeless task of writing laws with the requisite specificity to cover endless special circumstances across the entire policy landscape, or in the alternative, to abdicate its law-making function to the executive branch and independent agencies. To choose the former leaves major national problems unresolved; to opt for the latter risks unaccountable policymaking by those not elected to fill that role.[43]

Do you agree?

---

43. White, J., dissenting, *INS.v. Chadha*, 462 U.S. 919, 968 (1983).

Part IV: Expedited ("Fast Track") Procedures

What Are Expedited Procedures?

History. — Expedited procedures, also known as "fast track procedures" or "congressional priority procedures", were first placed into statutes pre-*Chadha* as a means for Congress to exercise the legislative veto provisions of those statutes in a timely way. Despite the invalidation of the legislative veto by the *INS* v. *Chadha* decision, those procedures continue to be used where the veto mechanism was later amended to substitute "joint resolution" or "bill" for a concurrent, simple, or committee resolution, as the case may be.

Today expedited procedures are customarily attached to any statutory provision that conditions an Executive action upon the enactment of a joint resolution or bill approving or disapproving the action. In fact, drafting a condition that is fulfilled by the enactment of a bill or joint resolution only makes sense where procedures are available to expedite that legislation. Without those procedures, the condition would be merely a futile attempt to bind a future Congress and would be unnecessary to state.

Expedited Procedures Defined. — The term "expedited procedures" means special procedures that Congress establishes by statute to govern the consideration by Congress at a future date of a specific legislative measure to ensure that a final vote[44] will be taken on the measure.

Purpose. — Expedited procedures provide Congress with a short time frame, usually ranging between 30 to 60 days, within which to disapprove or approve a proposed Executive action. By ensuring a prompt vote, the procedures enable Congress to exercise oversight and control of the executive branch.

Limited Applicability. — The number of legislative measures entitled to expedited procedures in any year is very small. There are no expedited procedures that provide for a general override of the "regular order" of the Senate or the House of Representatives in its consideration of all legislation. To do so would impose a strait jacket on the legislative process that would hinder compromise through the amendment process.

Legal Basis. — Congress enacts expedited procedures as an exercise of its power under the Constitution to "determine the Rules of its Proceedings".[45] There is no Constitutional requirement that legislative rules made by the Houses of Congress must be applied uniformly to all bills and resolutions.

Parliamentary Terminology. — A joint resolution or bill that is entitled to expedited procedures is usually referred to in the House of Representatives as "highly privi-

---

44. *See* Appendix A for an explanation of why final votes on legislative measures are not guaranteed.

45. US Const., art. I, § 5, cl. 2,

leged" and in the Senate as "privileged". Whether any particular joint resolution or bill is entitled to expedited treatment is determined in the House of Representatives by the Speaker, in consultation with the House Parliamentarian, and in the Senate by the Presiding Officer, in consultation with the Senate Parliamentarian.

Joint Resolutions Preferred Over Bills. — Most expedited procedures call for the use of joint resolutions rather than bills. This is consistent with the general usage of joint resolutions in situations that are of an extraordinary or emergency nature, but this usage is not required by the Constitution.

Frameworks for Using Expedited Procedures

Two Approaches to Using Expedited Procedures. — Expedited procedures may be used to expedite the passage of (1) legislation that blocks the exercise of an executive branch authority that has previously been delegated by statute (known as "disapproval legislation"), or (2) legislation that permits the exercise by the executive branch of an authority the exercise of which has previously been prohibited by statute (known as "approval legislation").

Framework of Disapproval Legislation Provisions. — A statutory provision providing for expediting disapproval legislation consists of the following:

(1) A delegation of authority.

(2) A requirement of a report, certification, or other notification to Congress from the executive branch proposing a specific exercise of the authority.

(3) A waiting period between the date of congressional notification and the date on which the authority may be exercised.

(4) A statement that disapproval legislation enacted within the waiting period will block the exercise of the authority.

(5) A statement making any qualifying disapproval legislation eligible for expedited procedures.

Example of Legislative Framework for Disapproval Legislation:

The [executive branch official] shall not exercise the [cited authority] if Congress, within __ days after receipt of a certification [describing the proposed Executive action] by the [official], enacts a joint resolution stating in substance its disapproval of the certification. Any such joint resolution shall be considered in the Senate or the House of Representatives in accordance with the [referenced expedited procedures].

Framework of Approval Legislation Provisions. — A statutory provision providing for expediting disapproval legislation consists of the following:

(1) A prohibition on action by an executive branch official.

(2) A requirement of a report, certification, or other notification to Congress from the executive branch requesting a waiver of the prohibition.

(3) A statement that approval legislation enacted within a specified period of time after the executive branch request will waive the prohibition, thereby authorizing the action.

(4) A statement making any qualifying approval legislation eligible for expedited procedures.

Example of Legislative Framework for Approval Legislation:

The prohibition [on Executive action] shall cease to apply if—

(1) the [executive branch official] submits to Congress a certification stating _____; and

(2) Congress enacts a joint resolution stating in substance its approval of the certification.

Any such joint resolution shall be considered in the Senate or the House of Representatives in accordance with the [referenced expedited procedures.

Choosing the Approach Best Designed to Protect Congressional Interests. — The enactment of a joint resolution of approval to waive a statutory prohibition usually serves the institutional interests of Congress better than the enactment of a joint resolution of disapproval to block the exercise of Executive authority.

In the former case, the President is almost certainly committed to signing any passed joint resolution since the President did request the waiver. The result will be that both branches of government will be acting in concert. In the latter case, on the other hand, the President will almost certainly veto the joint resolution because the enactment of the resolution would constrain already authorized Executive action. Unless Congress musters a two-thirds vote to override the veto, no joint resolution of disapproval is likely to be enacted. The result will be a confrontation between the two branches of government that Congress will lose.

Elements of Expedited Procedures

In General. — Although there is no uniformity in expedited procedures in statutory law, each set of expedited procedures tends to address the same parliamentary obstacles to speedy passage of legislation.

Issues in Writing Expedited Procedures. — Model expedited procedures address each of the following issues:

(1) **Identification of the Privileged Legislation.** — Privileged legislation is identified by either stating the exact text of the legislation or by stating that the privileged legislation is a joint resolution or bill "stating in substance" its approval or disapproval of the proposed Executive action. Reciting the exact

language reduces the chance that the Speaker or the Presiding Officer of the Senate will deny expedited treatment to the legislation.

(2) **Method of Introduction of the Privileged Legislation.**—Most procedures apply to any legislation introduced by any Member of Congress within a specified number of days after a particular report, certification, or other notification is received by Congress. This allows the remote possibility that no legislation will be expedited for lack of sponsorship. In certain cases where an executive branch official is seeking urgent authority to act, this possibility is unacceptable, and so the expedited procedures will require the introduction of the privileged legislation by either a Leader of a House of Congress or a chairman of a specified congressional committee.

(3) **Calculation of the Time Period for Expedited Procedures.**—Expedited procedures available to any specific joint resolution always expire. This must be so because otherwise Congress would be continuously setting aside regular business to attend to privileged resolutions. However, it defeats the purpose of having the expedited procedures if they expire during a congressional adjournment. Consequently, most procedures exclude from the calculation of the time period for the availability of the procedures those adjournments of Congress of more than three days, although other formulations are possible.

(4) **Choice of Committee of Referral.**—Most expedited procedures permit the privileged legislation to be referred to a single specified committee in each House of Congress. A multiple referral would be unnecessarily dilatory.

(5) **Limited Committee Action.**—This type of provision provides for the discharge from committee of the privileged legislation after a short period, either automatically or by motion, to ensure that the legislation will not expire in committee.

(6) **Limited Floor Action.**—This requirement limits the number of hours permitted for debate on the floor of a House of Congress and imposes sublimits on the consideration of any motions, appeals, amendments, or conference reports.

(7) **Amendments.**—A choice is required as to whether or not to allow amendments and, if so, whether to require the amendment to be germane and relevant. The adoption of any amendment will require a reconciliation of the text between the two Houses, usually through a committee of conference, thereby necessitating the inclusion of a provision on the consideration of conference reports. This gets quite messy as there is no procedural way to force a compromise in conference committee. Accordingly, expedited procedures ordinarily establish a point of order against the consideration of any amendment, thereby ensuring that the final vote will be an "up or down" vote on the proposition stated in the privileged legislation, as introduced.

(8) Deference to the First House to Act.—This type of provision requires that a House of Congress first receiving the passed privileged legislation of the other House must act on that legislation and not lay it aside while it acts on its own privileged legislation. This is essential to expedite the legislative process.

Model Expedited Procedures

The following is an example of expedited procedures set forth in a legislative section:

SEC.____. *EXPEDITED PROCEDURES.*

(a) Joint Resolution Defined.—*In section ____, the term "joint resolution" means only a joint resolution introduced not later than __ days after the date on which the President [makes a certification] [submits a report] under section ____, the matter after the resolving clause of which is as follows: "That, pursuant to section ____ of the _____ Act of 20__, Congress [approves] [disapproves] the [certification made][report submitted] under section ____ of the _____ Act.".*

(b) Referral of Joint Resolutions.—*A joint resolution described in subsection (a) introduced in the House of Representatives shall be referred to the Committee on _____ of the House of Representatives. A joint resolution described in subsection (a) introduced in the Senate shall be referred to the Committee on _____ of the Senate. Such a joint resolution may not be reported before the eighth day after its introduction.*

(c) Discharge of Committees.—*If the committee to which is referred a joint resolution described in subsection (a) has not reported such resolution (or an identical resolution) at the end of fifteen calendar days after its introduction, such committee shall be discharged from further consideration of such resolution and such resolution shall be placed on the appropriate calendar of the House involved.*

(d) Floor Procedures.—

(1) Motion to Proceed to the Consideration of a Joint Resolution.—*When the committee to which a resolution is referred has reported, or has been deemed to be discharged (under subsection (c)) from further consideration of, a resolution described in subsection (a), notwithstanding any rule or precedent of the Senate, including Rule 22, it is at any time thereafter in order (even though a previous motion to the same effect has been disagreed to) for any Member of the respective House to move to proceed to the consideration of the resolution, and all points of order against the resolution (and against consideration of the resolution) are waived. The motion is highly privileged in the House of Representatives and is privileged in the Senate and is not debatable.*

The motion is not subject to amendment, or to a motion to postpone, or to a motion to proceed to the consideration of other business. A motion to reconsider the vote by which the motion is agreed to or disagreed to shall not be in order. If a motion to proceed to the consideration of the resolution is agreed to, the resolution shall remain the unfinished business of the respective House until disposed of.

*(2) **Debate.**—Debate on the resolution, and all debatable motions and appeals in connection therewith, shall be limited to not more than ten hours, which shall be divided equally between those favoring and those opposing the resolution. A motion further to limit debate is in order and not debatable. An amendment to, or a motion to postpone, or a motion to proceed to the consideration of other business, or a motion to recommit the resolution is not in order. A motion to reconsider the vote by which the resolution is agreed to or disagreed to is not in order.*

*(3) **Vote on Final Passage.**—Immediately following the conclusion of the debate on a resolution described in subsection (a), and a single quorum call at the conclusion of the debate is requested in accordance with the rules of the appropriate House, the vote on final passage of the resolution shall occur.*

*(4) **Appeals from Decisions of the Chair.**—Appeals from the decisions of the Chair relating to the application of the rules of the Senate or the House of Representatives, as the case may be, to the procedure relating to a resolution described in subsection (a) shall be decided without debate.*

*(e) **Receipt of Other House's Resolution Before Final Passage.**—If, before the passage by a House of Congress (in this section referred to as the "first House") of a resolution of that House described in subsection (a), that House receives from the other House (in this section referred to as the "second House") a resolution described in subsection (a), then the following procedures shall apply:*

(1) The resolution of the second House shall not be referred to a committee.

(2) With respect to a resolution described in subsection (a) of the first House—

(A) the procedure in the first House shall be the same as if no resolution had been received from the second House; but

(B) the vote on final passage shall be on the resolution of the second House.

(3) Upon disposition of the resolution received from the second House, it shall no longer be in order to consider the resolution originated in the first House.

*(f) **Subsequent Receipt of Other House's Resolution.**—If the first House receives from the second House a resolution described in subsection (a) after the first House has disposed of a resolution that originated in the first House, the action of the first House with regard to the disposition of the resolution that orig-*

inated in the first House shall be deemed to be the action of the first House with regard to the resolution that originated in the second House.

(g) Exercise of Rulemaking Powers. — This section is enacted by Congress—

(1) as an exercise of the rulemaking power of the Senate and the House of Representatives, respectively, and as such it is deemed a part of the rules of each House, respectively, but applicable only with respect to the procedure to be followed in that House in the case of a resolution described in subsection (a), and it supersedes other rules only to the extent that it is inconsistent with such rules; and

(2) with full recognition of the constitutional right of either House to change the rules (so far as relating to the procedure of that House) at any time, in the same manner and to the same extent as in the case of any other rule of that House.

Test Your "Formalizing" Skills

Drafting Exercise No. 2-A

For each of the following legislative proposals, choose the most appropriate legislative vehicle, including its House-of-origin designation, and explain your choice:

(1) In the Senate: To require a phased withdrawal of the United States Armed Forces from hostilities in a foreign country.

(2) To establish a Senate committee on the budget deficit.

(3) In the House of Representatives: To express the sense of Congress regarding nuclear weapons talks with a foreign country.

(4) In the House of Representatives: To reorganize and consolidate Federal agencies in the executive branch of Government.

Check your answers in Appendix C.

Drafting Exercise No. 2-B

Using the appropriate, complete resolution form, format the following language for introduction in the Senate by Senator Softy:

The devastating 7.0 magnitude Haitian earthquake of January 12, 2010, resulted in more than 230,000 deaths and left more than 1,000,000 Haitians homeless. Haiti desperately needs both short-term humanitarian aid and long-term development aid. Aid to Haiti from the international community has fallen far short of Haiti's needs. It is the sense of

Congress that the President should seek to obtain more aid for Haiti from the international community.

Check your answer in Appendix C.

Drafting Exercise No. 2-C

Please prepare perfecting "floor" amendments to be offered by Senator Flats, *en bloc*, to fictional bill S. 5079 to make the following changes:

- Substitute Haiti for Afghanistan.
- Include medicines in the definition of humanitarian assistance.
- Substitute $200,000,000 for $100,000,000.
- Add the same level of funding for fiscal year 2020.

Check your answers in Appendix C.

115th Congress	page 1	Calendar No. 1
1st Session	S. 5079	

IN THE SENATE OF THE UNITED STATES

January 3, 2017

Mr. Mountain, from the Committee on Foreign Relations, reported the following bill, which was read twice and placed on the Calendar.

A BILL

To authorize humanitarian assistance for Afghanistan, and for other purposes.

1   *[Page 1:] Be it enacted by the Senate and House of Representatives of the United States*
2   *of America in Congress assembled,*
3   **SECTION 1. SHORT TITLE.**
4   This Act may be cited as the "Afghanistan Humanitarian Assistance Act".
5   **SEC. 2. DEFINITION.**
6   In this Act, the term "humanitarian assistance" means the provision of food and
7   clothing.
8   **SEC. 3. AUTHORIZATION OF ASSISTANCE.**
9   The President is authorized to provide humanitarian assistance for Afghanistan.
10   **SEC. 4. AUTHORIZATION OF APPROPRIATIONS.**
11   There is authorized to be appropriated to the President $100,000,000 for each of
12   the fiscal years 2018 and 2019 to carry out the provisions of this Act.

Chapter Three

How to Relate to Existing Law

"It usually takes a hundred years to make a law; and then, after it has done its work, it usually takes a hundred years to get rid of it."[1]

Step Three: "Integrate!"

The third basic step in converting a legislative proposal to a draft bill or joint resolution[2] is to integrate, in the most appropriate way, the law being newly created with existing Acts of Congress or the United States Code (in this chapter collectively referred to as "existing law"). The ways to do this vary from the simplistic to the highly complex and technically demanding.

Part I: Three Approaches

Introduction

New law should be related to existing law by one of the following three approaches:

(1) **Statutory Construction.**—Do nothing and rely on statutory construction.

(2) **Override.**—Override ("supersede") conflicting, inconsistent existing law.

(3) **Statutory Amendment.**—Amend the existing law.

The approach the drafter takes will depend on the particular natures of the two laws and may vary within the new law on a provision-by-provision basis.

---

1. Henry Ward Beecher, 1858, quoted in *Life Thoughts: Extemporaneous Discourses of Henry Ward Beecher* (Edna Dean Proctor, ed.) (1860).

2. Chapter Three is not applicable to the drafting of a concurrent or simple resolution except in the rare circumstance where the new legislation relates to the existing rules or internal operations of Congress.

Statutory Construction

Description. — The easiest approach is to do nothing and instead to rely on the courts to sort out the relationship between new law and existing law through the use of statutory construction. The courts use two principal canons of statutory construction for doing this, as follows:

(1) **Later-in-Time Supersedes Earlier-in-Time.** — Later enactments of Congress prevail over earlier enactments.

(2) **The Specific Supersedes the General.** — Specific provisions of law prevail over general provisions of law.

Where Properly Used. — This approach makes sense mainly where the later enacted law is so time-limited or subject-matter limited that nothing is gained by integrating such a parochial law with the earlier general and permanent law. Given time, the later enacted law will become obsolete and inapplicable, withering on the vine, if you will.

Examples of a time-limited provision include any provision containing an expiration date or any provision limited to a specific fiscal year or series of fiscal years such as an appropriation, an authorization of appropriations, or a budgetary control provision.

Examples of a subject-matter provision include any provision that addresses a specific political subdivision or geographic area such as a State, locality, or foreign country and any provision that is limited to a specific governmental program or project.[3]

For all those kinds of provisions, the drafter simply does nothing, relying on the Federal agencies and courts to apply the two canons described above.

Advantages. — When used in the very limited situations described, this approach has the advantage of keeping general and permanent law from becoming cluttered with parochial or obsolete provisions. Also, involving no work whatsoever, this approach is well suited to the lazy drafter!

Disadvantages. — Many lazy drafters, however, will not restrict their use of this approach to the very limited situations described but apply the approach more generally. Where a specific provision amounts to an exception from a more general, earlier provision that is neither referenced nor amended, and where the provision relies for its effectiveness on judge-made interpretation, transparency in reading the law is lost. The law becomes scattered and difficult to find, with the result that it becomes hard to connect the various provisions addressing the same subject matter, and Congress abdicates its lawmaking power to the judiciary by effectively requiring judges to make sense out of the mess that Congress has created.

---

3. An example of both a time-limited and subject matter limited provision is any bar on aid to a specific foreign country for a specific fiscal year. Such a provision carves out an exception to the worldwide foreign aid program without amending or even referencing the worldwide program.

Overriding Existing Law

Description. — A second approach is to override existing law. Overriding existing law (also known as "superseding") is the pro-active way to ensure that a particular provision of law prevails over an earlier, conflicting law without having to amend the earlier law. Most frequently[4] this is done by beginning a legally binding sentence with "Notwithstanding any other provision of law," or "Notwithstanding section _____ of _____ Act,". The "notwithstanding" phrase immediately alerts the reader to the intent of Congress that the sentence in which the phrase appears should prevail over any conflict.

The addition of this phrase, however, may make a sentence so long that a better choice would be to give the override its own sentence, as follows:

This provision [or referenced provision] supersedes any other provision of law. OR

This provision [or referenced provision] supersedes section _____ of ___ Act.

Where Properly Used. — Like the statutory construction (or "do nothing") approach, overrides should be used sparingly. An override should be used only if any of the following applies:

(1) Where there are so many existing, conflicting provisions that amending them all would be overly burdensome.

(2) Where the drafter cannot identify all the possible existing, conflicting provisions in order to amend them.

(3) Where the existing, conflicting provision is parochial and, therefore, the entire nature of the provision would change if it were amended by a general and permanent provision — kind of like an elephant sitting on a mouse.

(4) Where the earlier-in-time provision is a specific prohibition or restriction of a limited subject matter and the later-in-time provision is an authorization of the same type of subject matter but on a time-limited basis. In this last situation, the two canons of statutory construction described above are at loggerheads and of no use.

Advantages. — This approach involves very little work or research and, as with the "do nothing" approach, is well suited for the lazy drafter. In addition, the approach feeds the psychic need of the drafter to do some "lawyering". Not surprisingly, then, overrides are the preferred choice of many hard-pressed Members of Congress and their staffs!

Disadvantages. — As with the statutory construction (or "do nothing") approach, overrides must not be used indiscriminately. Overrides are particularly susceptible

---

4. When the override needs to appear at the end of a sentence, the phrase "without regard to ___ " is used instead of "notwithstanding ___ ".

to misuse and abuse by giving the drafter the false sense of security that the drafter has "done something" to relate new law to existing law. By using an override where amending existing law is the better choice, the drafter misses the opportunity to integrate the law into a single, comprehensive expression. This is a major drafting error. The result will be a public policy existing in two or more places in the law books, scattered as in a patchwork quilt, with the earlier expression read in total ignorance of the modification to come.

Amending Existing Law

Description. — An amendment to existing law (in this manual referred to as a "statutory amendment"[5]) is made by striking, inserting,[6] or striking and inserting[7] a word, phrase, or block of text of an earlier enacted statute. Statutory amendments do not use other terms such as "deleting", "omitting", "replacing", or "substituting", as statutory amendments parallel the terminology of legislative amendments.

A statutory amendment is easy to identify in a bill or joint resolution because the language being amended almost always appears within quotation marks. These are usually the only quotation marks in the legislation other than in the sentence containing the short title. As with legislative amendments, it is unnecessary to identify the quoted matter as being a "word" or "phrase". *See* Figure 3-1.

Figure 3-1

		Function or Mode	
		"Freestanding"	Amendatory
Legislation	Bill	Yes	Yes
	J. Res.	Yes	Yes
	Con. Res.	Yes	No[a]
	Res.	Yes	No[b]
	Amdt.	*	*

[a] May amend prior concurrent resolutions.
[b] May amend prior "simple" resolutions.

---

5. The usual term is "amendatory language", but the term does not answer the question: "Amendment to statute or amendment to pending legislation?" The dual uses for the word "amendment" have prompted the author to create the new terms "legislative amendments" and "statutory amendments".

6. When the insertion would be made at the end of a statutory subdivision, such as a section or paragraph, "by adding" is substituted for "by inserting".

7. Note that "striking and inserting" is now favored over the more legalistic "striking out and inserting in lieu thereof".

Statutory amendments are treated in detail in Parts II, III, and IV of this Chapter.

Where Properly Used.—Amending existing law is the approach that is generally preferred for relating new law to existing law for it is the only approach by which a single, fully integrated text may be realized. The drafter should always seek to amend except in the special circumstances where the statutory construction ("do nothing") or override approach retains an advantage.

Advantages.—Amending existing law promotes cohesiveness and unity of the law and minimizes the opportunities for conflict among statutory provisions. It forces the drafter to find the right fit for a new policy within existing statutes and, therefore, aids the development of policy as well.

Disadvantages.—There are no major disadvantages to making statutory amendments except that it involves work—sometimes a great deal of work—but that is why we have professional legislative drafters! In addition, the method of amendment calls for the exercise of some judgment, as you will see in the more detailed explanation in Part II.

What Is the Role of Freestanding Language?

Freestanding Language Described.—Legislative language that does not amend a statute or a previously adopted resolution is referred to as "freestanding language". In other words, "freestanding" and "amendatory" cover the entire universe of possible ways in which legislative language may be displayed. Freestanding language never appears within quotation marks and may be found in any bill or resolution. *See* Figure 3-1.

Where Properly Used.—Freestanding language is appropriate for legislation (1) where the drafter has chosen to relate new law to existing law by either the statutory construction ("do nothing") or override approach, or (2) where the legislative provision has no bearing whatsoever to existing law, that is, where a completely new statutory or legislative regime or rule is being created. Not surprisingly, the early statutes of the United States were largely written as freestanding language and, as the number of totally new statutory regimes decreases over time, the number of statutory amendments will increase.

Examples of Freestanding Language.—Despite this trend toward statutory amendments, there continues to be a role for freestanding language in statutory writing. Time-limited statutes such as appropriations Acts, or subject-matter limited statutes such as country-specific foreign affairs statutes, consist almost entirely of freestanding language. In addition, nonbinding provisions and "housekeeping" provisions are almost always written in freestanding language. But it is wrong to say, as many on Capitol Hill do, that all bills are freestanding. On the contrary, the typical bill or joint resolution is a hybrid, containing both freestanding and amendatory language.

Part II: Statutory Amendments

Seven Basic Rules

There are seven basic rules for drafting statutory amendments, as follows:

Rule No. 1: Make the Law the Subject of the Sentence

It is the law being amended, not the words being amended, that should be the subject of the sentence. This contrasts with legislative amendments, where the amending action always appears first.

Note also that since statutes are not published with line numbers (and the United States Code is periodically republished, which would throw off any line reference), it is wrong to cite statutory provisions by page and line numbers.

Incorrect Example:

Strike "Secretary of State" and insert "Secretary of Defense" in section ___ of the ____ Act.

Correct Example:

Section ___ of the _____ Act is amended by striking "Secretary of State" and inserting "Secretary of Defense".

Rule No. 2: Amend the "True" Version of the Law

Amend only the authoritative, "true" version of the law, as found using the directions in Part IV of this Chapter. This is the primary legal citation for the amendment drafter. Secondary citations to less authoritative versions of the law may be inserted parenthetically after references to the "true" law.

Example:

Section 101(a)(15) of the Immigration and Nationality Act (8 U.S.C. 1101(a)(15)) is amended by _____.

Rule No. 3: Identify the Target Law with Specificity

The law that is the target of the amendment must be identified with sufficient specificity so that the reader may avoid having to search large amounts of verbiage for the targeted text.

Incorrect Example:

The _____ Act is amended by striking "Secretary of State" and inserting "Secretary of Defense".

Correct Example:

Section 2(a)(1)(A) of the _____ Act is amended by striking "Secretary of State" and inserting "Secretary of Defense".

Rule No. 4: Choose the Appropriate Method of Amending

A statutory amendment may be expressed either as a "cut and bite" or as a "restatement", with each method having an advantage and disadvantage. *See* the relevant segments of this Part to determine how to choose between the methods.

Rule No. 5: Amend Punctuation and Connectors, if Necessary

Whenever making a statutory amendment would otherwise add redundant punctuation or connecting words such as "and" or "or" to a statute, thus creating a confusing text, the drafter needs to make adjustments in the amendment to avoid this and to "clean up" the changes being made.

The goal should always be to make the new language fit seamlessly into the existing law. Some drafters wrongly believe that this "clean up" is not their responsibility and will be taken care of by some unknown clerk whose job it is. There is no such person. It is beyond the authority or expertise of the Enrolling Clerk to "adjust" existing law, and it would violate the separation of powers doctrine for the President to do it. Under the Constitution, Congress is the exclusive law-writing branch of Government. Consequently, any clerical errors that are created by a statutory amendment must be corrected by that amendment or later by the enactment of a "corrections" bill or joint resolution.

Consider the following three most common situations in which punctuation or connectors require amending in a three-paragraph section:

Example of Adding to a Series:

Section _____ (a) of the _____ Act is amended—

(1) by striking "and" at the end of paragraph (2);

(2) by striking the period at the end of paragraph (3) and inserting "; and"; and

(3) by adding at the end the following new paragraph:

"(4) _____".

Example of Striking from a Series:

Section _____ (a) of the _____ Act is amended—

(1) in paragraph (1), by adding "and" at the end;

(2) in paragraph (2), by striking "; and" and inserting a period; and

(3) by striking paragraph (3).

Example of Inserting in a Series:

Section _____ (a) of the _____ Act is amended—

(1) by redesignating paragraph (3) as paragraph (4);

(2) by striking "and" at the end of paragraph (2); and

(3) by inserting after paragraph (2) the following:

"*(3) _____; and*".

Rule No. 6: Redesignate Provisions of Existing Law, if Necessary

The redesignation of provisions is required whenever a provision is inserted into, or struck from, any part of an existing statutory structure except at the very end. Where more than one provision is redesignated, "respectively" is added at the end of the redesignations to ensure that the new designations properly correspond to the old provisions.

Example:

Section ___ is amended —

(1) by striking subsection (a); and

(2) by redesignating subsections (b), (c), and (d) as subsections (a), (b), and (c), respectively.

Whenever a redesignation of one statutory provision occurs, the drafter should be vigilant to correct any cross-reference elsewhere in the legislation to the original designation. This is done by making a conforming amendment to each provision containing the cross-reference.

In the case of a redesignation of *sections*, an alternative is to "squeeze" the new section between the existing sections as a new section ___ A, but this should not be done unless (1) the number of cross-references are so great that to change them all would be too burdensome, or (2) there simply is not available an extra section number in the series of sections. The downside to this approach is that at a later time the new section may get overlooked.

Rule No. 7: Refer to the Amended Law in the Long Title

Whenever a statutory amendment is included in a bill, the long title of the bill should be modified to begin as follows: "To amend _____" [the blank to be filled in with the short title of the Act of Congress, or the number of the positive law title of the United States Code, being amended]. The reference to the targeted law serves to aid the Parliamentarian in referring the bill to the proper committee of jurisdiction. Consequently, when the drafter has a choice of laws to amend, the drafter's decision to amend a particular law may influence the bill's referral and should be made carefully, in close consultation with the bill's sponsor.

"Cut and Bite" Amendments

In General. — "Cut and bite" amendments strike, insert, or strike and insert only the particular words or phrases that are the targets of the amendments and nothing else.

Examples of "Cut and Bite" Amendments:

Section _____ of the _____ Act of 20__ is amended—

> *(1) by striking "_____";*

> *(2) by inserting "_____" after "_____"; and*

> *(3) by striking "_____" and inserting "_____".*

[OR]

Section _____ of title ____, United States Code, is amended—

> *(1) by striking "_____";*

> *(2) by inserting "_____" after "_____"; and*

> *(3) by striking "_____" and inserting "_____".*

Advantages of "Cut and Bite" Amendments. — "Cut and bite" amendments offer a couple of advantages that make this the preferred method of making statutory amendments. First, "cut and bite" amendments precisely highlight the text that is being amended. The reader has the chance to compare on a word-by-word basis how the proposed new language differs from the existing statutory language. Secondly, "cut and bite" amendments do not produce unintended consequences by rewriting words or phrases that are not the target of the amendments. Every statute is the embodiment of a political negotiation, overt or implied, and that political bargain is reopened when changes are made to the statute's text. To rewrite text where not strictly required runs the risk of incurring the opposition of the authors of the statute being amended.

Disadvantages of "Cut and Bite" Amendments. — The principal disadvantage of "cut and bite" amendments is readability. They require some brainpower to piece together how the new law will read. Consequently, although the change in individual words or phrases is highlighted, the overall change in legal effect is often obscured. This, unfortunately, contributes to the reputation of legislation as lacking transparency.

A second disadvantage of making "cut and bite" amendments is that they involve a fair amount of work, for each amendment requires the drafter to refer specifically to the provision of the existing statute that is the target of the amendment. The greater the number of amendments the more the drafter has to move back and forth between the amending legislation and the target statute, with all the inconvenience that entails.

"Restatement" Amendments

In General. — In contrast to "cut and bite" amendments, a "restatement" amendment rewrites a whole block of text, usually a section, subsection, paragraph, or other unit of the statute, or even merely a whole sentence. In a restatement amendment there is at least one word stricken that is reinserted by the amendment. A restatement amendment, therefore, reuses some of the same statutory text that it seeks to replace. To avoid the awkwardness of appearing to strike and reinsert the same unit of a statute, restatement amendments use the following language: "[Referenced provision of law or sentence] is amended to read as follows:".

Example of a Restatement Amendment:

Section ____ (a)(1) of the _____ Act of 20__ is amended to read as follows:

    "(1) _____

    _____

    _____.".*

Advantage of Restatement Amendments. — The advantage of restatement amendments is simply that they avoid the disadvantages of "cut and bite" amendments. They are easy to read and easy to make.

Disadvantages of Restatement Amendments. — Restatement amendments run the risk of reopening, unintentionally, the settled political bargains of legislators reflected in the statute that is the target of the amendment. This may mean that political fights already won must be refought. In addition, a restatement amendment buries the actual wording change in the restated text, thus leaving the reader totally unaware of what the precise change in the law is. In short, the ease of reading the new text is offset by a total lack of transparency in understanding the differences between the new law and the "old" law. So "transparency", it turns out, is a relative term and does not always equate with readability.

Where Properly Used. — As a consequence of its disadvantages, an amendment should only be framed as a restatement amendment if either of the following applies:

(1) When the changes to be made within a single section, subsection, paragraph, or other unit of the target text are so numerous that to make the changes as "cut and bite" amendments would be too burdensome.

(2) When there is a paramount political need to make the legislation highly readable or to bury the precise changes being made to the original statutory text.

Statutory Amendments vs. Repeals

A "repeal" is the term used to represent an amendment to strike an entire statute or a title or section of a statute. In addition, it is sometimes used to strike a subsection. Repeals must not, however, be used to strike individual words, phrases, sentences, or small units of text such as clauses or paragraphs. The term "repeal" should always be used in this technical sense and not as a description of an override.[8]

---

8. The use of "repeal" has not always been so limited, which prompted some courts to assert that "repeals by implication are not favored".

It is not the practice in the United States to repeal an Act solely to replace it with a similar, but rewritten, newer enactment. To repeal and replace is equivalent to making a sweeping restatement amendment whose readability, unfortunately, is far outweighed by the political cost involved in reenacting a previously enacted policy. Only where the prior law is so technically flawed or politically discredited should a repeal and a replacement be chosen over making statutory amendments revising the prior law.

Statutory Amendments vs. Legislative Amendments

So far we have seen that statutory amendments are very different animals than legislative amendments,[9] but the two kinds of amendments may overlap. A legislative amendment *may* make a statutory amendment, in which case the drafter faces the same choices as if the drafter had included the statutory amendment in the bill initially, that is, what version of the law to amend[10] and whether to make the amendment "cut and bite" or a restatement. (*See* Figure 3-2.)

Figure 3-2

Draft an "Amendment"!

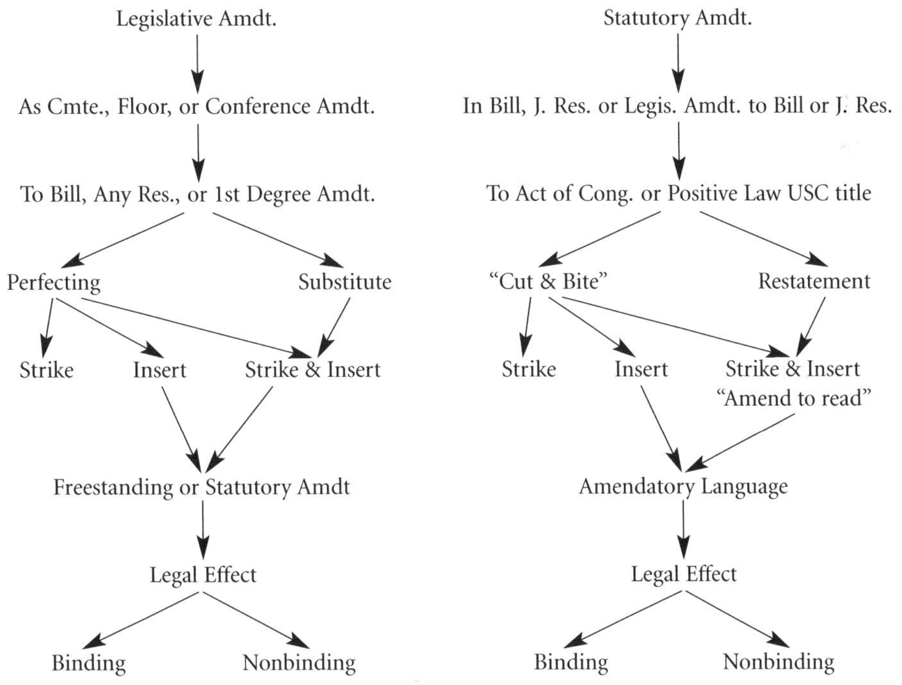

---

9. *See* Chapter Two, Part II, *supra*.
10. *See* Part IV of this Chapter, *infra*.

In short, the word "amendment" masks several possibilities. So, the next time a Member of Congress demands that you "draft an amendment" your reply should be "Would you be more specific, please?"

"Execution" of Statutory Amendments

The "Empty Shell" Concept. — An important legal transformation occurs once a statutory amendment is enacted and takes effect: the amendment is no longer considered part of the statute that carried the amendment into law. This leaves the provision of the statute that contained the amendment as an empty shell to which any further reference would be meaningless. Instead, the amendment is deemed "executed", and the text of the target statute is considered to have been rewritten in accordance with the directions of the amendment, as if by magic!

How Statutory Amendments Are Executed. — Where the target of the amendment is a provision of the United States Code, the execution of the amendment will be made by the Office of the Law Revision Counsel of the House of Representatives and changes made by the amendment will appear seamlessly in the next reprinting of the United States Code. Where the target of the amendment is an Act of Congress not reflected in the United States Code, the execution of the amendment is nothing more than a legal fiction since the amendment is never physically integrated in the earlier Act as it appears in the Statutes at Large. However, unofficial compilations of that Act, if any, may integrate the changes made by the amendment with the earlier text in order to give the reader a current, composite view of the Act.[11]

It follows from this that any attempt to repeal a provision that did not qualify for inclusion in the United States Code cannot "clean up" the statute books since the repeal would not actually result in the removal of the earlier provision. When a repeal is made, no Government functionary tears out a page from the statute books!

Legal Effect of a Repeal of a Repeal. — The "empty shell" concept has ramifications for both repeals and amendments to strike. A repeal of a repealer provision, or a strike of an amendment to strike, or any combination of the two, does not cause the restoration of the original text that was repealed or stricken, as the case may be. The reason is that the first repeal or first strike was "executed"; the first repealer or amendatory provision is effectively devoid of substantive content at the time of the second repeal or strike. The horse is already out of the barn!

---

11. Two publishers of unofficial compilations of uncodified Acts are congressional committees and lobbying firms. In the foreign affairs field, for example, the primary compilation is the multivolume *"Legislation on Foreign Relations"*, prepared by the Congressional Research Service of the Library of Congress under the auspices of the congressional foreign relations committees.

Part III: "Clean Up"; Transitions; Effective Dates

Introduction

Whenever a bill or joint resolution contains a statutory amendment, the drafter should consider whether or not the bill or resolution requires the addition of a specialized provision to make the amendment fully effective. Such specialty provisions may include any of the following:

- A "cleaning up" of related provisions of existing law.
- A transition from the earlier law to the later, newly amended law.
- An effective date different from the date of enactment.

Whether or not any such provision is necessary depends on the nature and timing of the statutory change desired. In this Part, therefore, let us see how these considerations influence a drafter's choice of (1) "clean up" provisions, (2) transition provisions, and (3) effective dates.

"Clean Up"

In General

Whenever a statutory amendment renames an agency or official position of the Government, substantially alters an existing statutory scheme, or simply redesignates a provision of law, it is like breaking eggs. There is a great deal of cleaning up to do. The "clean up" may be done by drafting a series of technical, clerical, or conforming amendments or occasionally by drafting a "references" provision, or both.

Technical, Clerical, and Conforming Amendments

In General. — Just as a legislative amendment to a bill may necessitate "clean up" amendments to that bill so, too, may an amendment to a statute require a technical, clerical, or conforming amendment to be made to that statute or another statute. While the terms "technical", "clerical", and "conforming" are not mutually exclusive, they tend to describe certain types of amendments, as follows:

Technical Amendments. — Although having the broadest meaning of the three terms — meaning anything nonsubstantive — the term "technical amendments", paradoxically, is used more narrowly to describe only nonsubstantive *corrections* to existing law.

Example:

(_) Technical Amendment. — Section 105 of title 1, United States Code, is amended by striking "June 30" and inserting "September 30". [Correcting an

obsolete reference to the ending date of a fiscal year as in effect before the change to the current system of October 1–September 30 fiscal years.]

Clerical Amendments.—Clerical amendments are typically amendments that change the table of contents of an Act of Congress, the table of chapters or sections of a positive law title of the United States Code, or any misspelling or other misprint in a statute.

Example 1:[12]

(_) Clerical Amendment.—The table of contents of the Immigration and Nationality Act is amended by inserting after the item relating to section 274A (as added by section 101(c)), the following new item:

"Sec. 274B. Unfair immigration-related employment practices.".

Example 2:[13]

(_) Clerical Amendment.—The table of chapters for part III of title 5, United States Code, is amended by adding at the end the following new items:

"Subpart J—Immigration Affairs Agency Personnel

"96. Personnel flexibilities relating to the Immigration Affairs Agency ... 9601.".

Conforming Amendments.—Conforming amendments are largely directed at changing references or cross-references in existing law in order to conform to a change made by a statutory amendment elsewhere in a bill. A conforming amendment may also make a substantive change in order to conform to a substantive statutory amendment. A single amendment to a statute may require scores of conforming amendments to existing law.

Examples:[14]

(b) Section 212 of the Foreign Relations Authorization Act, Fiscal Years 1992 and 1993 (22 U.S.C. 1475h) is amended—

(1) by striking "United States Information Agency" each place it appears and inserting "Department of State";

(2) in subsection (a), by inserting "for carrying out overseas public diplomacy functions" after "grants";

(3) in subsection (b)—

(A) by striking "a grant" the first time it appears and inserting "an overseas public diplomacy grant"; and

---

12. Section 102(c) of the Immigration Reform and Control Act of 1986 (Pub. L. 99-603).

13. Section 201(b) of S. 2444 of the 107th Congress (as introduced in the Senate).

14. Section 1355(b) of the Foreign Affairs Reform and Restructuring Act of 1998 (division G of Public Law 105-277), which made conforming amendments necessary to incorporate the functions of the United States Information Agency into those of the Department of State.

(B) in paragraph (1), by inserting "such" before "grant" the first place it appears;

(4) in subsection (c)(1), by inserting "overseas public diplomacy" before "grants";

(5) in subsection (c)(3), by inserting "such" before "grants"; and

(6) by striking subsection (d).

References in Law

Conforming Amendments Preferred. — The preferred method of changing obsolete references in law is to amend them using conforming amendments, as described above. Where all the conforming amendments address the same statute, the drafter should precede the amendments with the following provision, which enables the amendments to be made without repeated mentions of the target Act:

SEC.___. REFERENCES IN ACT.

Except as specifically otherwise provided, whenever in this Act an amendment or repeal is expressed as an amendment or repeal of a provision, the reference is deemed to be made to the _____ Act.

"References" Provisions. — A "references" provision creates a legal fiction, using such verbs as "to be deemed" or "to be considered", that all existing references to a certain matter now refer to something different. This is the "quick and dirty" alternative to drafting conforming amendments. When drafting time is short, or when existing references are too numerous or difficult to identify easily, a "references" provision is a Godsend to the drafter.

It is also a crutch that the drafter should only use as a last resort because a references provision presents all the disadvantages of the override approach of relating new law to existing law. By leaving unamended a multitude of references in the statute books, a references provision does nothing to alert an unaware reader who rummages through the older statutes that the references the reader is viewing are incorrect.

Despite these drawbacks, a references provision may serve as a useful stop-gap measure until the drafter has enough time to prepare conforming amendments for inclusion in a subsequent statute. The drafter may get a head start on this process by preparing the easy conforming amendments initially, together with a references provision to catch the rest of the references.

Example:

SEC.___. REFERENCES.

Except as otherwise provided in this Act, any reference before the effective date of this Act in any statute, reorganization plan, Executive order, regulation, agreement, determination, or other official document or proceeding to the Di-

rector of the United States Information Agency shall, on or after that date, be deemed to refer to the Secretary of State.

Transition Provisions

In General.—Whenever a law is repealed or significantly amended, a question arises as to whether additional provisions are required to transition from the earlier state of the law to the current law.[15] Transition provisions may include the following freestanding provisions with respect to the functions and assets of government officials and bodies under the targeted law:

(1) A transfer of functions.

(2) A transfer of personnel and other resources.

(3) Determinations with respect to the functions and resources transferred.

(4) Allocations of the resources transferred.

(5) Transitional funding.

(6) Savings provisions.

Of these provisions, the least customized and most like "boilerplate" are the savings provisions, which will be the focus of this segment.

Savings Provisions.—Savings provisions, popularly known as "grandfather" provisions, continue into effect the litigation, administrative actions, and other actions under the law as the law was in effect before being repealed or amended. The object of savings provisions is generally to mitigate against the unfairness that would occur if the break with the earlier law was immediate and complete, although some "grandfather" provisions are clearly nothing more than exemptions of special interests from newly instituted reforms.

Example of Savings Provisions:

SEC.___. SAVINGS PROVISIONS.

(a) Continuing Effect of Legal Documents.—*All orders, determinations, rules, regulations, permits, agreements, grants, contracts, certificates, licenses, regulations, privileges, and other administrative actions*—

(1) that have been issued, made, granted, or allowed to become effective by the President, any Federal agency or official thereof, or by a court of competent jurisdiction, in the performance of functions that are transferred under this Act, and

---

15. Transition provisions may be useful outside the context of statutory amendments. Whenever terms of office are being staggered, for example, a transition provision is initially required. *See, e.g.,* U.S. Const., art. I, §3, cl. 2, relating to the staggering of the terms of United States Senators.

(2) that are in effect at the time this Act takes effect, or were final before the effective date of this Act and are to become effective on or after the effective date of this Act,

shall continue in effect according to their terms until modified, terminated, superseded, set aside, or revoked in accordance with law by the President, the head of the [transferee agency] or other authorized official, a court of competent jurisdiction, or by operation of law.

(b) Proceedings Not Affected. —

(1) Pending Proceedings. — The provisions of this Act shall not affect any proceedings, including notices of proposed rulemaking, or any application for any license, permit, certificate, or financial assistance pending before [the transferor agency] at the time this Act takes effect, with respect to functions transferred by this Act but those proceedings and applications shall be continued.

(2) Orders. — Orders shall be issued in those proceedings, appeals shall be taken from those orders, and payments shall be made under those orders, as if this Act had not been enacted, and orders issued in any such proceeding shall continue in effect until modified, terminated, superseded, or revoked by a duly authorized official, by a court of competent jurisdiction, or by operation of law.

(3) Statutory Construction. — Nothing in this subsection prohibits the discontinuance or modification of any such proceeding under the same terms and conditions and to the same extent that the proceeding could have been discontinued or modified if this Act had not been enacted.

(c) Suits Not Affected. — The provisions of this Act do not affect suits begun before the effective date of this Act, and in all those suits, proceedings shall be had, appeals taken, and judgments rendered in the same manner and with the same effect as if this Act had not been enacted.

(d) Nonabatement of Actions. — No suit, action, or other proceeding begun by or against [the transferor agency], or by or against any individual in the official capacity of such individual as an officer of [the transferor agency], shall abate by reason of the enactment of this Act.

Effective Dates

In General. — Like any other legislative provision, a statutory amendment may be given an effective date that differs from the date of enactment. If the drafter wants the statutory amendment to take effect retroactively or on a delayed basis, the drafter must expressly so provide in a freestanding effective date provision.

Specific Referencing of Statutory Amendments. — Wherever statutory amendments are made by a bill containing a prospective or retroactive effective date, the effective date must reference the "amendments made by this Act", together with "this Act". Otherwise the statutory amendments would take effect by default on the date of enactment, a different date from that of the freestanding provisions of the Act. This is not likely to be the desired result.

> **Example.** — An example of an effective date section that references statutory amendments is the following:

> *SEC. 11. EFFECTIVE DATE.*

> *This Act, and the amendments made by this Act, take effect ___ days after its date of enactment.*

When to Use a Prospective Effective Date. — Whenever there is a need for a statutory amendment to take effect on a delayed basis, for whatever reason, a prospective effective date provision is required. Two situations that cry out for such a delay are (1) where the statutory amendment affects levels of appropriations or authorization of appropriations for a future fiscal year, and (2) where there is a need to allow executive branch officials sufficient time to carry out any transition provisions set forth in a statute.

> **Example:**

> *(_) The amendment made by section 5(a) takes effect on October 1, 20__.* [Note: The Federal fiscal year begins on October 1 of each year.]

When to Use a Retroactive Effective Date. — A retroactive effective date for a statutory amendment is necessary where the drafter seeks to bar any chance that a public official or private person might take steps to evade the policy contained in the amendment before it can take effect. In this situation, the effective date works to ensure that there is no transition; the provision "freezes" the legal landscape in place. A retroactive effective date is written using verbs of legal fiction such as "deemed" or "considered".

> **Example:**

> *(_) The amendment made by section 5(a) is deemed to have become effective on the date of enactment of the Illegal Immigration Reform and Immigrant Responsibility Act of 1996.* [Referencing the retroactive date of September 30, 1996 indirectly by citing the "date of enactment" of the prior Act.]

When No Effective Date Included. — If the legislation is silent and there is no effective date provision applicable to the statutory amendment, the presumption is that the statutory amendment is intended to take effect on the date of enactment of the bill or joint resolution.[16]

---

16. *See* Chapter Five, Part IV, *infra*, for a full explanation of the presumption.

Part IV: Finding the "True" Law to Amend

Introduction

There is no more vexing problem in Federal legislative drafting for the beginner or occasional drafter than finding the authoritative, "true" version of the law to amend.[17] This is due to the complexity of Federal law: Federal statutory law suffers from a double dichotomy; the law is split both in its layout in the statute books and in its legal status. Most American lawyers, heavily schooled in case law, are unaware of these distinctions, much to their detriment.

General Principle

The only legitimate target for a statutory amendment is an Act of Congress[18] or a positive law title of the United States Code.[19] Conversely, repealed Acts of Congress and the remainder of the United States Code may not be amended. A constant challenge to the would-be amender is to find an up-to-date statutory text of the "true" law. To do this, the amendment drafter needs to understand some basic terminology and the significance of the double split in Federal law.

Public Laws and Acts of Congress

Public Laws Described. — After a bill or joint resolution is enacted into law, the new Act of Congress is assigned a Public Law number consisting of both the number of the Congress and the numerical sequence of the enactment within that Congress.[20] The new Public Law is first printed as a separate document referred to as a "slip law" and then, when a sufficient number of Public Laws within a Congress have been enacted, bound together with those other laws in a new volume of the Statutes at Large. The new Public Law is usually cited by its short title (for example, the "Foreign As-

---

17. This problem applies not only to the drafting of statutory amendments but also to the cross referencing of existing law within a statute.

18. In most instances, the provision of the Act of Congress being amended will be a provision of a general and permanent nature. This is so because of the availability of alternatives to amending existing law, that is, the statutory construction and override approaches with respect to time-limited and subject matter-limited provisions. *See* Part I of this Chapter.

19. *See* this Part: Split Legal Status of the Code, *infra*, for a discussion of positive law titles.

20. The date of enactment of a bill or joint resolution will be the earliest of (1) the date of approval of the legislation by the President, (2) the date of expiration of the 10-day period (excluding Sundays) after the presentation of the legislation to the President, if the legislation remains on the President's desk, or (3) the date on which the second House of Congress overrides, by a two-thirds vote, any veto of the President.

sistance Act of 1961"). Its Public Law number or Statutes at Large citation may be provided as a secondary citation in parenthesis although a United States Code citation, when available, is preferable.

Act of Congress Defined. — An Act of Congress[21] is the freestanding text and the unexecuted statutory amendments[22] of any Public Law, plus any changes in the text of the Act made by later enacted statutory amendments, and is always cited by the short title of the Public Law in which the Act first appears, unless that short title is later amended.

How Acts of Congress Differ from Public Laws. — Every Public Law is an Act of Congress, but any Act of Congress may transcend the boundaries of the original Public Law that brought the Act of Congress to life. Unlike a Public Law, whose text remains as it was enacted, unchanged through eternity, an Act of Congress is a dynamic text, always evolving with each additional amendment. Because any Act of Congress may amend another Act, the text of every Act of Congress may be more or less than the text of the static Public Law in which the Act first appears.

The Effect of Executed Amendments. — When a later enacted Act of Congress amends an earlier enacted Act, the wording of the prior Act evolves and usually expands[23] beyond the text of the Public Law that brought the prior Act to life. At the very moment that the prior Act is expanding, the later Act is contracting since it has "executed" its statutory amendments and lost language. The text of the later Act is now less than the text of the Public Law that brought the later Act to life, consisting of the text of that Public Law minus its executed statutory amendments.[24] Occasionally, where a new Public Law is comprised solely of freestanding language and there are no further amendments, the texts of the new Public Law and the Act of Congress remain identical. Unfortunately, because of the omnipresence of those pesky statutory amendments, this is never true of major laws and even rarely true of many laws of lesser importance.

Citation of Acts of Congress. — For these reasons, the drafter is always wrong to insert "as amended", after the short title of an Act of Congress. An Act of Congress is always presumed to be the current legally effective text of the Act, that is, the Act *plus* all amendments made to the Act and *minus* all amendments executed by the Act to any prior statute. On the other hand, in the rare case where the drafter must make an historical reference to an Act before it was subsequently amended, the drafter

---

21. In some statutory provisions, a reference to an Act of Congress refers only to an enacted bill and thus requires enacted joint resolutions to be listed separately.

22. Amendments are unexecuted when there is an effective date linked to the amendments that has not yet been reached.

23. The text might contract if the amendments made by the later enacted Act were predominantly amendments to strike.

24. Because most statutory amendments are executed upon the date of enactment of the Act carrying the amendments, most Acts of Congress "lose" their amendatory language immediately.

should attach to the short title of the Act the phrase ", as in effect on _____," [the past date to be filled in].

Finding the Act of Congress Text. — In summary, the current wording of an Act of Congress may not exist in any single place but may have to be pieced together by reviewing all enactments later than the original Public Law in which the Act of Congress first appeared. This job is made easier by consulting the source note at the end of each prima facie law title of the United States Code, which lists all the subsequent enactments.[25]

The Statutes at Large

General Description. — The Statutes at Large is a series of statute books in which all the Public Laws are bound in the chronological order of their enactment. The Statutes at Large is a comprehensive collection containing all Public Laws dating back to the First Congress in 1789.

Revisions Not Made. — The Statutes at Large does not attempt to execute the various statutory amendments scattered throughout the Public Laws. In other words, no attempt is made to piece together the various amendments to achieve a single, revised text that would comprise an Act of Congress. Rather, the Statutes at Large is simply an historical record of each enactment. It is frequently the case, therefore, that two statutes on the same subject are separated in the Statutes at Large by many pages. Consequently, nothing is gained by reprinting the entire Statutes at Large. Like the accretion of sedimentary layers in the Grand Canyon, the Statutes at Large grows slowly, one new volume at a time.

The United States Code

General Description. — The United States Code is just a part, though an important part, of all Federal statutory law. (*See* Figure 3-3 on the next page.) The Code sets forth all the general and permanent laws of the United States[26] arranged by subject matter. The Code consists of 54 titles,[27] with each title dedicated to a major field of Federal law.

Provisions of Acts of Congress excluded from the Code include:

- Time-limited provisions such as appropriations.
- Subject matter-limited provisions such as country-specific foreign affairs provisions and "private" laws.
- Nonbinding provisions.
- Repealed provisions.

---

25. *See also* this Part, *infra*, "Value of Prima Facie Law Titles for Finding Acts of Congress".

26. The phrase "general and permanent laws of the United States", as used in the United States Code, does not include any provision of a treaty or Federal regulation.

27. Two of the titles are currently vacant.

Figure 3-3

The United States Code within Statutory Law

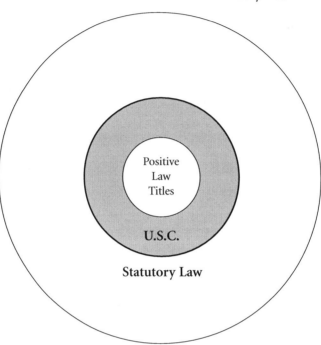

Positive
Law
Titles

U.S.C.

Statutory Law

Classification and Reenactment. — The arrangement of statutory provisions in the United States Code occurs in two stages. First, each eligible section of an Act of Congress is classified to the appropriate title and section of the Code. Later, each title of the Code will be revised, consolidated, codified, and reenacted by Congress. Currently, this latter stage is proceeding slowly and is not expected to be completed until a distant, unknown date.

Classification of Acts of Congress. — A classification to the Code usually involves dividing an Act of Congress by sections. First, provisions of a general and permanent nature are separated from subject matter-limited and time-limited provisions. Secondly, provisions of a general and permanent nature are divided by topic. So, for example, all immigration-related provisions will be classified to title 8 of the Code, all foreign affairs provisions will be classified to title 22, etc. It is not unusual for provisions in lengthy Acts of Congress or in Acts of Congress containing nongermane provisions to fall into several different titles of the Code.

Periodic Revisions of the Entire Code. — Because the general and permanent laws of the United States may be amended by an Act of Congress at anytime, the entire Code is subject to change and must be reprinted periodically. Since 1934, the entire Code has been reprinted every six years. In addition, the United States Code is annually updated by the publication of supplemental volumes that contain the changes made to all the titles of the Code during the previous year.[28] These changes are included in a restatement of the pertinent part of the Code.

Publication of the Code.—The Office of the Law Revision Counsel of the House of Representatives[29] prepares and publishes the United States Code. To perform its work, the Office will (1) review each provision of every Act of Congress to determine if the provision is of a general and permanent nature and what subject matter of law the provision addresses, (2) classify qualifying provisions to the Code, conforming the provisions to Code structure and style and making clerical corrections, and (3) prepare the reenactment bills described below.

Searching the Code Online.—Two of the best on-line Internet sites for searching the United States Code are the following: *www.congress.gov* and *http://uscode. house.gov.*

How the Code Differs from Acts of Congress

Different Structure.—The United States Code is organized by title, chapter, subchapter, and section in contrast to Acts of Congress that are organized mainly by sections but occasionally by titles and subtitles as well. This means that when a provision of an Act of Congress is classified to the Code, the cross-references in the provision will change. So, for example, a cross-reference in a provision of an Act of Congress to "this Act" may become a cross-reference in the Code to "this chapter". In addition, the section numbers in the Act of Congress are not likely to correspond to the section numbers in a title of the United States Code and this, too, will require a change in cross-references.

Different Style.—The United States Code also has a different style from Acts of Congress, especially in the style of headings. For example, in the preparation of title 50 of the Code, "§ 1702. **Presidential authorities**" was substituted for the Act of Congress heading "SEC. 203. PRESIDENTIAL AUTHORITIES.".[30] In addition, all subsection headings in the Code appear in lowercase boldface unlike in an Act of Congress where they appear in a combination of upper and lower-case Roman type.

Different Text.—The text of a Code provision *may* differ from its corresponding provision in an Act of Congress for any of several reasons. First, because incorporation in the Code requires a reprint of the original Act of Congress provision, the Code may contain clerical errors. Secondly, the Code may correct the clerical errors in the Act of Congress and provide an improved but divergent text. Thirdly, just before a title

---

28. An easier and more informative way to read the Code is through the United States Code Annotated (U.S.C.A.), whose numbering corresponds exactly with that of the Code.

29. The Office is headed by the Law Revision Counsel, who is a nonpartisan appointee of the Speaker of the House of Representatives.

30. Section 203 of the International Financial Institutions Act (50 U.S.C. 1702).

of the Code is reenacted, the House Law Revision Counsel may make further technical changes to improve the text.

Split Legal Status of the Code

In General.—A part of the United States Code duplicates Federal law found in the Acts of Congress and the Statutes at Large. The remainder of the United States Code, on the other hand, is an exclusive source of Federal law[31] not found elsewhere but in repealed, unusable Acts of Congress. What follows is an explanation of why this legal distinction is important.

Prima Facie Law Titles.—Slightly less than one-half of the United States Code titles[32] is merely prima facie evidence of the law. In other words, for purposes of citation before a court of law, there is a rebuttable presumption that the text in these titles is the law.[33] Each provision of a prima facie law title of the Code duplicates the text of a provision in an Act of Congress, subject to the minor differences noted above between Code provisions and Acts of Congress. *A drafter must never directly amend a prima facie title of the Code.* Instead, the statutory amendment should be made to the corresponding provision of an Act of Congress, which remains in effect. Among the prima facie law titles of the Code are titles 8 and 22 relating to immigration and foreign relations, respectively.

Positive Law Titles.—Slightly more than one-half of the United States Code titles[34] has a higher legal status than mere prima facie law. These titles are positive law, which means they are conclusive evidence of the law, authoritatively prescribed by government and suitable for citation before a court of law.[35] Positive law, derived from "posited", is distinguishable from natural law[36] or any unofficial source of law. *Statutory amendments to the Code may be made only to a positive law title of the Code.* An example of a positive law title of the Code is title 18 relating to Federal criminal law.

---

31. All Federal "general laws of permanent interest" enacted before December 1, 1873, were codified in the Revised Statutes of the United States (1875 edition), but because of numerous technical errors this codification was terminated. A section of the Revised Statutes (1875 edition), however, remains an exclusive source of Federal law where it has not been incorporated into the positive law portion of the United States Code.

32. Twenty-five titles as of this writing.

33. 1 U.S.C. § 204 (2012). The less than authoritative legal status of the prima facie law titles is understandable when one considers that the classification of Acts of Congress as prima facie law Code titles by the Office of the Law Revision Counsel, a subgroup of one House of Congress, does not meet the Constitutional standards for lawmaking. *See INS v. Chadha*, 462 U.S. 919 (1983).

34. Twenty-seven titles as of this writing.

35. 1 U.S.C. § 204 (2012). Positive law is sometimes referred to as "legal evidence" of the law.

36. *See,* Thomas Hobbes, *Leviathan, or the Matter, Forme & Power of a Common-Wealth Ecclesiastical and Civil* (1651), for an exposition of natural law and its distinction from positive law.

Identification of Code Titles by Legal Status.—A listing of each title of the United States Code that is positive law may be found at the end of section 204 of title 1 of the Code. For the current listing of both positive law and prima facie law titles, *see* Figure 3-4 on the next page.

Legal Status of Code Appendices.—Several positive law titles of the Code have an appendix or appendices. These appendices are, however, merely prima facie evidence of the law and may not be directly amended.[37]

Finding the Code Provision That Corresponds to an Act of Congress Provision.—When the drafter knows the short title of an Act of Congress, the drafter may easily find the corresponding citation in the United States Code for a provision of that Act by referring to the "Popular Names Table" at the end of title 50 of the United States Code, or in the "Popular Names Table" at the end of the United States Code Annotated (U.S.C.A.), where the short titles of Acts of Congress are listed alphabetically. Of the two tables, the USCA table is the more user-friendly because it is a cumulative, revised table while the USC table is divided between the table for the main volumes and for the annual supplements.

Congressional Goal.—United States Code law is in transition. The long-term goal of Congress is to revise and codify each prima facie law title as a positive law title of the Code. When that conversion is accomplished, all the general and permanent laws of the United States will be found entirely in the United States Code and not at all in the Statutes at Large. After that date, almost all statutory amendments will target only Code provisions. The way in which this conversion is accomplished is through the reenactment of the Code, title-by-title. (*See* Figure 3-5.)

The "Holding Pen".—Until reenactment occurs, the prima facie law titles may be imagined to exist in limbo in a "holding pen". Nevertheless, their presence in the Code provides a convenient reference tool for reading an integrated text of the various underlying Acts of Congress. While there are no strict guidelines to determine which prima facie title to reenact next, the prospect of cooperation from the Federal agency or agencies whose charter Acts are affected, together with a dearth of new legislation in the field during the reenactment process, are factors favoring the reenactment of a title.

Reenactment.—A prima facie law title becomes positive law upon the reenactment of the title by Congress. This occurs when there is enacted into law a bill that restates a "cleaned up" version of a prima facie law title, without making substantive changes to the Acts of Congress that underlie that title.[38]

---

37. Among the most useful appendices are those to title 5 of the United States Code, which include the Federal Advisory Committee Act and the Inspector General Act of 1978, which of course may be amended as Acts of Congress.

38. The "clean up" involves the revision and correction of the title to eliminate redundancies, contradictions, and ambiguities.

Figure 3-4

Titles of the United States Code

* This title has been enacted as positive law. However, any
Appendix to this title is not positive law.

*1. General Provisions.

2. The Congress.

*3. The President.

*4. Flag and Seal, Seat of Government, and the States.

*5. Government Organization and Employees; and Appendix.

6. Domestic Security.

7. Agriculture.

8. Aliens and Nationality.

*9. Arbitration.

*10. Armed Forces; and Appendix.

*11. Bankruptcy; and Appendix.

12. Banks and Banking.

*13. Census.

*14. Coast Guard.

15. Commerce and Trade.

16. Conservation.

*17. Copyrights.

*18. Crimes and Criminal Procedure; and Appendix.

19. Customs Duties.

20. Education.

21. Food and Drugs.

22. Foreign Relations and Intercourse.

*23. Highways.

24. Hospitals and Asylums.

25. Indians.

26. Internal Revenue Code; and Appendix.

27. Intoxicating Liquors.

*28. Judiciary and Judicial Procedure; and Appendix.

29. Labor.

30. Mineral Lands and Mining.

*31. Money and Finance.

*32. National Guard.

33. Navigation and Navigable Waters.

34. [Navy]. [Merged with title 10].

*35. Patents.

*36. Patriotic and National Observances, Ceremonies, and Organizations.

*37. Pay and Allowances of the Uniformed Services.

*38. Veterans' Benefits; and Appendix.

*39. Postal Service.

*40. Public Buildings, Property, and Works.

*41. Public Contracts.

42. The Public Health and Welfare.

43. Public Lands.

*44. Public Printing and Documents.

45. Railroads.

*46. Shipping; and Appendix.

47. Telegraphs, Telephones, and Radiotelegraphs.

48. Territories and Insular Possessions.

*49. Transportation.

50. War and National Defense; and Appendix.

*51. National and Commercial Space Programs.

52. Voting and Elections.

*54. National Park Service and Related Programs.

Figure 3-5

Reenactment as Positive Law

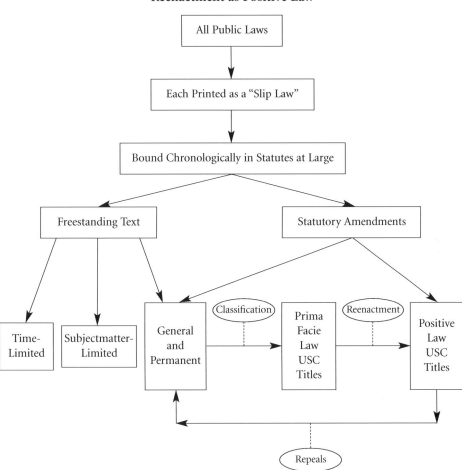

Preparation of Reenactment Bills. — The so-called "reenactment bill"[39] is prepared by the Office of the Law Revision Counsel of the House of Representatives. In preparing the bill, the Office revises and restates the prima facie law title by removing "ambiguities, contradictions, and imperfections".[40] Once prepared, the bill is introduced and referred to the Judiciary Committee of the House of Representatives. If the Judiciary Committee approves the bill, the Committee will report the bill to the House Calendar, where it continues its legislative journey like any other bill seeking to become law.

---

39. An example of a reenactment bill enacted into law was Public Law 111-314, approved on December 18, 2010, which established a new title 51 of the United States Code (relating to national and commercial space programs).

40. Section 101(1) of the Supplemental Appropriations Act (2 U.S.C. § 285b; Public Law 93-554).

Example of the First Section of a Reenactment Bill:[41]

That title 18 of the United States Code, entitled "Crimes and Criminal Procedure" is hereby revised, codified, and enacted into positive law, and may be cited as "Title 18, U.S.C., § _____", as follows:

[Text of title 18 inserted here].

Repeals. — Upon the enactment of a "reenactment" bill, the Acts of Congress (or the corresponding provisions of those Acts) underlying the new positive law title of the Code are repealed, making the new positive law title the sole source of the law on that subject matter. After repeal, it is error to make any cross-reference or direct amendment to the repealed provision.[42]

Value of Prima Facie Law Titles for Finding Acts of Congress

The disqualification of prima facie law titles of the Code as objects of direct amendment does not mean that those titles are without value to the amendment drafter.

First, United States Code citations for those titles may be used in legislative drafting as secondary citations. The following is a correct example of primary and secondary citations in a statute: *Section 101 of the Immigration and Nationality Act (8 U.S.C. 1101).*

Secondly, at the end of each section of a prima facie law title, there is a source note listing each Public Law section that comprises the text of the Code section. By researching the first Public Law listed, a drafter will find the Act of Congress that is the target of the drafter's amendment, including the short title of the Act and the original section numbers, cross-references, and printing style employed.

Thirdly and most importantly, a prima facie law title is highly readable as an integrated text, which enables the drafter to arrive quickly at the target text of an Act of Congress by working backwards and converting the section number, cross-references, and styling of the prima facie law provision to the corresponding section number, cross-references, and styling of a provision of an Act of Congress. This saves the drafter from having to stitch together multiple statutory amendments, scattered through a variety of Acts, to form a composite text of a single statutory provision.

---

41. Public Law 80-772; 62 Stat. 683.
42. *But see* Chapter Four, Part I: Short Title: Mistakes in Use, *infra*.

Test Your "Integrating" Skills

Drafting Exercise No. 3-A

For each of the following legislative proposals in Year 2, indicate which approach you would use to establish the relationship of the proposal to the existing law in Year 1:

Legislative Proposal No. 1:

Year 1 Law: The President is authorized to provide assistance to any African country.

Year 2 Proposed Legislation: No assistance may be provided to the Government of Sudan for the Fiscal Year 3.

Legislative Proposal No. 2:

Year 1 Law: No assistance may be provided to Sudan.

Year 2 Proposed Legislation: Humanitarian assistance may be provided to the victims of ethnic violence in Africa.

Legislative Proposal No. 3:

Year 1 Law: The President is authorized to provide humanitarian assistance to any country suffering from a natural disaster.

Year 2 Proposed Legislation: The President is authorized to provide humanitarian assistance to any country suffering from a natural disaster or ethnic strife.

Check your answers in Appendix C.

Drafting Exercise No. 3-B

Title 50 of the United States Code contains the following section and legal source note:

§ 1601. Termination of existing declared emergencies

(a) All powers and authorities possessed by the President, any other officer or employee of the Federal Government, or any Executive agency, as defined in section 105 of Title 5, as a result of the existence of any declaration of national emergency in effect on September 14, 1976 are terminated two years from September 14, 1976. Such termination shall not affect—

(1) any action taken or proceeding pending not finally concluded or determined on such date;

(2) any action or proceeding based on any act committed prior to such date; or

(3) any rights or duties that matured or penalties that were incurred prior to such date.

(b) For the purpose of this section, the words "any national emergency in effect" means a general declaration of emergency made by the President.

(Pub. L. 94-412,[43] Title I, § 101, Sept. 14, 1976, 90 Stat. 1255.)

Please draft a section to amend, correctly, the text to eliminate the "saving" in subsection (a)(3) of the rights, duties, and penalties before September 14, 1976.

Check your answer in Appendix C.

---

43. The short title of Public Law 94-412 is the "National Emergencies Act".

Chapter Four

How to Organize the Legislative Text

"The law is or should be treated as a science."[1]

Step Four: "Organize!"

Having drafted the intended legal effect, chosen the legislative vehicle, and drafted any overrides or statutory amendments, the drafter is now ready to prepare the layout of the legislation. This fourth step, "organization", is all about presentation and has become highly systematized since the advent of legislative drafting as a professional field. There is, however, still room for creativity, as this Chapter makes clear.

Legislative Organization, Generally

The System.—There is a system in Federal legislation that is generally accepted both for structuring bills and resolutions and for organizing each section. While there is no legal penalty for deviating from the system, its many benefits have made the system more widely accepted and applied today than ever before.

Purposes of the System.—The purposes of the system include all of the following:

(1) **Readability.**—To promote the readability of the text by labeling and designating legislative provisions.

(2) **Amendability.**—To facilitate the drafting of legislative and statutory amendments by designating each provision of the targeted text so that it may be easily identified.

(3) **Ease of Reference.**—To make a statute usable as an easy reference tool through the creation of a standard, uniform arrangement of sections.

(4) **Policy Development.**—To encourage the filling in of gaps in legislative policy by requiring the logical sequencing and grouping of provisions.

---

1. John Bassett Moore, *Foreword to the Office of the Legislative Counsel*, 29 Colum. L. Rev. 379 (1929).

Part I: Organizing a Bill

Subpart A: "Simple Bills"

Organizing a "Simple Bill"

A "simple bill"[2] is a bill that addresses a cohesive subject matter and is relatively short, ordinarily less than 20 pages. The text of a simple bill takes a basic structure comprised solely of sections and excluding titles or other larger units of organization.

The typical simple bill consists of several numbered sections with each section serving a unique function and arranged in a predictable sequence. The functions progress through the legislation much as one finds in any well organized writing, with a distinct beginning, middle, and end. (*See* Figure 4-1.) Each function, in turn, determines the type of legislative language that is appropriate for the section. What follows is a description of the function and language of each section in the order of its appearance in a simple bill:

Short Title

Function. — The first section (always designated "**SECTION 1.**") is usually a short title, which serves both as a legal citation and as a popular name for the statute. Unlike the long (or "official") title, the short title is not required to reflect the purpose of the statute. Accordingly, the wording of a short title is usually driven by the political needs of the bill's sponsor, who is preoccupied with "marketing" the bill. In making that choice, the sponsor will most likely want to express the short title in an unobjectionable, appealing way that will enable the sponsor to characterize any opposition to the bill as unreasonable.

Language. — A short title of a bill never uses the word "Bill" but uses "Act" or, sometimes, in the case of a bill proposing statutory amendments, "Act Amendments". In addition, the modern trend is to insert a reference to the year of enactment after "Act". Occasionally, a clever drafter will devise a short title that creates an acronym to shorten further the short title! For example, note the acronym within the following short title: *The Support East European Democracy (SEED) Act of 1989.* Popularly, this Act is referred to as the "SEED Act".

Location of Section. — Short titles did not exist in early statutes. Later, short titles were located as the last section of the bill or statute. This was hardly the best place to market or popularize a bill. Today, short titles are uniformly made the first section

---

2. The author's term.

Figure 4-1

Organization of a "Simple Bill"

SECTION 1. SHORT TITLE.

SEC. 2. CONGRESSIONAL FINDINGS.

SEC. 3. PURPOSE.

SEC. 4. DEFINITIONS.

SEC. 5. [GENERAL AUTHORITY].

      (a) [General Rule].—

      (b) [Exception].—

SEC. 6. [LIMITATIONS].

      (a) [Prohibition] [or] [Restriction].—

      (b) [Exception]

      (c) [Waiver]

SEC. 7. [ADMINISTRATIVE PROVISIONS].

      (a) [Reporting Requirements]

      (b) [Special audits][?]

      (c) [Powers][?]

SEC. 8. SENSE OF CONGRESS.

SEC. 9. AUTHORIZATION OF APPROPRIATIONS.

SEC. 10. EFFECTIVE DATE[?] or TERMINATION DATE[?].

---

except in the case of appropriations Acts where they remain anachronistically—to the chagrin of the professional drafter—as the last section.

Mistakes in Use.—The popularity that a short title attains may become so great that the demand for the short title continues even after the codification of the statute and the repeal of the underlying statute such as the "Freedom of Information Act" (codified in 5 USC 552). It is, however, technically wrong to cite a short title of an Act of Congress that has been codified. If the short title must be used in such a case, the citation should be set forth as follows: *section 552 of title 5, United States Code (also known as the "Freedom of Information Act").*

Another mistake is to include a short title in a bill that consists entirely of statutory amendments. This is technically unnecessary and useless since once the amendments are executed what remains will be an "empty shell" to which no further citation may be made.

Example.—An example of a short title section is the following:

SECTION 1. SHORT TITLE.

This Act may be cited as the "_____ Act of 20__". [Fill in the second blank with the year of enactment.]

Congressional Findings

Description. — A "congressional findings" section (also known as a "findings" section) is a recitation of the facts that support the enactment of the bill.[3]

Function. — Congressional findings play a role in bills analogous to that of preambles in resolutions, but, unlike preambles, findings are part of the text. At their best, a few short findings may help to explain the need for the bill by providing useful background information.

Courts rarely resort to congressional findings to construe statutes.[4] This is so because findings, in describing a policy "problem", tend not to shed any light on the goals of a bill. Nor may they "cure" an unconstitutional remedy chosen by Congress.[5] Findings reflect the general motivations of the legislators, not specific legislative purposes.

Language. — Findings may be written in any tense but should never express the imperative, permissive, or hortatory moods. Rather, this is the one place in the bill where narrative-type language is acceptable.

Deference to Bill Sponsors. — Because of the limited legal value of findings, the wording may be largely left to the policymakers. This is advantageous since the findings section, like the short title, helps to market the bill. Legislative drafters who attempt to demonstrate their creative writing skills by rewriting findings do so at their peril. There is hardly anything more likely to annoy the drafter's political client.

Misuse of Findings. — The only danger with findings is their overuse. The more findings that are included the greater the likelihood of factual errors. This is particularly so where statistics are employed that require continual updating. There are other means by which a legislator may make findings of fact, including floor statements, committee reports, and press releases. Including in a bill too many findings puts the reader in the position of consuming too many appetizers before the entrée arrives!

Example. — An example of a congressional findings section is the following:

---

3. In the case of a joint, concurrent, or simple resolution, the role of the findings section is performed by the preamble. The inclusion in a resolution of a preamble is optional with the drafter. *See* Chapter Two, Part I.

4. *But see* Chapter Five, Part IV.

5. "When Congress finds that a problem exists, we must give that finding due deference; but Congress may not choose an unconstitutional remedy.", *Citizens United* v. *Federal Election Commission*, 558 U.S. 50, 95 (2010).

SEC. 2. CONGRESSIONAL FINDINGS.

> *Congress makes the following findings:*
>
>> *(1)* _____*.*
>>
>> *(2)* _____*.*
>>
>> *(3)* _____*.*

Purpose

Description.—The "purpose" (or "purposes") section expresses the goals or objectives of the bill. In other words, a purpose section is the aspirational section of a bill.

Function.—A purpose section serves the important functions of both narrowing the scope of a bill and providing a useful cross-reference ("the purposes of this Act") to shorten later provisions in the bill such as general authorities, reporting requirements, and authorization of appropriations.

Language.—A purpose section should be written in the self-executing language of the present tense.

Since the long title must state the purposes of a bill, the wording of a purpose section may parallel the long title. The need for brevity that applies to long titles, however, does not apply here, and where the opportunity presents itself the drafter is well advised to make the purposes section a greater elaboration on the goals of the bill than is found in the long title. This is particularly true where the long title is unable to state all the goals of the bill and uses the catchall phrase "and for other purposes". It is never appropriate to use that catchall phrase in the section. Instead, the purposes should be specifically stated.

Mistake in Use.—Elaboration of purposes should not result in referencing the specific duties, delegations, and rights conferred by the bill. The specific actions called for by a bill should not be merged with its goals.

Example.—An example of a purposes section is the following:

SEC. 3. PURPOSES.

> *The purposes of this Act are—*
>
>> *(1) to meet the humanitarian needs of Haitians; and*
>>
>> *(2) to promote sustainable development in Haiti.*

Definitions

Function.—The definitions section is arguably the most important section of a bill because the legal scope of the bill depends on the meanings given to its key terms. A term is eligible for inclusion in a definitions section if the term appears in two or more sections of the bill. Otherwise, the definition of the term should be made in the section where the term is found.

A word or phrase should be defined if either of the following applies:

(1) **Where a Specialized Meaning is Intended.** — Whenever the word or phrase is intended to have a more specialized meaning than its plain, dictionary meaning, the word or phrase should be defined.

(2) **Where Word Economy is Sought.** — Whenever a group of words, such as the title of an official or government body, is used repeatedly and may be shortened, however minimally, a definition is required. In addition, a definition is useful even where the term appears just once if the use of the term would significantly shorten a sentence.

Language. — A definition section employs "housekeeping" wording, usually "means", but occasionally "includes" where only an illustrative meaning is available.

Definitions themselves may be shortened by the inclusion of defined terms.

Definitions should be listed in alphabetical order for ease of reference.

Location of Section. — The modern practice is to locate the definitions section immediately before the substantive legal sections, which confer duties, delegations, or rights. This makes it convenient for the reader to learn the definitions before encountering the substantive law.

Historically, however, most definitions sections were located at the end or very near the end of the bill or statute. This proved unwise because it was not always evident to the reader that there were defined terms and because, in long statutes bound together in a statute book, it was difficult to find the end of the statute. Nevertheless, the practice of placing definitions at the end persists in the legislation of some foreign countries.

Mistakes in Using Definitions. — For a description of the many types of mistakes that may be made with definitions, *see* Chapter Five, Part II.

Definitions Incorporated by Reference. — Not all definitions require original wording. Where a suitable definition exists in another statute, and where the definition is long, it makes no sense to repeat the entire definition in the new bill. Rather, the drafter should insert the following phrase in the definitions section: *The term "_____" has the same meaning given the term in section _____ of _____ [Act] [USC title].*

Example. — An example of a definitions section, illustrating three ways of expressing a definition, is the following:

SEC. 4. DEFINITIONS.

In this Act:

(1) [Term]. — The term "_____" means _____.

(2) [Term]. — The term "_____" includes _____.

(3) [Term]. — The term "_____" has the same meaning given the term in section _____ of _____. [complete the last blank with an Act of Congress or United States Code positive law title].

General Authority

Function. — General authority is the generic description for a section or sections that set forth all duties, delegations, and entitlements carrying out the primary purposes of the bill. Whenever a section establishes a governmental entity or position, that, too, would be considered a general authority and located at this place in the bill.

Language. — Accordingly, general authority provisions are the legally substantive provisions at the heart of the bill and may use the entire range of binding language except for housekeeping language. Exceptions to general authority, however, are best written in the indicative mood.

Distinguished from Other Provisions. — While seemingly as important to the bill as general authorities, certain specialized provisions using binding language are always kept apart from general authorities. These include any legislative oversight, administrative, or funding provision.

It is especially tempting, but wrong, to combine a general authority with a funding provision. The reason for this may be found in the need to provide new funding every year or two without jeopardizing the "permanent" legal authorities.

Organization of Section. — A general authority section or sections accords each duty, delegation, or entitlement its own provision. Any exemption, waiver, or override is also drafted as a separate provision within a general authority section. By ensuring that each sentence seeks to achieve not more than one legal effect, readability is enhanced. In addition, whenever a general rule is followed by an exception (also known as an "exemption"), a reference should be made in each provision to the other provision to ensure that both provisions are read together.

Mistake in Use. — A common mistake made is to merge a general authority with a definition. Definitions should never include legal authorities. A warning that this has happened is when the definition appears to define a verb and not a noun.

Generic Heading Not Used. — "General Authority" is seldom used as a section heading; each section heading, instead, should reflect the particular legal operation of that section.

Example. — An example of a general authorities section is the following:

SEC. 5. AUTHORITIES OF THE SECRETARY OF STATE.

(a) In General. — Except as provided in subsection (b), and subject to subsection (c), the Secretary of State may _____.

(b) Exception. — Subsection (a) does not apply to _____.

(c) Waiver. — The Secretary may waive the application of subsection (a) if the Secretary determines _____ .

Limitations

Prohibitions and Restrictions. — A "limitation" is a provision that either prohibits or restricts an activity. A "prohibition", popularly known as a "sanction" or "bar", blocks an activity entirely. A "restriction" differs from a prohibition in that a restriction couples a prohibition on an activity with a condition, either precedent or subsequent, using such words as "if", "unless", or "until" to introduce the conditional phrase.

Function. — Like a definition or an exception, a limitation is an important device for narrowing the scope of a statute. A section on limitations is particularly necessary where the activity being limited is authorized by more than one section. Consequently, limitations always follow general authorities and form part of the substantive core of a bill.

Language. — Language used in drafting a prohibition typically employs "shall not", "may not", or "none of". A limitation may also be expressed as an override by the introductory phrase "Notwithstanding section _____," or as a separate sentence stating that the provision "supersedes section _____", with the blanks filled in with a citation to the provision that is being overridden. Overrides must be used sparingly,[6] primarily where what is being overridden appears in more than one section.

Distinguished from Exceptions. — Where the proposed limitation relates to only one section, however, a question arises as to whether, instead of a limitation, an "exception" is required. Where the provision simply negates the general authority with respect to a particular activity, then an exception is called for. Where, on the other hand, the provision denies benefits under a general authority to a class of recipients, a prohibition would seem more appropriate. The drafting decision here may call for the exercise of judgment.

Example No. 1. — An example of a limitation section is the following section 6:

SEC. 5. AUTHORIZATION OF ASSISTANCE.

The President is authorized to provide assistance for Yemen.

SEC. 6. PROHIBITION.

Notwithstanding section 5, the President may not provide assistance to any terrorist organization.

Example No. 2. — In contrast, an example of an exception is the following section 5(b):

---

6. *See also* Chapter Three, Part I, *supra.*

SEC. 5. AUTHORIZATION OF ASSISTANCE.

(a) In General. — Except as provided in subsection (b), the President is authorized to provide assistance to religious charitable organizations in the Middle East.

(b) Exception. — Subsection (a) does not authorize the furnishing of food assistance.

Administrative Provisions

Function. — Administrative provision is the generic description of any section that sets forth a duty or other authority incidental to the administration of a general authority.

Legislative Oversight Provisions. — Among these authorities is any provision by which Congress maintains oversight of the executive branch's implementation of the statute, in other words, a legislative oversight provision. Legislative oversight provisions impose duties on executive branch officials to provide information to Congress[7] and, consequently, almost always employ mandatory language.

Mistake in Use. — A mistake commonly made with administrative provisions is to include them in a general authority section. Although both types of provisions use binding language, and an administrative provision is a type of authority, it is best to keep the minutiae of the administrative provisions from cluttering up the more important general authorities.

Common Administrative Provisions. — The following are several common types of administrative provisions:

Reporting Requirements

In General. — Requiring an executive branch official to prepare and transmit to Congress a report on a matter of public policy is the most common type of legislative oversight provision. While the requirement may be burdensome, and the report may not be read, a reporting requirement is a useful tool to hold the executive branch accountable as it forces an official to "go on the record".

Contents. — Every reporting requirement includes the following:

(1) **A Deadline for Submission.** — For a one-time report, a date fixed to the date of enactment, or a calendar date. For a periodic report, a date beginning at an interval after the date of enactment and at specified intervals of time thereafter.

---

7. The President has an "executive privilege" to withhold information, based in part on the separation of powers doctrine, but the privilege is not absolute and is subject to a balancing of the interests of the branches of Government. *See United States v. Nixon*, 418 U.S. 683 (1974).

(2) **An Appropriate Sender.**—The President or a Federal agency head, as appropriate.

(3) **An Appropriate Recipient.**—A choice between Congress as a whole,[8] the congressional leadership,[9] or congressional committees. Where referral of the report within Congress might be in doubt, congressional committees are the best choice. A useful drafting shorthand is to define the term "appropriate congressional committees" to mean the recipient committees.

(4) **Transmittal Language.**—Use the verb "submit", which implies a written report, and avoid "shall report", which may be oral.

(5) **Contents.**—Use descriptive verbs and avoid calling for a "report on" a subject, which does not describe the actual requirement.

Example of a Reporting Requirements Provision:

SEC. 7. REPORTS.

(a) One-Time Report.—Not later than ___ days after the date of enactment of this Act, the Secretary of State shall submit to the appropriate congressional committees a report describing _____.

(b) Periodic Reports.—Beginning ____ days after the date of enactment of this Act, and every ____ days thereafter, the Secretary of Defense shall submit to the appropriate congressional committees a report describing _____.

Special Audits

Where Properly Used.—Another legislative oversight provision is a requirement for the Comptroller General, who heads the Government Accountability Office (GAO), an arm of the Legislative Branch, to conduct a special investigation and audit of a Federal program. This provision is only necessary where an inspector general[10] within a Federal "establishment" has not performed a financial audit or evaluation sought by Congress or where Congress does not trust the executive branch to audit or evaluate a particular program that it administers. In most cases, Congress will want a performance audit, rather than a financial audit, of a Federal program.

Example of Special Audit Provision:

SEC. 7. AUDIT BY THE GOVERNMENT ACCOUNTABILITY OFFICE (GAO).

(a) Definitions.—In this section:

(1) The term "appropriate congressional committees" means—

---

8. The constitutionally-recognized officers of Congress are the Speaker of the House of Representatives and the President and President *pro tempore* of the Senate.

9. The congressional leadership consists, at a minimum, of the constitutionally-recognized officers of Congress, plus the Majority and Minority Leaders of each House of Congress.

10. Appointed under the Inspector General Act of 1978 (5 U.S.C. App. 3).

(A) the Committee on _____ of the Senate; and

(B) the Committee on _____ of the House of Representatives.

(2) The term "Comptroller General" means the Comptroller General of the United States.

(b) In General. — The Comptroller General shall conduct in accordance with generally acceptable accounting principles an audit of _____.

(c) Access to Papers, Things, and Property. — The representatives of the Government Accountability Office shall have access to all books, accounts, records, reports, files, and all other papers, things, or property pertaining to such expenditure and necessary to facilitate the audit.

(d) Report. — Not later than _____, 20__, the Comptroller General shall submit to the appropriate congressional committees a report setting forth the findings of the audit.

"Powers" Provisions, Generally

Where Required. — Wherever general authorities include the establishment of a governmental entity or position, the administrative provisions must also include a "powers" section, which enumerates the ministerial powers that are being *authorized* for the entity or the official occupying the position. Accordingly, "powers" provisions are necessarily discretionary and use authorizing language. Such powers may include the power to hold hearings, subpoena documents and witnesses, appoint and compensate personnel,[11] allow travel expenses, hire consultants, lease vehicles, exercise the postal frank, and possess a Federal agency seal.

Example of Hearings and Subpoena Provisions:

SEC. 7. POWERS OF_____.

(a) Hearings. — The _____ may hold such hearings and sit and act at such times and places, take such testimony, receive such evidence, and administer such oaths as may be necessary to carry out the purposes of this Act.

(b) Subpoenas. —

(1) In general. — The _____ may require, by subpoena or otherwise, the attendance and testimony of such witnesses and the production of such books, records, correspondence, memoranda, papers, and documents, as the _____ may determine advisable.

(2) Enforcement. — In the case of contumacy or failure to obey a subpoena issued under paragraph (1), the United States district court for the judicial district in which the subpoenaed person resides, is served, or may be found,

---

11. *See* the follow-on segment entitled "Hiring and Compensation of Government Personnel" for a discussion of these types of provisions.

or where the subpoena is returnable, may issue an order requiring such person to appear at any designated place to testify or to produce documentary or other evidence. Any failure to obey the order of the court may be punished by the court as a contempt of that court.

[Fill in the blanks with the appropriate Government body]

"Powers" Provisions: The Appointment and Compensation of Government Personnel

In General. — The typical bill generally does not require specific "powers" provisions to provide for the hiring and compensation of Government personnel to implement the bill's provisions.

Exceptions. — The general rule stated above does not apply to the following situations:

Establishment of a New Federal Agency. — Whenever a bill establishes a new department or agency of the Federal Government, the bill must confer upon the agency head the authority to appoint and compensate personnel.

High-Level Political Appointees. — Whenever a bill provides for a Presidential appointment to be made, "by and with the advice and consent of the Senate",[12] the compensation of that officer must be expressly provided in the bill.

Example:

[Principal officer's title] shall be compensated at an annual rate of basic pay payable to individuals occupying positions at level III of the Executive Schedule under section 5314 of title 5, United States Code.

Alternative (preferred):

Section 5314 of title 5, United States Code, is amended by adding at the end the following:

"[Principal officer's title].".

Exemption from Civil Service Hiring Rules. — Whenever the appointment of Government personnel is sought to be exempted from otherwise applicable Civil Service rules, the special treatment must be expressly provided in the bill.

Example:

(_) Appointment and Compensation. — The [head official] may appoint and fix the compensation of such personnel as may be necessary to enable the [Government entity] to carry out its functions, without regard to the

---

12. This is the requirement of Senate confirmation, a necessary precondition to the appointment of any principal officer of the United States. U.S. Const., art. I, §2, cl. 2.

provisions of title 5, United States Code, governing appointments in the competitive service, and without regard to the provisions of chapter 51 and subchapter III of chapter 53 of such title relating to classification and General Schedule pay rates, except that no rate of pay fixed under this subsection may exceed the equivalent of that payable for a position at level __ of the Executive Schedule under section 53__ of title 5, United States Code.

Special Travel Expenses; Special Consultant Services. — Whenever the intent is to allow travel expenses and a "per diem in lieu of subsistence" at a higher rate than applicable under existing law, or whenever the intent is to pay consultants at a higher rate than applicable under existing law, then the bill must expressly so provide.

Examples:

(_) Travel Expenses. — The officers and employees of the [agency] shall be allowed travel expenses, including per diem in lieu of subsistence, in the same manner as persons employed intermittently in the Government service are allowed expenses under section 5703(b) of title 5, United States Code.

(_) Consultant Authority. — To carry out _____, the [agency head] is authorized to procure the services of experts and consultants in accordance with section 3109 of title 5, United States Code, but at rates not to exceed the daily rate paid a person occupying a position at level IV of the Executive Schedule under section 5315 of title 5, United States Code.

Sense of Congress

Function. — The substantive core of the bill behind us, it is now appropriate to consider the inclusion of any nonbinding expression of policy. In an oft-derided term, this section is referred to as a "Sense of Congress" provision. Ideally, the sense of Congress relates to the subject matter of the bill but not always. Congress has an insatiable need to express its sentiments and does not always care if those sentiments are germane to the bill.

Language. — In any event, a "sense of Congress" is always a nonbinding expression. This is called for (1) where a binding statement would otherwise lie outside the legislative jurisdiction of Congress and would violate the separation of powers doctrine or the Federal-State allocation of powers, or (2) where Congress, for political reasons, chooses not to bind the Executive. To ensure that a "Sense of Congress" section is nonbinding, the language of the section almost always uses the hortatory helping verb "should". Although it would seem unnecessary, it is customary to begin these sentences with the phrase "It is the sense of Congress". Note also that "sense" provisions may also be labeled as "statements of policy".

Mistake of Referring to a Single House of Congress. — One of the most common mistakes made with this type of provision is for the House of Congress originating the bill to confine this "sense" language to an expression of that House alone. Occasionally, a legislative staff member believes that writing a "sense of the Senate" or "sense of the House of Representatives" provision will be more politically expedient than writing the broader-phrased provision. This tactic almost always backfires, as the excluded House will demand to know in conference committee why it was excluded and, in some conferences, it may be beyond the scope of the conference to broaden the language.

Mistake of Excessive Detail. — Another mistake, common to nonbinding expressions, is to write a provision in such detail that the policy expressed by Congress is guaranteed not to be fully carried out. For that reason, "sense of Congress" language is best expressed in general terms.

Example. — An example of a sense of Congress section is the following:

SEC. 8. SENSE OF CONGRESS.

It is the sense of Congress that the President should notify the Government of _____ of the opposition of the United States to _____.

Authorization of Appropriations

Function. — Whenever a statute mandates or authorizes any significant government activity, thereby adding to the duties or other responsibilities of Federal officials, the additional spending necessary will require a new appropriation[13] or the use of an existing appropriation. Before an appropriation may be enacted, however, House[14] and Senate[15] rules require the enactment of legal authority for the appropriation — in essence a two-tiered enactment system. An authorization of appropriations section, which provides both legal authority and a ceiling for the amount of the appropriation, satisfies the requirement for the first tier.

Where an existing appropriation is already available to cover the purposes of the additional spending, no authorization of appropriations section is necessary. This may require, however, that the existing appropriation be specifically authorized for the additional purposes. An example of a reauthorization of an existing appropriation is as follows: *Funds available to the Department of State shall be made available to pay the expenses of the Advisory Committee.*

Recipient of the Appropriations. — Appropriations are ordinarily made to a Federal department, agency, or other entity, not to a Federal official, except where legal authorities are vested soleiy in the President, in which case the appropriations are

---

13. U.S. Const., art. I, § 9, cl. 7 (requiring that no money may be drawn from the Treasury except pursuant to law).

14. Rule XXI(2) of the House of Representatives.

15. Rule XVI of the Standing Rules of the Senate.

made expressly to the President.[16] Consequently, the recipient of an authorization of appropriations must also be a Federal entity or the President, as the case may be.

Amount and Duration of the Appropriations. — Generally, an authorization of appropriations is made in a specific amount for a specific fiscal year. In order to facilitate readability, dollar amounts are always set forth in Arabic numerals and never spelled out. Occasionally, an indefinite appropriation is desired, effectively giving the Committees on Appropriations a blank check on arriving at an amount. This is done by substituting the phrase "such sums as may be necessary" for the actual amount.

Purpose of the Appropriations. — An authorization of appropriations must specify the purpose for which the appropriations would be made. In most bills, this is expressed by cross-referencing the "purposes of this Act". Where, however, the purposes of the Act are either not expressed or ill-defined, the authorization of appropriations is expressed as being made to carry out the "provisions of this Act".

"Carryover" Language Optional. — Generally, funds unobligated at the end of the fiscal year automatically revert to the general funds of the Treasury and are lost to the account to which originally appropriated.[17] To avoid this result, a drafter must add "carryover" language that authorizes the amount appropriated "to remain available until expended" ("no-year funds") or "through" the end of a later fiscal year, as the case may be.

Revolving Funds. — A way to circumvent the automatic reversion of miscellaneous receipts to the Treasury is to establish a revolving fund. A revolving fund is a mechanism that guarantees a stream of funding for a Government program without the need for an appropriation and, therefore, without the need for an authorization of appropriations. Because a revolving fund removes funds from the annual appropriations process, such a fund runs counter to the goals of the Congressional Budget Act of 1974 (2 U.S.C. 601 et seq.) and should rarely be drafted.

Example:

SEC.   . REVOLVING FUND.

    (a) Establishment. — There is established in the Treasury of the United States the _____ Fund, which shall be available without fiscal year limitation for the purposes of _____.

    (b) Amounts Credited. — The Fund shall be credited with —

        (1) such amounts as may be received under section _____;

---

16. An example of the exception is foreign assistance appropriations, which are made directly to the President in whom is statutorily vested the administration of the foreign assistance program.

17. 31 U.S.C. § 3302(b) (2012). *See also West Virginia Association of Community Health Centers, Inc. v. Heckler*, 734 F. 2d 1570, 1576 (D.C. Cir. 1984).

(2) interest or other receipts on the investments of the Fund; and

(3) such amounts as may be appropriated for the Fund.

Earmarks Possible but Disfavored. — While there is no legal or technical reason why an authorization of appropriations may not include an earmark, the Appropriations Committees of Congress do oppose their inclusion, arguing that earmarks set "floors" on spending and that only appropriations may include "floors",[18] authorizations being limited to "ceilings". Substituting "is authorized to be available for" for the earmark language "shall be available only for" should satisfy the appropriator's objections as the former phrase does not technically set aside funds.

Mistakes in Using Appropriations Language. — A provision making appropriations without an authorization or in excess of the authorized amount is subject to a point of order.[19] It is also error to combine an appropriation with an authorization of appropriations. House and Senate rules[20] effectively require that these two lawmaking acts occur in separate bills.

Example. — An example of an authorization of appropriations section is the following:

SEC. 9. AUTHORIZATION OF APPROPRIATIONS.

(a) In General. — There is authorized to be appropriated to the Department of Justice $_____ for the fiscal year 20___ to carry out the purposes of this Act.

[(b) Availability of Funds. — Amounts appropriated under subsection (a) are authorized to remain available until expended.] **[Optional]**

Effective Dates and Termination Dates

In General. — A bill may contain an effective date section, a termination date section, both sections, or neither section. The majority of bills do not require either section.

Function of Effective Dates. — An effective date section is necessary wherever the provisions of the bill are required to take effect on a date other than the date of enactment. The effective date may be either a prospective date or, where constitutionally permissible, a retroactive effective date. In all other cases, a legislative provision is strongly presumed to take effect on the date of its enactment.[21]

---

18. *See, e.g.,* 135 Cong. Rec. S1511-1524 (November 16, 1989). The logic of these arguments is to make the earmarking power the exclusive preserve of the Appropriations Committees.

19. *Supra* at notes 14 and 15.

20. *See, e.g.,* Rule XXI(2) of the House of Representatives and Rule XVI of the Standing Rules of the Senate.

21. *See* Chapter Five, Part IV, *infra,* for a full explanation of the presumption.

Function of Termination Dates. — A termination date section is required where the bill establishes a government body intended to be temporary or, rarely, when the duties, authorities, or rights established by the bill are to be extinguished on a specific date. A termination date is not necessary where a section of the bill will become obsolete through the natural carrying out of its terms. A single termination date section is also not advisable where the bill contains provisions requiring more than one deadline. In that latter case, each deadline should appear within the corresponding substantive provision.

Language of Effective and Termination Dates. — In drafting an effective date or termination date, the preferred language is the present tense, indicative mood, which exemplifies "housekeeping language". If statutory amendments are made by the bill, then the effective date should reference those amendments, together with "this Act".[22]

If the intent behind a termination date section is to terminate statutory amendments previously made, then those amendments need to be reversed by additional amendments or repeals in order for the termination to be effective. This is another example, if one is needed, that an amendment, once "executed", cannot be undone by nullifying the law that brought the amendment to life.

Common Mistakes. — The most common drafting mistake made with an effective date or termination date section is to include the section unnecessarily. A minor mistake with respect to termination date sections is to refer to them as "sunset" provisions. While colorful, "sunset" is a slightly less accurate description than "termination date".

Examples. — Examples of effective date and termination date sections are the following:

SEC. 11. EFFECTIVE DATE.

This Act, and the amendments made by this Act, take effect ____ days after its date of enactment.

SEC. 11. TERMINATION DATE.

The Commission shall terminate _____ days after the date on which the final report [described in section _____] is required to be submitted.

Subpart B: "Complex Bills"

Organizing a "Complex Bill"

In General. — A "complex bill"[23] is a bill that addresses a collection of loosely connected subjects, which tend to make the substantive core of the bill lengthy and un-

---

22. *See* Chapter Three, Part III, *supra,* for a full explanation of the relationship of statutory amendments to effective dates.

23. The author's term.

wieldy or require customized "housekeeping" provisions on a title-by-title basis. "Complex bills" may amount to hundreds of pages, but they also may be short. The hallmark of a complex bill is any bill comprised not only of sections but also of titles. (*See* Figure 4-2.)

Where Required.—A bill requires a complex structure whenever its general authorities may be subdivided into several common subject matters, loosely related to one another.

Subject Matter Groupings.—A common subject matter around which a title may be arranged in a complex bill includes any of the following:

Figure 4-2

Organization of a "Complex Bill"

SECTION 1. SHORT TITLE; TABLE OF CONTENTS.
       (a) Short Title. __
       (b) Table of Contents. __ The table of contents of this Act is as follows:

                  [INSERT TABLE ITEMS]

SEC. 2. CONGRESSIONAL FINDINGS.
SEC. 3. PURPOSES.
SEC. 4. DEFINITIONS.

          TITLE I—[FIRST SUBJECT MATTER]

SEC. 101. SHORT TITLE. [Title I Only]
SEC. 102. DEFINITIONS. [Title I Only]
SEC. 103. GENERAL AUTHORITY. [Title I Only]
SEC. 104. LIMITATIONS. [Title I Only]

          TITLE II—[SECOND SUBJECT MATTER]

          Subtitle A—[First Part of 2nd Subject Matter]

SEC. 201. SHORT TITLE. [Subtitle A Only]
SEC. 202. DEFINITIONS. [Subtitle A Only]
SEC. 203. GENERAL AUTHORITY. [Subtitle A Only]
SEC. 204. LIMITATIONS. [Subtitle A Only]

          Subtitle B—[Second Part of 2nd Subject Matter]

SEC. 211. SHORT TITLE. [Subtitle B Only]
SEC. 212. DEFINITIONS. [Subtitle B Only]
SEC. 213. GENERAL AUTHORITY. [Subtitle B Only]
SEC. 214. LIMITATIONS. [Subtitle B Only]

          TITLE III—GENERAL PROVISIONS.

SEC. 301. LIMITATIONS. [Both Titles I and II]
SEC. 302. REPORTING REQUIREMENTS. [Both Titles I and II]
SEC. 303. SENSE OF CONGRESS. [Both Titles I and II]
SEC. 304. AUTHORIZATION OF APPROPRIATIONS. [Both Titles I and II]
SEC. 305. EFFECTIVE DATE. [The Act and any amendments made by the Act]

• **Charter Acts.** — A "charter" (or "organic") Act, which provides the basic authorities of a Federal agency or program, to which several statutory amendments are being made.

• **Federal Agencies.** — A Federal department or agency whose programmatic or personnel authorities are being modified.

• **Federal Programs.** — A Federal program whose authorities are being modified.

• **Public Policy Issues.** — An issue of public policy not limited to a specific Federal program.[24]

• **Major Functions of the Bill.** — Any collection of administrative or transition provisions or any expedited procedures governing the consideration of future legislation.

Section Numbering. — In a complex bill, sections are arranged by title, and the content of each section is never duplicated. There is an accepted system for the numbering of sections in titles that begins title I with section 101, title II with section 201, and so forth. This has the double advantage of creating "gaps" that allow room for adding new sections to the title through the amendment process while also facilitating the search for particular sections by title and function, such as a "definitions" section.

Duplication of Overall Bill Structure Within a Title. — The organization of each title resembles that of a simple bill in miniature, that is, each title mimics the section labeling and sequencing of a simple bill but with the important difference that each section must relate only to the subject matter of that title, and all cross-references internal to the title will refer to "this title", not "this Act".

For example, a title may include its own short title, findings, purposes, definitions, and sense of Congress language if the content of those sections pertains only to the subject matter of the title. This raises the possibility that a particular provision of a complex bill may be cited by either of two short titles, one for the overall Act and one for the title — an undesirable drafting result but politically useful inasmuch as a legislator may take credit for "an Act", which in reality is only a title of an Act.

Treatment of Provisions Applying to More Than One Title. — Wherever a section applies to more than one title, the section must not be placed in a substantive title. The short title for the entire bill and the findings, purposes, and definitions should precede title I. The administrative provisions, general limitations, authorization of appropriations, and effective date or termination date provisions, when applicable to the entire bill, should comprise a final title, usually entitled "General Provisions". Occasionally, the effective date is given its own title.

---

24. In the foreign relations field, examples include groupings by region of the world, international organization, or a United States foreign policy issue such as nuclear nonproliferation.

Table of Contents Required.—Every complex bill requires a table of contents.[25] This contrasts with simple bills for which table of contents are optional. A table of contents is customarily bundled together with the short title of the overall bill within the same section, giving that section a dual function. The font size for lettering in the table of contents is reduced from that of the rest of the bill's text.

Omnibus, "Mega" Bills.—Occasionally, a complex bill spans totally unrelated subjects and amounts to hundreds of pages. This legislative monster is most likely to surface near the end of a session of Congress, when two or more very different bills may be bundled together into a single, omnibus "mega" bill to expedite their enactment. In that event, 10 titles covering sections 1 through 999 are insufficient to organize the voluminous legislative text. The correct drafting solution is to create "divisions", grouping the text of each major bill or comprehensive subject matter as a "division" and subdividing each division by titles. Each division is then designated A, B, C, etc., with the first section of division A designated as section 1001, the first section of division B as section 2001, etc., and subsequent sections numbered in the same manner as in a less complex bill consisting solely of titles.

Part II: Organizing a Section

Introduction

Sections are the building blocks of legislation, with each section performing a particular function. The exact content of a section, however, is not preordained. While the United States Code requires each section to "contain, as nearly as may be, a single proposition of enactment",[26] the vagueness of this standard permits the drafter a wide latitude of interpretation. Although performing only one function, a typical section sets forth more than one duty, delegation, entitlement, or internal rule, and each distinct legal effect must be kept separate within the section in order to promote readability. Proper section organization does exactly that.

Subdividing a Section

Subsets or Itemizations.—A section may be subdivided by either of the following two methods, or any combination of the two:

(1) **By Whole Sentences.**—In its entirety, forming neat subsets of whole sentences.

---

25. *See* Appendix B(3)(F), *infra*, for how to start a table of contents.
26. 1 U.S.C. § 104 (2012). There is no enforcement provision for a violation of section 104.

(2) **By Grammatical Clauses.** — In fragments, by itemizing the section's grammatical clauses.

Nomenclature of the Subdivisions of a Section. — A section is subdivided in descending order using alternating alphabetical and numerical designations, as follows:

Subsections: (a), (b), (c), etc.

Paragraphs: (1), (2), (3), etc.

Subparagraphs: (A), (B), (C), etc.

Clauses: (i), (ii), (iii), etc.

Subclauses: (I), (II), (III), etc.

The designation system in United States legislation is an arbitrary system that is useful only if applied consistently. Alternative systems may easily be imagined but the system described above has near universal acceptance in United States Federal legislative drafting. Treaty texts and the legislation of many parliamentary democracies, however, use different systems.[27]

"Noah's Ark Principle". — For each level of subdivision, there must be at least two items, meaning that if the drafter wishes a subsection (a), then the drafter must at least provide for a subsection (b), and so forth down the hierarchy of subdivisions.[28] The failure to designate at least a second item in a level of hierarchy means that subdivision at that level is not possible and that the expression should remain with the next higher level of the hierarchy. This basic principle of subdivision seems to elude many novice drafters who insist on stranding a single subsection, paragraph, subparagraph, or clause without a partner. For this reason the author refers to the concept as the "Noah's Ark Principle" of section organization in an attempt to shame the drafter into compliance, but of course Noah would object as there may be more than two items at any one level!

Example of Incorrect Organization:

SEC.___. NATIONAL INTELLIGENCE ADVISORY COMMITTEE.

(a) Establishment. — There is established the National Intelligence Advisory Committee.

(1) Inapplicability of the Federal Advisory Committee Act. — The Federal Advisory Committee Act shall not apply to the Committee.

(b) Responsibilities. — The Committee may advise the President regarding United States intelligence activities.

Example of Correct Organization:

SEC.___. NATIONAL INTELLIGENCE ADVISORY COMMITTEE.

(a) Establishment. __

---

27. In many countries the system is as follows: Subsections: (1), (2), (3), etc.; Paragraphs: (a), (b), (c), etc.; Subparagraphs: (i), (ii), (iii), etc.

28. Note that this principle is not applicable to sections themselves; a one-section bill or resolution is acceptable and is commonplace.

(1) In General. — *There is established the National Intelligence Advisory Committee.*

(2) Inapplicability of the Federal Advisory Committee Act. — *The Federal Advisory Committee Act shall not apply to the Committee.*

(b) Responsibilities. — *The Committee may advise the President regarding United States intelligence activities.*

Hierarchical Position, Not Grammar, Determinative. — Except as noted below, it is the hierarchical position that determines the designations that are used without regard to whether the text that follows is a whole sentence containing a subject and a verb, an independent clause containing a subject and a verb, or a dependent clause containing a sentence fragment. In other words, the nomenclature that applies to a class of designations is purely arbitrary and may not be an apt description of the grammatical structure that follows. For example, it is entirely acceptable to use a "clause" designation such as (i), (ii), or (iii) in front of a whole sentence, which grammatically is not a clause.

Exception to the Hierarchical Position Rule. — "Subsection" designations such as (a), (b), or (c) must always precede a whole sentence. They are reserved exclusively for the creation of large subsets within a section. This means that a section comprised of only a single sentence may never contain subsections but may, of course, itemize its constituent clauses, if any, beginning with "paragraph" designations such as (1), (2), and (3) and proceeding through the rest of the subdivision nomenclature, as needed. In short, the first level of subdivision has been skipped over.

"Tax Style"

In General. — "Tax Style"[29] is a style of drafting that is applied to the formatting of sections that originated with the tax drafters of the House Legislative Counsel's Office in the 1960s and gained widespread acceptance by congressional drafters by the mid-1980s. "Tax Style" is applied not only to freestanding text but also to statutory amendments, even where those amendments are being made to Acts of Congress or positive law titles of the United States Code that were not originally written using "Tax Style".[30] This may result in two different styles appearing within the same statute but it would be presumptuous and overly burdensome to rewrite a whole statute for style reasons alone. Hopefully, these mixed-style statutes will become more uniformly "Tax Style" as the older sections are amended and rewritten.

Purpose. — The purpose of "Tax Style" is to promote the transparency and predictability of the text. Not only does "Tax Style" facilitate the reader's ability to find

---

29. "Tax Style" is not the most attractive term in light of the complexity of tax law, but the drafter needs to overlook the historical origins of the style, as it is applicable to any subject matter.

30. The prevalent style before "Tax Style" used a "center cap" heading floating above a section, designated as "Sec.", with no further headings in the section and margin indents only for grammatical clauses.

a specific provision but also enhances the ability of the drafter to think through the contents of a section while drafting the language. Disciplined use of "Tax Style" will readily expose any gaps in the logic or coverage of a legislative provision.

Elements of "Tax Style".— "Tax Style" consists of all of the following:

(1) **Captions.**— Captions inserted between subdivision designations and whole sentences. A caption consists of not more than three or four words that describe the contents of a unit of subdivision, followed by a point and a dash. Virtually every whole sentence, without regard to its particular designation, will be preceded by a caption.

(2) **Margin Indents.**— Margin indents that precede each subdivision with a caption and that become greater as the hierarchy of subdivisions descends.

(3) **Typeface Changes.**— Typeface changes on captions that vary with the level of subdivision within a section. For example, the lettering of subsection captions takes large and small capitals, with initial letters taking large capitals. For paragraph and subparagraph captions, the lettering should be made entirely in small capitals except for the first letter of the first word, which should take a large capital.

A Tale of Three Sections

When "Tax Style" is combined with the rules for the subdivision of legislative text, three different types of section organization emerge. All three types may appear in the same bill, and most drafted sections will reflect one of the three types. Consider, then, each of the following hypotheticals:

Hypothetical No. 1: A Single Sentence Section with Grammatical Clauses

Many sections consist of only one sentence, which may or may not contain grammatical clauses. Where there are grammatical clauses, these should be designated and indented to promote readability. The section should not contain any "Tax Style" caption since the section contents are adequately covered by the section heading, and captions may not precede a grammatical clause as this would interrupt the flow of the sentence. *See* Figure 4-3 on the next page.

Hypothetical No. 2: A Multi-Sentence Section with No Grammatical Clauses

The second case is a section consisting of multiple sentences, grouped in descending order of designation in order to achieve the further subdivision of the concepts covered by the section. Each designation will take a "Tax Style" caption, and each level of designation will have the same margin indents. Note that the first whole sentence is preceded by several levels of captions, each level without any text. *See* Figure 4-4 on the next page.

Figure 4-3

Hypothetical No. 1: Single Sentence Section with Grammatical Clauses

SEC.___. HEADING.
  Text—

    (1) text; [and] [or]
    (2) text—

        (A) text; [and] [or]
        (B) text—

            (i) text; [and] [or]
            (ii) text.

Figure 4-4

**Hypothetical No. 2: Multi-Sentence Section with No Grammatical Clauses
(Five Whole Sentences)**

SEC.___. HEADING.

  (a) Heading.—

    (1) Heading.—

      (A) Heading.—

        (i) Heading. — Text.
        (ii) Heading. — Text.

      (B) Heading. — Text.

    (2) Heading. — Text.

  (b) Heading. — Text.

Hypothetical No. 3: A Hybrid Section Combining Hypotheticals Nos. 1 and 2

The third and final illustration of section organization is a hybrid of the first two hypotheticals. This hybrid quality should not trouble the reader for there is no requirement of structural purity. It is the contents of the section that dictate the organization and not the reverse. There is no reason why a section may not contain both sentences with grammatical clauses and sentences without. Hybrid sections are common.

In hypothetical no. 3, subsection (a) reflects the organization of hypothetical no. 1, and subsection (b) reflects the organization of hypothetical no. 2. Of course, in an actual section there may be any number of subsections or other units of subdivision. *See* Figure 4-5.

Figure 4-5

Hypothetical No. 3: Hybrid Section Combining Hypotheticals Nos. 1 and 2 (Five Whole Sentences)

SEC.___. HEADING.

    (a) Heading.—Text—

        (1) text; [and] [or]
        (2) text—

            (A) text; [and][or]
            (B) text—

                (i) text; [and][or]
                (ii) text.

    (b) Heading.—

        (1) Heading.—

            (A) Heading.—

                (i) Heading.—Text.
                (ii) Heading.—Text.

            (B) Heading.—Text.

        (2) Heading.—Text.

The Confusion of Sections Making Statutory Amendments

The organization of a section may seem most confusing when the section contains a statutory amendment. This is so because the statutory amendment may add or "amend to read" a subsection, paragraph, or clause,[31] which will be interspersed among the subsections, paragraphs, and clauses of the new bill section making the amendment.

The result is a jumble of section subdivisions, some freestanding and others amendatory, with the designations *apparently* out of sequence. In actuality, the section is operating on two levels, each of which must be kept distinct in the drafter's mind and organized separately. This may be easily done simply by viewing the quoted (amendatory) text apart from the non-quoted (freestanding) text and organizing the quoted text only in relation to the law being amended. The rules of section organization do not change; they are merely applied with two different frames of reference in mind, creating a 2-tiered track. Stay focused and don't be fooled!

Example:[32]

SEC. 907. TECHNICAL AMENDMENTS.

(a) In General.—Section 599C of the Foreign Operations, Export Financing, and Related Programs Appropriations Act, 1991, is amended—

(1) in subsection (a), by adding at the end of the first sentence "during fiscal year 1991";

(2) in paragraphs (3) and (4) of subsection (b), by striking "During" each place it appears and inserting "Except as provided in paragraph (5), during";

(3) by adding at the end of subsection (b) the following new paragraph:

"(5) For purposes of the application of paragraphs (3) and (4) to United States hostages captured in Lebanon, the period of entitlement of benefits, subject to the availability of funds, shall be _____.";

(4) in subsection (d), by amending paragraph (4)(B) to read as follows:

"(B) the term 'United States hostages captured in Lebanon' means _____."; and

(5) in subsection (e), by amending paragraph (2) to read as follows:

"(2) Funds allocated under paragraph (1) are authorized to remain available until expended.".

---

31. The same confusion may occur, but less often, with respect to titles and sections.

32. The example is a revised and abridged version of section 907 of S. 1433 of the One Hundred Second Congress (as reported by the Committee on Foreign Relations of the Senate) (relating to foreign relations authorizations, fiscal years 1992 and 1993).

(b) Effective Date. — The amendments made by subsection (a) are deemed to have become effective as of the date of enactment of the Foreign Operations, Export Financing, and Related Programs Appropriations Act, 1991 (Public Law 101-513).

In the example, note that the paragraphs specifically mentioned in the text refer to paragraphs within subsections (b), (d), and (e) of section 599C, the target of the amendments, and do not refer to the paragraphs within section 907(a), the section making the amendments.

Making Connections Within a Section

There are two different ways of displaying grammatical clauses, however designated, within a section. The principal technique employs "and" and "or" and may be referred to as "Connector Style". Alternatively, the same clauses may be listed without the use of connectors in what may be referred to as "List Style". In "List Style", the relationship between the clauses is established in the introductory language above the clauses. Although a drafter must avoid creating a hybrid style that mixes elements of both Connector Style and List Style within the same provision, the drafter is free to use both styles within the same bill, as it may be more inviting to use a particular style with one type of provision and not with another.

"Connector" Style

In General. — Connector Style requires the use of an "and" or an "or" after the semicolon (or occasionally, comma) at the end of the next to the last clause in a series of clauses. There is no need to repeat the connector at the end of each clause, as this adds nothing to meaning.

Use of "And". — "And" in common parlance is ambiguous; it may mean joint and indivisible or joint and several. The presumption in legislative drafting, which favors singular subjects and singular objects, is that where "and" appears it is intended to mean joint and indivisible.

The President shall sell defense articles and defense services to Colombia and Peru literally means both defense articles and defense services must be provided to each country. If one country does not receive both types of assistance, then the provision is violated.

Use of "Or". — "Or" also is ambiguous in common parlance; it may mean the disjunctive, namely, setting forth exclusive alternatives or it may mean the conjunctive, namely, setting forth inclusive alternatives, that is "either A or B or both". The presumption in legislative drafting is that "or" is intended as a conjunction and therefore the phrase "or both" is implied and not stated.[33]

---

33. By custom, however, in criminal penalty provisions "or both" is inserted after the statement that the crime is punishable by a fine or imprisonment.

For example, *The President may provide assistance to Colombia or Peru* means that either country or both may receive assistance.

Avoid "And/Or".—Lawyers who write using plural subjects or objects, when a singular subject or object would suffice, are tempted to use "and/or" to paper over the ambiguity that they have created. This practice, of course, serves no other purpose than to lock in the ambiguity. Consequently, "and/or" should never be used; the drafter must choose between the two connectors and in doing so will be compelled to make conforming changes to the sentence. As a result, the sentence will be much more clearly expressed.

Use of Case and Punctuation.—Grammatical clauses that are displayed in Connector Style are always preceded by text ending in a dash. Each grammatical clause ends in a semicolon except for (1) the next to the last clause, which ends with a semicolon and the connector, and (2) the last clause, which ends with a period. The initial word of each grammatical clause begins in lower case (except for proper nouns).

Example.—An example of Connector Style is the following:

The President may do—

   (1) x;

   (2) y; and

   (3) z.

"List" Style

"List Style", Generally.—List Style does not use any connectors but simply lists the grammatical clauses. The relationship between the clauses is established in the introductory text immediately preceding the listing.

Where List Style is Used.—List Style is used where the drafter wishes to highlight the grammatical clauses. It is a more emphatic means of presentation. Congressional findings and definitions sections are particularly helped by application of this style.

Use of Case and Punctuation.—Grammatical clauses that are displayed in List Style are always preceded by text that indicates that further matter "follows", or is "following", and a colon. Each grammatical clause ends in a period. At the beginning of each grammatical clause, the drafter may insert a caption[34] but, in any event, must begin the first word of the clause in upper case.

Example.—An example of list style is the following:

The President may do any of the following:

   (1) X.

---

34. The insertion of captions is customary when list style is used in definitions sections.

(2) Y.

(3) Z.

Part III: Cross-References

What Is a Cross-Reference?

A cross-reference is a shorthand way of incorporating the meaning of another legislative or statutory provision without reciting the full language of the provision.

Why Make a Cross-Reference?

Purpose.—The purpose of any cross-reference is to shorten the length of a sentence.

Advantages.—The use of cross-references has the following advantages:

(1) **Word Economy.**—Enhancing the readability of a sentence by shortening the sentence.

(2) **Comprehensiveness of Meaning.**—Ensuring the comprehensiveness of meaning of the sentence.

Disadvantage.—The use of cross-references has the disadvantage of making a sentence less transparent by virtue of omitting words from a sentence that must be found elsewhere.

Rules for Drafting Cross-References

In drafting cross-references, the drafter should apply the following rules:

(1) **Use of "Described In".**—Precede the cross-reference by "described in", not "referred in".

(2) **Level of Unit Designation.**—Cite the highest unit of organization sufficient to identify the referenced text but no higher. Since section numbers are never duplicated within the same Act of Congress, where a single section is the only target of the reference, it is unnecessary to cite higher units such as subtitles, chapters, or parts.

(3) **Choice of Unit Designation.**—When the referenced text is buried within several levels of units of organization, begin the cross-reference by citing the most encompassing unit that is essential to identifying the provision.

(4) **No Abbreviations.**—Spell out the name of the legislative or statutory unit and include its alphabetical or numerical designation in parentheses.

(5) **Lower Case.**—Cite all words in a cross-reference in lower case, except—

(A) a reference to "this Act", "the United States Code", or a short title; or

(B) a reference that begins a sentence.

(6) **No "Third Person" References.** — Never cite the unit of organization in which the drafter is writing (or a higher legislative unit that contains the unit in which the drafter is writing) by its alphabetical or numerical designation; cite it as "this ____" [name the unit]. To do otherwise would be like referring to yourself in the third person.

(7) **Same Rules as Apply to Statutory Amendments.** — When drafting cross-references to existing law, the primary reference must be to a unit of an Act of Congress or a positive law title of the United States Code. Do not make primary cross-references to Public Laws, the Statutes at Large, or titles of the Code that have not been reenacted and are merely prima facie evidence of the law. These less satisfactory references may, however, be used inside parentheses as secondary references. In other words, apply the same rules for cross-references as are applicable to identifying the "true" version of the law to amend.

Definitions as Alternatives to Cross-References

A definition may be substituted for a cross-reference if both of the following apply:

(1) The meaning covered by the reference may be described by a single word or a very short phrase.

(2) The definition will be used at several places in the text.

This alternative to the creation of cross-references is available rarely since the language being incorporated by a cross-reference is frequently difficult to characterize or, even if it may be easily described, may only be incorporated at one or two places in the bill, thus not justifying a definition. Wherever creating a definition is an option, however, it should be taken because a defined term is infinitely more transparent than a cross-reference.

Example:

> In this Act, the term "democratically elected government in Cuba" means the government determined by the President to have met the requirements of section 206.[35]

Note how creation of the definition makes unnecessary any cross-reference to section 206 (and its 14 word lead-in) throughout the Act.

---

35. The example is drawn from section 4(6) of the Cuban Liberty and Democratic Solidarity (LIBERTAD) Act of 1996 (22 U.S.C. 6023(6)).

Test Your "Organizing" Skills

Drafting Exercise No. 4-A

Please organize (and reorganize) the following sentences into a complete bill for introduction in the Senate:

> Effective October 1, 2030, there is established within the Office of Personnel Management the Office of Regulatory Drafting, which shall be headed by the Regulatory Counsel, appointed by the President, by and with the advice and consent of the Senate. The Regulatory Counsel may assist any Executive agency (as defined in 5 U.S.C. 105) seeking to write regulations in plain English in order to promote the goal of transparency in Government. Not later than one year after the establishment of the Office, the Director of OPM shall submit to Congress a report on the activities of the Office. This Act may be cited as the "Plain English Regulatory Drafting Act of 20__". Funding of the Office is up to $10,000,000 for fiscal year 2031, to remain available until expended.

Check your answer in Appendix C.

Drafting Exercise No. 4-B

The italicized cross-references in the following two sections are incorrectly drafted. For each incorrect reference, substitute the correct reference in the blank after the reference.

SEC. 107. IRAN AND NUCLEAR WEAPONS.

(a) Report. — Not later than 30 days after the date of enactment of this Act, the President shall submit to Congress a report on the Iranian nuclear weapons program.

(b) Contents. — The report described in *subsection (a) of this section of this Act* _____ [1] shall include ___

  (1) an estimate of the date on which Iran will become a nuclear-weapon state; and

  (2) a description of the steps the United States has taken to prevent Iran from becoming the state described in *subsection (b)(1)* _____ [2], including a description of ___

    (A) all United States diplomatic efforts; and

    (B) all economic sanctions imposed on Iran.

(c) Termination of Sanctions.—The economic sanctions described in *subparagraph (b)(2)(B)* _____ [3] shall cease to apply if the Government of Iran halts its nuclear weapon program.

SEC. 108. PROHIBITION ON IMPOSITION OF SANCTIONS IN CASES OF HUMANITARIAN NEED.

Notwithstanding *Sec. 107 of this Act* _____ [4], no economic sanctions may be imposed that would withhold food, medicines, or clothing from the people of Iran.

Check your answers in Appendix C.

Chapter Five

How to Achieve Clarity

"The difference between the almost right word and the right word is really a large matter — 'tis the difference between the lightning-bug and the lightning."[1]

Step Five: "Clarify!"

The fifth and final step in drafting legislation is to clarify the text. On Capitol Hill, this is commonly referred to as "wordsmithing", and politicos often view the time consumed by this process negatively as an unnecessary indulgence in creative writing delaying the legislative process. In fact, the time the drafter spends in clarifying the text is time well spent, as this Chapter will reveal. "Tweaking" a draft to ensure clarity is an essential part of legislative drafting. And what's the harm if it is fun, too?

Part I: Objectives

Confronting Twin Evils

The drafter typically confronts two obstacles to writing clearly: ambiguity and imprecision. While different, they are not mutually exclusive. Ambiguity is a problem of multiple meanings, and imprecision is a problem of scope of application. If not avoided or dealt with, these twin evils mean the legislative text will produce unintended consequences. This is the worst nightmare of the drafter, for the drafter's overarching goal is to carry out the intent of the legislator. Nothing more, nothing less. By writing clearly, the drafter ensures that the text carries out the legislator's intent and achieves predictable results.

Eliminating Ambiguity

In General. — Language is ambiguous if it may be construed to have two or more meanings. Ambiguity is Public Enemy Number 1 of the legislative drafter because

---

1. Samuel L. Clemens ("Mark Twain") in a letter to George Bainton, October 15, 1888.

the consequences of ambiguity are so dire and yet it is such an easy pitfall. Ambiguity may occur as easily as making a poor word choice or misplacing a modifier. Ambiguous legislative text, of course, is totally unacceptable to the drafter, if unintended consequences are to be avoided. While following certain rules of clear expression will lessen the risk of ambiguity, there is no guarantee of unambiguous writing except through a careful reading and rereading of the text.

Occasional Use as a Political Tactic.—Congressional staffers may be attracted to ambiguous legislative text believing that a little bit of ambiguity is politically necessary to bring opposing legislators together to pass the legislation. This is politics gone amuck! The enactment of ambiguous text locks in a future legal dispute that will be decided not by Congress but by the executive branch or the judiciary. As such this approach represents an abdication of legislative power. In effect, Congress has decided to punt. A drafter should never punt.

Eliminating Imprecision

Overbreadth.—The most common form of imprecise language is the word, phrase, or sentence that is overbroad. An overbroad rule is one that applies to persons or things not intended to be covered. More than 200 years of lawmaking in the United States makes it difficult to draft a totally new legislative rule that is not overbroad. Virtually every new rule implicates an existing statute and must be drawn narrowly within the confines of the definitions and scope of that statute. In the rare case where the proposed rule is novel and fills a gap between existing statutes, the drafter must also draw the rule narrowly simply to avoid collision with those statutes.

Underinclusion.—A rule is underinclusive if it is drawn too narrowly, failing to include all the intended individuals or objects. Underinclusion is just as much a form of imprecision as overbreadth, but, perhaps because of the adverse political consequences of failure to cover all the intended beneficiaries of a new program, underinclusion is not as common as overbreadth.

What to Do about Vagueness

Vagueness Described.—Unlike ambiguity, which is characterized by two or more different, clear meanings, vague language has only one meaning but that meaning is so general and fuzzy that the boundary lines for its application are uncertain. A general standard accompanying authorizing language is a common example of a vague phrase such as when the President is authorized to act if the President "determines that it is in the national interest of the United States to do so".

Intentional Vagueness.—Vagueness is not always a drafting mistake. There are situations where vagueness in a statute is desirable. Where Congress does not have the expertise or will to narrow the scope of application of a statutory provision, Congress may intentionally draft the provision using vague language. This is an invitation to an executive branch official to issue regulations to implement the provision. The draft provision may go one step further and include a directive for implementing regulations by adding the following sentence: *The [official] shall prescribe such regulations as may be necessary to carry out [a referenced provision].*

Void for Vagueness Doctrine

Vagueness in certain statutory provisions constitutes a violation of the Due Process Clause of the United States Constitution.[2] When a statute imposes a criminal or civil penalty for an act or omission, due process requires, at a minimum, that a person committing the violation may only be penalized if the person had reason to know that the statute prohibited the act or omission. This, of course, is not a requirement that the person have actual knowledge but merely that the person should have known. A vague word, phrase, or sentence, whose application is uncertain, does not afford an individual adequate notice of the inclusion of their act or omission in the class of proscribed conduct and, consequently, violates the Due Process Clause. United States courts refer to this rule as the "void for vagueness doctrine". Of course, most statutory provisions are not penal provisions.

Part II: Twelve Rules for Drafting Clearly

Introduction

To draft clearly takes practice, lots of practice, but there are some basic rules that will help the drafter to achieve clarity. The following rules attempt to correct the 12 most common legislative drafting errors:

Rule No. 1: Present Tense

Rule. — Draft all legally binding text in the present tense. Write each legislative provision as if it were being applied currently even though its application, if any, will occur in the future.

Reason. — As a matter of statutory construction, the perspective of a sentence is viewed as of its date of application, not as of its date of drafting or enactment.[3]

Exception No. 1. — In "findings" sections and "Whereas" clauses, the drafter may employ any grammatical verb tense. Not surprisingly, the recitation of background or historical information frequently requires the use of the past tense.

---

2. U.S. Const., amend. V and amend. XIV, § 1.
3. Reed Dickerson, *The Fundamentals of Legal Drafting*, 2d ed. (1986), § 8.17, at 185.

Exception No. 2.—The use of the future tense will be necessary where the sentence describes an assurance or prediction of a future event expressed as a condition.

Common Mistake.—Drafters should resist the temptation to use the future perfect tense, which combines a future tense of the verb "to have" with a participle.

Examples:

Incorrect: Whenever the President *will determine [or shall have determined]* X, the President may do Y.

Correct: Whenever the President *determines* X, the President may do Y.

Rule No. 2: Active Voice

Rule.—Draft in the active voice.

Reason.—Use of the passive voice omits the subject of the action entirely or refers to the actual subject indirectly in a prepositional phrase beginning with "by" after the use of the verb. Either way, readability is sacrificed and, quite possibly, accountability as well.

Exception.—The passive voice is acceptable where the sentence is written as a prohibition and specifying a single subject of the sentence would make the prohibition ineffective for being drawn too narrowly.

Example: *No United States Armed Forces may be deployed* is more legally effective than *The Secretary of Defense may not deploy United States Armed Forces* because both the President and the Secretary of Defense share authority over the Armed Forces, and in the latter, more narrow phrasing the President may circumvent the intent of the prohibition by directly ordering the deployment.

Common Mistake.—The passive voice most commonly occurs whenever the verb is a form of "to be", together with the past participle of another verb, and the actual subject of the sentence appears after the past participle, following the word "by". Virtually every legislative sentence that contains the word "by" signals the use of the passive voice.

Examples:

Incorrect: Whenever *a determination of X is made by* the President, Y *may be done by* the President.

Correct: Whenever the President *determines* X, the President *may do* Y.

Rule No. 3: Singular Subjects

Rule.—Draft each sentence using a singular subject.

Reason.—Doing this will avoid the ambiguity found in plural subjects as to whether or not any legal duty, requirement, or entitlement is intended to be applied collectively or individually. A statutory stipulation that the plural includes the singular and *vice versa* does not remove the ambiguity.[4]

Exception.—A sentence may require a compound subject consisting of two or more actors. When the drafter intends a collective application, as where 2 or more officials are intended to cooperate in carrying out a legal duty, the drafter should specify that the action is carried out jointly.

> **Example:** The Secretary of State and the Secretary of Defense, *acting jointly*, shall submit a report to the President. Absent the italicized language, two reports might be required.

Common Mistake.—There is a strong temptation to begin a sentence using a plural subject because the sentence will contain fewer words since words such as "each", "any", "a", "an", and "every" are absent. What is gained by the economy of words, however, is more than offset by the ambiguity created. Drafting in the plural is the preferred style of the lazy drafter and is wrong.

Examples:

> **Incorrect:** *The reports* shall include *descriptions* of X, estimates of Y, and listings of Z.

> **Correct:** *Each* report shall include *a* description of X, *an* estimate of Y, and *a* listing of Z.

Rule No. 4: Place Modifiers Side-by-Side with Modified Text

Rule.—Place each modifying word or phrase as closely as possible to the word or phrase being modified.

Reason.—The correct placement of modifiers will ensure that the reader may easily identify the proper antecedent for each modifying phrase and avoid the ambiguity created where two or more antecedents are possible.

Common Mistake.—A common mistake is to misplace a modifier in order to avoid awkwardness in the way a sentence sounds. Consider the example of the former Speaker of the House of Representatives who, boasting of his legislative work during the Cold War with the Soviet Union, said that he "helped lead the effort to defeat communism in the Congress".[5] What he meant to say of course was the slightly more awkward statement that he "helped lead the effort in the Congress to defeat communism". A similar choice in the arrangement of words presents itself regularly to legislative drafters, and the correct choice is to opt for clarity despite any awkwardness.

---

4. *See, e.g.,* 1 U.S.C. § 1 (2012). To say that a particular expression includes its opposite is to say nothing at all.

5. Newt Gingrich in a television interview aired by FOX News on December 1, 2011.

Examples:

Incorrect: "the President shall certify the determination regarding ___ *to Congress*".

Correct: "the President shall certify *to Congress* the determination regarding ___".

Rule No. 5: Avoid Long Sentences

Rule.—Do not draft long sentences. Prefer the sentence lengths of Ernest Hemingway over those of William Faulkner!

Reason.—The longer the sentence, the less readable its text, especially if buried within the sentence are several grammatical clauses.

Exception.—A long sentence that consists of two or more properly indented and designated clauses is permissible because the clauses may be easily identified and cross-referenced, and the sentence is more readable.

Common Mistake.—In writing a short sentence, the novice drafter is tempted to express an incomplete thought, omitting a crucial qualifier that would limit the scope of the sentence. The result is a sentence that is overbroad. A reader should not have to interpret, unaided, a sentence "in context".

One way to achieve precision in a short sentence is to insert an introductory phrase that alerts the reader that the sentence is specifically linked to, and qualified by, another sentence or provision. Such phrases include "Except as provided in _____," and "Subject to _____," with the blanks filled in by a cross-reference to a specific sentence or provision.

Another way to keep a sentence short is to define one or more of its terms.

Examples:

Incorrect: *The President may act whenever the President determines that the Government of ___ is complying with applicable United Nations Security Council resolutions and the continued imposition of sanctions against that country would not be in the interests of the United States.*

Correct: *The President may act whenever the President determines that—*

(1) the Government of ___ is complying with applicable United Nations Security Council resolutions; and

(2) the continued imposition of sanctions against that country would not be in the interests of the United States.

Rule No. 6: Avoid Combining Legal Concepts

Rule.—Do not combine two or more distinct legal concepts in the same sentence.

Reason.—The merger of two or more legal concepts in the same sentence makes it difficult, at a later time, to cross-reference or amend any one concept.

Examples:

Incorrect: *For each country the President shall determine whether the country has done X and, if so, the country may not be eligible for assistance.*

Correct: *(a) For each country the President shall determine whether the country has done X.*

(b) Any country for which a determination is made under subsection (a) may not be eligible for assistance.

Rule No. 7: Define Terms

Rule. — Define each word or phrase where the intent is to convey a specialized meaning or where word economy is sought. When creating a definition, the defined term is bracketed by quotation marks, and the quoted matter never begins with "the", "a", or "an".

Reasons. — A specialty term requires a definition because applying the plain meaning of the term, the default rule under the canons of statutory construction, would be inadequate to the task. In addition, the repeated occurrence of a phrase in a text requires the use of a defined term that employs fewer words than the phrase itself in order to shorten sentences and, thus, to shorten the overall length of the text. Even where the defined term is used just once the definition is justified if it would significantly shorten a sentence and promote readability.

Common Mistakes. — There are six common mistakes made with definitions, as follows:

(1) **Failure to Define.** — It is easy to assume that the meaning of a word or phrase used in a piece of legislation is commonly understood because the drafter understands the context in which the word or phrase is being used. In fact, legislation is best written in a narrow, highly tailored way, and there is a great likelihood that the key terms of the legislation are intended to have meanings more narrow than their dictionary definitions. A failure to define terms intended to have specialty meanings is a major error and amounts to a congressional abdication of power since, in the absence of a statutory definition, any question about the scope of a term will be decided by the executive branch through regulations or by the judiciary.

Sometimes the most important terms to define are concepts, not individual words. For example, legislation that provides benefits to a foreign country, government, or individual might usefully define "eligible country", "eligible government", or "eligible individual", respectively. By prefacing the defined term with "eligible", "qualifying", or "covered", the drafter can create a definition that captures a complex concept and save repeating the verbiage throughout the text. Unfortunately, it rarely occurs to beginner drafters to do this.

(2) **Not Using a Defined Term.** — Just the opposite of the mistake described in paragraph (1) is the mistake of defining a term and then not using

the term again in the legislative text. This mistake is usually made by drafters whose desire to impress with a lengthy definitions section outweighs their interest in allowing the definition to do its job.

(3) **Burying a Definition Within a Substantive Provision.** — Historically, definitions were frequently buried within the substantive text of a bill inside a parenthetical phrase adjoining the term the first place it appeared, wherever that might be.

Example:

[word or phrase] X (in this Act referred to as "_____").

This practice is particularly poor drafting as it defeats transparency — a later occurrence of the defined term may appear many pages after the definition, with no quick way to find the definition in a long bill. The longer the bill, the greater the problem.

(4) **Burying a Substantive Provision Within a Definition.** — Sometimes a definition goes too far and includes the *application* of the term defined as well as its *meaning*. This effectively turns the definition into a substantive provision with the danger that a later use of the term in the legislation will amount to a nonsensical double application or, worse, that the term will not be used at all. A correctly drafted definition should always be limited to a neutral description of the thing itself, nothing more.

Examples:

Incorrect: *In this Act, the term "assistance" means any loan or grant provided by the President to a foreign country annually under an agreement with that country.*

Correct: *In this Act, the term "assistance" means any loan or grant.*

(5) **Defining a Term as a Legal Fiction.** — Another common mistake is to define a term to mean something completely unrealistic — not a narrowing of its plain meaning but a complete alteration. We might call this the "Alice in Wonderland Problem" from the famous remark by Humpty Dumpty that a word means "just what I choose it to mean".[6]

Incorrect: *In this Act, the term "President" means "Secretary of State".*

In effect, the drafter has created a legal fiction and, while this works for purposes of interpreting the legislation, it injects awkwardness into the text that is avoided simply by choosing to define a different, more realistic term. Where the creation of a legal fiction is absolutely necessary, this should be done outside the definitions section in a substantive legislative provision called a "deeming" provision.

---

6. Lewis Carroll, *Through the Looking-Glass* (1872) at 72.

Example of Deeming Provision: *For purposes of section 207 of the Immigration and Nationality Act (8 U.S.C. 1157), a Haitian national who seeks to flee Haiti on account of the earthquake devastation in that country is deemed to be a refugee.*

(6) Defining a Plainly Understood Word. — Resist the temptation to pad a definitions section with terms that do not require defining. These are words that would otherwise be accorded their plain, dictionary meanings under the rules of statutory construction in the absence of any definition and for which no specialized meaning is intended. Defining these words merely consumes space and raises question as to why other common words were not defined as well.

Examples:

Incorrect: *In this Act, the term "determines" means _____.*

Correct: *In this Act, the term "nuclear safeguards" means _____.*

Rule No. 8: Use Words Consistently

Rule. — Be consistent in the choice of words. Use the same word or phrase to capture the same meaning throughout the entire legislative text.

Reason. — As a matter of statutory construction, different words are presumed to convey different meanings.[7] So, if the same meaning is intended, then the same word must be used. Legislative drafting is not to be confused with creative writing and does not require a demonstration of the drafter's impressive vocabulary.

Exceptions. — None.

Common Mistake. — A tempting mistake in legislative drafting is to make the text sound interesting! When a piece of legislation sounds entertaining, the drafter has made a big mistake.

Examples:

Incorrect: Each *country* shall be eligible for assistance to meet the basic needs of the *nation's* poor.

Correct: Each country shall be eligible for assistance to meet the basic needs of the *country's* poor.

Rule No. 9: Choose Basic Words, Essential to Meaning

Rule. — Use only basic words that have a single, well understood meaning. Do not use any word that is unnecessary to meaning.[8] Specifically, do not use any word that is —

(1) pretentious or a longer form of a basic word (for example, "embedded");

(2) slang, colorful, or in vogue (for example, "freeze assets");

---

7. *See also* this Chapter, Part IV: Canons of Statutory Construction, *infra.*

8. "There is a useless lawsuit in every useless word of a statute". Elihu Root, *The Layman's Criticism of the Lawyer*, 39 American Bar Association Report, 386, 395 (1914).

(3) introductory or transitional (for example, "however", "therefore", or "consequently");

(4) indefinite in its reference (for example, "it", "they", or "them");

(5) a Latinism or a legalism (for example, "*inter alia*", "hereby", "hereafter", or "thereunder"); or

(6) any "problem word" discussed in Part III of this Chapter.

Reasons.—The goal of the drafter in choosing each word should be to promote readability and avoid confusion.

The text is more readable if each word is basic[9] and essential to the meaning being conveyed. In short, the goal ordinarily should be word economy. Confusion is also avoided if words having two or more meanings are omitted and if all references are made clear, leaving nothing to the reader's imagination.

Exception.—Where word economy causes confusion and loss of clarity, such as with the use of indefinite references, Latinisms, or legalisms, the goal of word economy must yield to the needs of clarity. In other words, a sufficient number of words must be used to convey the meaning intended.

Common Mistakes.—There are two sides to bad word choices. Some drafters choose words to make the text sound interesting. Others choose words to make the text sound "legalistic". A few particularly bad drafters manage to do both in the same bill. The good drafter should do neither.

Rule No. 10: Write Formally, Not Conversationally

Rule.—Do not write conversational, informal English in legislation. Avoid using any abbreviation, acronym, contraction, or possessive apostrophe or making any shortened reference to a title or place.

When a possessive is intended, the concept should be captured by a phrase containing the preposition "of". In addition, do not personalize the text in any way such as writing phrases like "*our* Nation" or "*their* constitution".

Reason.—Legislative drafting is formal writing. The drafter should never forget that a bill or resolution is an official, historical document and not a piece of journalism. If a law is not a suitable place in which to cite the full title of an official or agency, or to write proper, formal English, what document would be?

Exceptions.—Sometimes the use of a possessive apostrophe[10] is the best way to achieve gender neutrality. In addition, in Federal legislation, "United States" may be omitted in front of a title, as those words are implied by virtue of the origin of the legislation.

---

9. Modern English vocabulary that may be traced to a Saxon root is generally more readable than English vocabulary of Norman-origin. So, for example, prefer "begin" over "commence", "country" over "nation", and "before" over "ante".

10. *See* Rule No. 11, *infra*.

Common Mistake. — A common mistake is to use an acronym, like the NRA, assuming its meaning to be clearly understood. But does the NRA refer to the National Recovery Administration or the National Rifle Association? Even if there is only one current reference for an abbreviation, what would prevent the emergence at a later time of the same abbreviation to refer to something completely different?

When an abbreviation is used, a single mistyped letter might result in a vastly different meaning. The meaning of a legislative text should not be left to the mercy of a careless word processor or printer. Consider the difference in meaning between the abbreviations for the International Development Association (IDA) and the Islamic Development Bank (IDB). Do not use acronyms.

An acronym may be made a defined term, of course, but turning the text into an alphabet soup of acronyms is less readable than simply defining one of the constituent words of the acronym, such as "Association" in the case of IDA.

Example:

Incorrect: *the Defense Secretary's determination that the UN can't do*

_____.

Correct: *the determination of the Secretary of Defense that the United Nations cannot do* _____.

Rule No. 11: Gender-Neutral Expression

Rule. — Write in a gender-neutral way that omits "he", "she", "him", "his", and "her". To achieve gender neutrality where a noun is desired, repeat the noun that is the correct reference. To achieve gender neutrality where the possessive is desired either (1) create a possessive phrase using "of" and the noun that is the correct reference, or (2) repeat the noun that is the correct reference and add an apostrophe "s".

Reason. — Writing that uses masculine-exclusive terms is offensive to women and raises unnecessary questions as to whether a law applies equally to all persons. Historically, equal application of the law to both genders while using solely masculine references was achieved by a statutory canon of construction, or by specific statutory provisions,[11] that deemed each masculine reference to include a feminine reference. While this legal fiction approach worked, stylistically the approach was offensive and should not now be used.

Exception. — None.

Common Mistake. — The most common mistake in drafting for gender neutrality is to include both masculine and feminine references at each place where a pronoun is desired. A legislative text that is replete with "he or she", "him or her", or, worst yet, "he/she" or "him/her" is a text that becomes difficult to read because it clutters sentences and distracts the reader from the verb action of the sentences.

_____

11. 1 U.S.C. § 1 (2012).

Examples:

Incorrect (Traditional): The Secretary of State shall submit to Congress a report containing *his* determinations on X.

Incorrect (Modern): The Secretary of State shall submit to Congress a report containing *his or her* determinations on X.

Correct: The *Secretary of State* shall submit to Congress a report containing the determinations of the *Secretary* on X.

Rule No. 12: Punctuate for Meaning

Rule. — Use punctuation and connecting words in a manner that is most likely to enhance meaning. Specifically, insert commas after every item in a series. Do not omit a comma after the next to the last item in the series as is customary in writing creative English. Correct series punctuation will necessarily require the correct use of "and" or "or" unless the series of items appears as an enumerated list.

In addition, quotation marks should usually appear inside the sentence punctuation. This, too, is at odds with the practice in creative writing but makes sense in legislative drafting. Any punctuation appearing within quotation marks will be strictly and literally interpreted as being included in the quoted text. In legislative drafting, the use of quotation marks most commonly occurs while making statutory or legislative amendments, and the inclusion or exclusion of punctuation within the quoted matter must be exact.

Reason. — Sloppy use of punctuation or a connecting word affects meaning and, consequently, statutory interpretation.

Exception. — None.

Common Mistake. — A common mistake is to attach a modifying phrase after the last item in a series without clearly indicating whether or not the phrase is intended to apply only to the last item or instead to apply to each item in the series. If modification of each item in the series is the intent, then the drafter may resolve the ambiguity by indenting and enumerating each item in the series but not indenting the modifying phrase.

Examples:

Incorrect: *The President shall submit to Congress a report on Afghanistan which shall include a description of the progress made, future plans and an exit strategy to ensure a stable, democratic country.*

Correct: *The President shall submit to Congress a report on Afghanistan, which shall include a description of—*

(1) the progress made,

(2) future plans, and

(3) an exit strategy,

to ensure a stable, democratic country.

In addition, the drafter must choose whether to leave the modifying phrase at the end of the sentence after the indented items or instead to work the modifying phrase into the beginning of the sentence leading up to the indented items. While either method works, a sentence generally reads more smoothly if the modifying phrase appears in the introductory language above the indented items.

Part III: "Problem Words"

Introduction

"Problem words" are words and phrases that should be avoided in legislative drafting, either entirely or in particular usages. All problem words should sound alarm bells with the drafter wherever the drafter first encounters them. They usually spell trouble. But not to worry. For every problem word (except one) there is an alternative. (*See* Figure 5-1 on the next page.)

"Above", "Below", "Aforementioned", "Heretofore", "Hereafter", "Thereafter", "Thereto", "Therefore"

Problem.—These words are shorthand references, some derived from Middle or Old English, to an earlier or later description or time mentioned in the text that the reader is expected to find. The problem is that what is being referenced may be hard to find, especially in long texts, or, when found, too vague or ambiguous to convey a useful meaning. In other words, they are legal gobbledygook!

Solution.—The solution is to substitute, using a proper legal citation, a cross-reference to the specific provision intended to be referenced or, where a date is the reference point, to substitute a specific date. A specific date may be a calendar date or the date of enactment or effective date of the Act.

Examples:

Incorrect: The authority of the President described *above* includes _____.

Correct: The authority of the President described *in section* ___ includes

_____.

"act", "state"

Problem.—Many drafters have an aversion to capitalizing the initial letter of the words "Act" and "State". Taking a minimalist view of capitalizations, consistent with creative writing principles, they want those words to appear entirely in lower case. However, the upper case or lower case of the initial letter is important to maintain the distinction between "Act [of Congress]" and "'act [or omission]", on the one hand, and between "State [of New York]" and "[mental] state", on the other. Do not, however, capitalize the initial letter of a subunit within an Act such as "title", "section", or "subsection".

Figure 5-1

Problem Words	Alternatives
above, below, aforementioned, heretofore, hereafter, thereafter, thereto, therefore	described in _____ [Use Specific Cross-Reference]
act, state	Act, State
assure, insure	ensure
authorities	[None]
by, within	not later than
commencing	beginning
currently, recently, soon	[specific date or reference to _____ days before or after date of enactment or effective date of the Act]
deems	determines
effects	affects
execute, implement	carry out
includes but not limited to	includes
person	individual
powers	authorities
prior to; subsequent to	before; after
program	authorities
: *Provided*, That	except, if, unless, until, or [separate sentence]
pursuant to	under
said, such	the, that, those
up to	not more than
which	that

Solution. — Maintain the capitalizations of the initial letters where an "Act" of Congress or "State" of the United States is being referenced.

Examples:

Incorrect: In this *act*, the term "assistance" means _____.

Correct: In this *Act*, the term "assistance" means _____.

"Assure", "Insure"

Problem. — Novice drafters often have trouble expressing the concept of a guarantee — a concept that recurs frequently in legislation. The temptation is to use a form of the verb "to assure" or "to insure". While these verbs are sometimes used in creative English writing to express a guarantee, the problem is that they have other, more prevalent meanings. "To assure" primarily means to make an assurance, commitment, or promise, usually as an oral statement. "To insure" primarily means to provide insurance under an insurance contract. In legislative drafting, words with more than one meaning should be avoided.

Solution.—Except in the limited circumstances where the drafter seeks to express the primary meanings of "to assure" or "to insure", the drafter should avoid using those verbs and instead use a form of the verb "to ensure".

Examples:

Incorrect: Before deploying troops to the Persian Gulf, the President shall *assure* the support of United States allies.

Correct: Before deploying troops to the Persian Gulf, the President shall *ensure* the support of United States allies.

"Authorities"

Problem.—"Authorities" is misleading since it appears to be limited to discretionary authorities, i.e., authorizing language. As used by legislative drafters, however, the word covers not only discretionary authorities but also legal duties.

Solution.—There is no solution for this unfortunate word usage, except to confine it to the plural form of the noun and not to extend the broader meaning to "authority". In Government reorganization provisions, "functions" is substituted for "authorities" but "functions" includes administrative delegations as well and is not recommended as a general substitute.

Correct Example:

The *authorities* of the President under this Act terminate 12 months after its date of enactment.

"By", "Within"

Problem.—When followed by a date or period of time, the words "by" and "within" are ambiguous. It is unclear whether the deadline day is included or excluded by the coverage of the sentence.

Solution.—This problem is easily resolved by substituting the phrase "not later than". The substitution makes it absolutely clear what days are covered and what days are not.

Example 1:

Incorrect: The President shall submit to Congress a report *by* December 31, 2012. [Unclear whether the report may be submitted on December 31.]

Correct: The President shall submit to Congress a report *not later than* December 31, 2012.

Example 2:

Incorrect: The letter of offer shall not be issued if Congress, *within* 30 days after receipt of the report, disapproves. [Unclear if Congress may disapprove on the 30th day.]

Correct: The letter of offer shall not be issued if Congress, *not later than* 30 days after receipt of the report, disapproves.

"Commencing"

Problem. — "Commencing" is a Latin-origin word that sounds pretentious to English speakers and impedes readability. Nevertheless, "commencing" is sometimes used by legislative drafters who want to sound lawyer-like, which is not a very good reason.

Solution. — The solution is simply to substitute the more ordinary "beginning".

Examples:

Incorrect: *Commencing* 30 days after the date of enactment of this Act, and every 30 days after that date, the President shall submit a report to Congress.

Correct: *Beginning* 30 days after the date of enactment of this Act, and every 30 days after that date, the President shall submit a report to Congress.

"Currently", "Recently", "Soon"

Problem. — "Currently", "recently", and "soon" are relative terms that, when inserted into legislation, raise more questions than they answer, because they are vague and are not tied to a specific date. Is the action referred to "current", "recent", or "soon" with respect to the date of drafting, enactment, or application of the statute?

Solution. — Time references in legislation need to be linked to a fixed, calculable date. Usually this means the "date of enactment of this Act", the "effective date of this Act", or a specific calendar date.

Examples:

Incorrect: The President shall keep the intelligence committees *currently* informed of each covert operation.

Correct: The President shall inform the intelligence committees of each covert operation *not later than 15 days after its date of conclusion*.

"Deems"

Problem. — The verb "to deem" has a proper, useful place in legislative writing. Properly used, "is deemed to be", "shall be considered to be", or "shall be treated as" are interchangeable phrases that create legal fictions that may be necessary to make a statute work, particularly in making provisions retroactive. The problem is that there is a temptation to take this passive voice, legal fiction usage of the verb and convert it into an active voice action verb. Since "deeming" is done by operation of law, it is impossible for an official of the executive branch, not possessing the lawmaking power, to "deem" anything. In short, the verb "to deem" is highly susceptible of misuse, with "deems" almost never having any proper use.

Solution. — When a legally binding finding by an executive branch official is sought to be used to "trigger" the operation of a legislative provision, the solution is to use "determines" rather than "deems". This accords the executive branch its proper role in implementing a statute rather than the improper role of making law by administrative decree.

Example:

Incorrect: Whenever the Secretary of State *deems* a country to be a state sponsor of international terrorism, the Secretary shall _____.

Correct: Whenever the Secretary of State *determines that* a country is a state sponsor of international terrorism, the Secretary shall _____.

"Effects"

Problem. — Some drafters, particularly Americans it seems, use "effect" as a verb to convey "to influence". This is incorrect.

Solution. — The verb the drafter apparently never learned in school but should be using in this case is "affect". There is a verb "to effect", meaning "to bring about", but there is rarely a need for this verb in legislation.

Examples:

Incorrect: The report shall describe how the actions of the foreign government *effected* United States foreign policy.

Correct: The report shall describe how the actions of the foreign government *affected* United States foreign policy.

"Execute", "Implement"

Problem. — Frequently, legislation requires a provision to be "executed" or "implemented" by a specified official of the executive branch of Government or in some specified way. The difficulty is that "to execute" sounds either harsh or laughable for the obvious reasons and "to implement" sounds a bit pretentious, awkward, or bureaucratic. "Execute" should make every drafter nervous for fear that it suggests the fate of the drafter!

Solution. — The problem is solved by substituting the more vernacular "to carry out". Although violating the principle of word economy by substituting three words for two, this substitution facilitates readability and is more pleasing to the ear.

Examples:

Incorrect: The President shall prescribe regulations *to execute* the provisions of this Act.

Correct: The President shall prescribe regulations *to carry out* the provisions of this Act.

"Includes but Not Limited to"

Problem. — Lawyers often insert the phrase "but not limited to" immediately after forms of the verb "to include" to guard against any inference that what is being specified in the sentence is an exhaustive listing. The problem is that "to include", by its plain meaning definition, is illustrative. One might even say it is inclusive! So the addition of this lawyerly phrase adds verbiage but no real meaning. The only value of the phrase is to justify a higher legal fee.

Solution. — The solution is easy. Omit "but not limited to" wherever a form of "to include" is written.[12] Not only will this improve readability but also, by promoting word economy, will shorten the legislation.

Examples:

Incorrect: The report shall *include, but not be limited to,* a description of X, Y, and Z.

Correct: The report shall *include* a description of X, Y, and Z.

"Person"

Problem No. 1. — "Person", as properly used in statutes,[13] includes both individuals ("natural persons") and "juridical entities", i.e., corporations, companies, associations, firms, and partnerships.[14] The error is to use "person" too broadly for the intended legal effect.

Solution. — Use "individual" where only natural persons are intended. In all other cases, as a precaution, define "person" to cover the broader meaning.

Example:

(_) Person. — The term "person" means —

(A) a natural person; and

(B) a corporation, business association, partnership, society, trust, any other nongovernmental entity, organization, or group, and any governmental entity operating as a business enterprise.

---

12. Note that the use of ", including _____" may be avoided entirely by first listing the included items followed by "and other _____", the blank to be filled in with the generic description of the class of items. This is a useful construct where the intention is to give the included items greater prominence.

13. Even the Constitution has been construed to protect the rights of corporations as well as individuals. *See, e.g., Citizens United v. Federal Election Commission*, 558 U.S.50 (2010) (holding that a statutory ban on the independent campaign expenditures of corporations violates the First Amendment.).

14. 1 U.S.C.§1 (2006).

Problem No. 2.—An additional problem occurs where the juridical entity must have a nexus to a particular country in order to establish the scope of the legislative provision. What is the appropriate nexus: the nationality of the ownership of the entity, the place where the entity is lawfully organized, or the place of doing business?

Solution.—To establish the nationality of a juridical entity, create a definition of "United States person" or "foreign person" in terms of the appropriate nexus. As a nexus, the nationality of the "beneficial" or "equitable" ownership, meaning capital stock ownership, is the most common.

Example:

(_) United States Person.—The term "United States person" means—

(A) a natural person who is a citizen of the United States or who owes permanent allegiance to the United States; and

(B) a corporation or other legal entity that is organized under the laws of the United States, any State or territory thereof, or the District of Columbia, if natural persons described in subparagraph (A) own, directly or indirectly, more than 50 percent of the outstanding capital stock or other beneficial interest in such legal entity.

"Powers"

Problem.—"Powers" has a broad, expansive meaning in plain English that does not carry over to legislative drafting. Drafters in the United States distinguish between the legally-sanctioned responsibilities of officials, on the one hand, and the capabilities of government entities, on the other hand, and do not use "powers" to cover both situations.

Solution.—To make this distinction, the word "powers" is reserved for the collective capabilities of government entities such as agencies, committees, commissions, and government corporations. Examples of these powers include the power to hold hearings, subpoena witnesses and documents, use a government seal, and to sue or be sued.[15] Where the drafter needs a term to encompass the duties and delegations of officials of the Government, that term is "authorities". Consequently, "powers" has a rather limited usage.

Examples:

Incorrect: The *authorities* of the Corporation include _____.

Correct: The *powers* of the Corporation include _____.

"Prior to", "Subsequent to"

Problem.—These are two-word, pretentious combinations that impede readability.

Solution.—There are readily available one-word substitutes in everyday English in "before" for "prior to" and in "after" for "subsequent to".

---

15. *See also* Chapter Four, Part I: Administrative Provisions, *supra.*

Examples:

Incorrect: *Prior to* obligating the funds, the President shall notify the Committees on Appropriations.

Correct: *Before* obligating the funds, the President shall notify the Committees on Appropriations.

"Program"

Problem. — A reference in a statute to a particular Government program presents the same problem as does a reference to a Government regulation. Just as the Executive may revoke any regulation so, too, may the Executive revoke or modify the regulation or regulations that comprise the Government program.

If, on the one hand, the drafter merely references a program in statute, then the statutory provision becomes obsolete and, arguably a nullity, in the event the Executive renames the program. If, on the other hand, the drafter establishes the entire program by statute, the drafter runs the risk of inadvertently omitting some of the legal authorities required to administer the program. Either way, programmatic language is a losing proposition.

Solution. — The easy solution is simply to avoid making any reference to a particular program and instead to refer only to the specific statutory authority or authorities involved. This permits the Executive to name the program by a regulation that cites those same statutory authorities. In any event, the Executive has no power to revoke authorities enacted by law.

Examples:

Incorrect: The President is authorized to carry out *the Economic Support Fund Program* with respect to _____.

Correct: The President is authorized to provide *assistance under chapter 4 of part II of the Foreign Assistance Act of 1961 (22 U.S.C. 2346 et seq.; relating to the economic support fund.)* with respect to _____.

"*: Provided,* That"

Problem. — The legislative proviso is a long-used device that has so much potential for making trouble that it should be completely eliminated. The proviso is inherently ambiguous since the reader cannot immediately determine whether or not an exception, condition, or independent thought is intended. In addition, a proviso may create a legal minefield wherever it disguises an independent thought since a failure to comply with the requirements of the proviso may be wrongly interpreted as vitiating the legal effect of the language preceding the proviso. In short, a proviso is a lawsuit waiting to happen.

Solution. — A substitute is always available for a proviso, depending only on what meaning is intended. If the drafter wishes to express an exception, then the proper substitute is ", except that" or a separate sentence setting forth the exception. If the intention is to express a condition, then the drafter should use "if", "unless", or "until". If, on the other hand, a completely independent thought is intended, then the drafter should create a new sentence out of the language of the discarded proviso.

Examples:

Incorrect: Amounts appropriated under this Act shall be available for disaster assistance for Haiti: *Provided,* That every 6 months the Secretary of State shall submit to Congress a report on _____. *[Failure to submit a timely report would seem to jeopardize the appropriation.]*

Correct: *Amounts appropriated under this Act shall be available for disaster assistance for Haiti. Every 6 months the Secretary of State shall submit to Congress a report on _____.*

"Pursuant to"

Problem. — There are thousands of places in United States statutes where "pursuant to" is used, either to refer to a specific legal authority or to compliance with a particular procedure. The problem, however, is that "pursuant to" now sounds harsh to the modern ear and looks a bit too much like the English of the 1600s. It distracts the reader from what is truly important in a sentence.

Solution. — Fortunately, the drafter may substitute the simple, unpretentious word "under" for "pursuant to" wherever "pursuant to" would precede a legal authority. In cases where "pursuant to" would precede a reference to a process or procedure, the phrase "in accordance with" appears to be the better substitute.

Example 1:

Incorrect: The President may act *pursuant to* section 301 of the ____ Act ...

Correct: The President may act *under* section 301 of the ____ Act ...

Example 2:

Incorrect: *Pursuant to* its adherence to the principle of nonintervention, the United States shall ...

Correct: *In accordance with* its adherence to the principle of nonintervention, the United States shall ...

"Said", "Such"

Problem. — "Said" and "such" are legalistic, stilted words that were once found useful as adjectives modifying nouns that were previously mentioned in the text. "Said" would precede a proper noun, and "such" would precede any other noun. Modern drafting practice dispenses with both words because they detract from readability and because there are alternatives that comport better with modern, conversational English.

Solution. — A good substitute for "said" is "the", which helps to explain why "said" disappeared from statutes several decades ago. "Such" has been more persistent and harder to eradicate. Modern drafters, however, substitute "that" when a singular noun is being modified and "those" when a plural noun is being modified. Better still is the substitution of "the" when the meaning is clear.

Example 1:

Incorrect: The Third Geneva Convention of 1946 does not bind the United States. *Said* Convention was never ratified by the United States.

Correct: The Third Geneva Convention of 1946 does not bind the United States. *The* Convention was never ratified by the United States.

Example 2:

Incorrect: The President shall submit to Congress a report on _____. *Such* report shall include _____.

Correct: The President shall submit to Congress a report on _____. *The* report shall include _____.

"Up To"

Problem. — The use of "up to" creates the same sort of ambiguity as does the use of "by" or "within", earlier discussed in this Part, except that "up to" is commonly used with quantities or amounts, especially dollar amounts, and thus requires a different alternative. The problem when "up to" is used is that it is unclear whether or not the last dollar or other last item in the amount is covered.

Solution. — Again the solution is easy. Simply substitute "not more than" for "up to".

Examples:

Incorrect: The President may use *up to* $1,000,000 of the funds for _____. [Unclear whether or not the one millionth dollar may be used.]

Correct: The President may use *not more than* $1,000,000 of the funds for _____.

"Which"

Problem. — A common mistake in English is to use "which" interchangeably with "that" to describe what follows a word. In fact, "which" and "that" have very different uses.

Solution. — The language that immediately follows "that" is indispensable to describing (and narrowing) the class of persons or objects that appear before "that". In contrast, the language that immediately follows "which" is always an incidental and legally unnecessary description of what precedes "which" and has no effect on narrowing any class of persons or objects. When used properly for these different purposes, a comma always precedes "which" but never precedes "that".

Examples:

Incorrect: The President may provide foreign assistance to any country *which* is friendly to the United States.

Correct: The President may provide foreign assistance to any country *that* is friendly to the United States.

Correct: The President may provide foreign assistance to Mexico, *which* is friendly to the United States.

Part IV: Outsmarting Statutory Interpretation

Introduction

To draft clearly it is not enough to apply common sense rules of clear expression and to avoid the pitfalls of "problem words". Whether or not a statute is clearly expressed depends in part on the eyes and ears of the consumer, and the primary consumer of a statute is a judge or administrator who is called upon to give it force. While ideally a drafter would like to avoid any need for statutory interpretation, this is an unrealistic goal. It is inevitable that over time gaps in the statutory scheme will be detected; the drafter simply cannot foresee all possible applications of draft language. In addition, clever lawyers will litigate based on supposed conflicts between one statutory provision and another. Where the volume of enacted laws is enormous, as in the United States, these conflicts are easy to find despite the drafter's best efforts to integrate new law with existing law seamlessly. Consequently, a drafter is well advised when drafting to take a moment to consider how a judge or administrator might interpret the language being drafted and to channel that interpretation in the drafter's favor.

American Theories of Statutory Interpretation in Brief

Intentionalism.—The traditional, predominant theory of United States statutory interpretation may be referred to as "intentionalism" or "purposive theory". The theory calls for the interpretation of statutory language based on what the legislature intended by the enactment of the statute.

"Legislative intent" may be gleaned from the statute itself or from sources outside the statute. These extrinsic sources, known in the United States as "legislative history", consist of the reports of the legislative committees, including the reports accompanying reported bills and resolutions and the joint explanatory statements of conferees ("statements of managers"), and the statements of the legislators.

If statutory language is unclear, the solution is to refer to legislative history. Intentionalists are divided, however, over whether or not to consider legislative history where the meaning of the statute is plain and unambiguous.[16] In either case, the theory calls for the courts to place themselves in the shoes of the legislature in interpreting the statute. The classic formulation of intentionalism is captured by the dicta that "a thing may be within the letter of the statute and yet not within the statute because not within its spirit, nor within the intention of its makers".[17] *See* Figure 5-2.

New Textualism.—While still a minority theory of statutory interpretation in United States courts, new textualism is growing in adherents. New textualism calls for the interpretation of statutes through the examination of the original meaning of the statutory text. Original meaning is determined by close scrutiny of the words and structure of the statute with extrinsic reference only to the way the same words are used in statutes enacted contemporaneously with the statute being interpreted. No resort to legislative history is made. New textualism freezes the interpretation of a statute as of its enactment and does not permit judicial speculation on how the legislature might have resolved the interpretive problem if the legislature had thought about it. The theory is best summarized by the observation of Justice Oliver Wendell Homes that "[w]e do not inquire what the legislature meant; we ask only what the statute means".[18] *See* Figure 5-2.

Figure 5-2

Aspects of Construction	Intentionalism	New Textualism
Guiding Principle	Intent of the Legislature	Original Meaning of Text
Legislative History	Yes	No, except to overturn absurd results
Plain Meaning Rule	Soft (overturnable by legis hist)	Hard, except to overturn absurd results
Extrinsic Aids	Legislative History	Contemporary statutes
Canons of Construction	Self-contradictory & useless	Commonsense grammar & logic rules
Structure of the Statute	Yes	Yes
Legal Theory	Law & Policy Inseparable	Law & Policy Separable

---

16. For an example of this dispute, *see United States v. Acker*, 361 U.S. 87 (1959), especially the dissenting opinion of Justice Felix Frankfurter at 95 arguing for resort to legislative history to trump plain meaning by saying that "[t]he Court's task is to construe not English but congressional English. Our problem is not what do ordinary English words mean, but what did Congress mean them to mean.".

17. *Rector of the Holy Trinity Church v. United States*, 143 U.S. 457, 459 (1892). In *Holy Trinity Church*, the Court construed a statute making it unlawful to import an alien "to perform labor or service of any kind" as excluding the employment services of a foreign cleric. *Id.*, at 458.

18. *Quoted in Schwegmann Bros. v. Calvert Distillers Corp.*, 341 U.S. 384, 397 (1951).

Which Theory Should the Drafter Prefer?—At first blush it would seem that the professional legislative drafter and the new textualist are kindred spirits. Both stress the importance of the plain meaning of the text. A drafter wants to see the text over which the drafter has labored countless hours given great deference. Most legislative drafters are all too familiar with the fragmentary and sometimes unreliable nature of legislative history prepared by harried congressional staffers, caught up in the pressure cooker of the legislative process, especially in the case of the "omnibus", mega-bills where:

> … legislative histories are either non-existent for many of the provisions or are highly suspect because you do not get a statement of managers that specifically reviews each of the provisions in the omnibus bill. Only the statement of managers, in my opinion, is worthy of great weight in the field of legislative history.[19]

On the other hand, the intentionalist's reliance on legislative history may serve to protect the drafter from the embarrassment of inevitable gaps in the statute caused by a failure to anticipate all the ways in which a draft might be applied. The intentionalist views the statute in the context of the entire legislative process and so seems to honor the legislative institution as a whole, of which the drafter is a part. The new textualist, in contrast, calls for the draft language to meet a high standard or else not be applied.

So this question is kind of like asking which parent do you love more: the parent who expects you to attend Harvard or the parent who does not care which school you attend, believing you to be a genius regardless? The answer is you love them both. Since many Federal judges like to show that the same result may be reached using either interpretive method, the drafter is well advised to choose words with both methods in mind.

Drafting for the Intentionalist Judge

Introduction.—While the legislative drafter cannot prevent an intentionalist judge from resorting to legislative history, the drafter may assist a judge in "finding" legislative intent intrinsically on the face of the statute by the way in which the drafter composes the long title and the findings, purposes, and definitions sections.

Long Title.—The long title is an abridged form of the "purposes" section and, thus, may become a source for determining the "intent of the legislature".[20]

Findings.—The way a findings section is worded may influence an intentionalist judge's search for legislative intent. Where, for example, the power of Congress to legislate is dependent on the finding of a real world "fact", such as whether or not a

---

19. Arthur J. Rynearson, *Office of the Senate Legislative Counsel, 1976–2003: Oral History Interviews, April 17–July 1, 2003*, at 135–136, Senate Historical Office, Washington, D.C. (2003).

20. *Rector of the Holy Trinity Church v. United States*, 143 U.S. 457, 462 (1892).

particular item moves in interstate commerce, the inclusion of a congressional finding on this matter in the text of the statute may sway the judge's opinion.[21]

Purposes.[22] — In legislative writing, the word "purpose" means "intent". So what better place for an intentionalist judge to seek legislative intent than the "purposes" section? Accordingly, the wise drafter will ensure that the purposes section is well written and strictly tailored to the drafter's understanding of the legislator's intent. A trick to doing this is to use the most basic words — words that serve as the lowest common denominator of what is being expressed. This will ensure that no unintended purpose is being captured.

Having done this, the conscientious drafter should take every opportunity to cross-reference to this section by using the phrase "to carry out the purposes of this Act" or the phrase "for the purposes of this Act" in the substantive provisions of the legislation. Use of either phrase will have the effect of limiting the scope of the duties, delegations, requirements, and entitlements made by the bill. This type of limitation is especially necessary in funding sections where appropriations must be made for a "purpose". A well-written purposes section will both facilitate the job of the intentionalist judge and also deter the judge from the urge to resort to legislative history.

Definitions. — Since the legislative process consists of several stages and each stage generates its own legislative history, the drafter at a later stage may incorporate in the latest draft the intent expressed in the legislative history surrounding an earlier draft. This is especially useful in the case of definitions. An interpretation, nuance, or "spin" that a legislative committee or legislator gives a word or phrase in a piece of legislation should, if possible, be included in the definitions section of the next draft of that legislation if that is acceptable to the proponents of the measure. By incorporating the added meaning on the face of the legislation, the drafter elevates its status from that of the work product of a legislative committee, a subgroup of Congress, to that of the work product of the entire Congress. This greatly enhances its interpretive value.

Drafting for the New Textualist Judge

Introduction. — How a new textualist judge views the text of a statute is quite different from that of an intentionalist judge. To appeal to a new textualist, the drafter will want to take special care with definitions, canons, and presumptions.

Definitions. — Because a new textualist judge will not resort to legislative history to determine the meaning of the text, whenever the drafter wishes a specialized meaning the drafter absolutely must achieve this through the definitions section. Conse-

---

21. *See, e.g., United States v. Lopez, 514 U.S. 549 (1995),* where the absence of a congressional finding relating to the effects upon interstate commerce of gun possession influenced the opinion of the Court.

22. For legislative systems outside the United States, "objectives" may be substituted for "purposes" if the former would better comport with previously enacted laws.

quently, there is more pressure on the drafter to make the definitions section a comprehensive collection of the specialized meanings than in the case of a statute reviewed by an intentionalist judge.

In the absence of a necessary definition, the new textualist judge will review the contemporary enactments of Congress to see how the term was defined or used in those enactments. In other words, the new textualist will attempt to determine Congress' word usage around the time of the enactment. The drafter may make this search moot by borrowing the definitions of contemporary enactments and incorporating them by cross-reference into the newer legislation. This cross referencing should take the following form: *In this Act, the term "_____" has the same meaning given the term in section ____ of _____ Act.*

Canons and Presumptions.—New textualists give more credence and weight to canons of statutory construction and make it harder to overturn presumptions than do intentionalists. To achieve clarity, in the case of canons, this enables the drafter to omit certain words and, in the case of presumptions, requires the drafter to insert "magic language". For more details, read the following two segments:

Canons of Statutory Construction

In the eyes of the new textualist, canons of statutory construction are common sense rules of grammar and logic.[23] Seven principal canons and what each one means to the drafter as a practical matter are as follows:

Plain Meaning Rule.—Unless specified otherwise and unless an absurd meaning would result, each word is construed in accordance with its plain ("dictionary") meaning.[24] This permits the drafter to leave most words undefined without fear of a contrary meaning creeping in through legislative history.

Whole Act Rule.—Unless specified otherwise, each provision of a statute must be given effect in a way that is harmonious with all other provisions of the statute.[25]

Application of the Whole Act Rule implies all of the following:

(1) Each provision shall be given effect.

(2) Different words shall be accorded different meanings.

(3) Later statements within the same legislative text prevail over earlier ones.

---

23. Antonin Scalia, *A Matter of Interpretation: Federal Courts and the Law* (1997), at 26. *But see* Llewellyn, *Remarks on the Theory of Appellate Decision and the Rules or Canons about How Statutes are to be Construed*, 3 Vand. L. Rev. 395 (1950). Intentionalists view the canons as meaningless and contradictory.

24. *2A Sutherland Statutes and Statutory Construction* (2007), 7th ed., revised by Norman J. Singer and J.D. Shambie Singer (1st–3d editions prepared by J.G. Sutherland), §46:1 at 137–141.

25. *Id.*, §46:5 at 189–190.

Useful as this rule is, the drafter should make explicit the relationship between different provisions where they are meant to interact through the use of such phrases as "subject to _____" and "except as provided in _____". This will help to guide the textualist judge.

Later Enactments Supersede Earlier Enactments.—A later, inconsistent statutory provision supersedes an earlier statutory provision to the extent of the inconsistency. While useful, application of this rule becomes moot where the later enactment amends the earlier enactment, as is frequently the case.

Special Rules Govern General Rules.—A special rule governs a more general rule. Again, the drafter may moot the application of this rule (1) by making a statutory amendment that creates an exception within the general rule, or (2) by expressing the general rule as an override of the special rule, usually by adding "notwithstanding any other provision of law" to the general rule.

Expressio Unius Est Exclusio Alterius.—The expression of the one is the exclusion of the other.[26] In short, words of exclusivity such as "only" or "solely" are unnecessary after most verbs. This eases the burden on the drafter considerably. Two examples may prove instructive, as follows:

(1) Where a sentence reads that "persons over the age of 64 are eligible for assistance", it is unnecessary to state that persons under the age of 65 are not eligible.

(2) Where it is stated that "the President is authorized to provide assistance for Cuba *if* Cuba establishes a democratic government", there is no need to say "only if" for it is implied that the absence of democracy will be insufficient to garner the assistance.

Noscitur A Sociis.—Each word is construed in the context of its surrounding words.[27] Rather than rely on "context", the drafter should handle word meanings in the definitions section.

Ejusdem Generis.—A general term included in a list of items is limited in scope to items of the same sort as the other items listed.[28] Reliance on this canon may be dangerous as it conflicts with the Plain Meaning Rule. A drafter who composes a series of words such as "pistols, rifles, machine guns, and other items" should not rely on the "other items" being interpreted as referring only to firearms but instead, by its plain meaning, should expect that all other items of any kind are covered. After all, who is to say that "firearms" is the limiting principle?

---

26. *Id.,* §47:23, at 404. "[A]ll omissions should be understood as exclusions".

27. *Id.,* §47:16, at 347–351. "[W]hen two or more words are grouped together, and ordinarily have a similar meaning, but are not equally comprehensive, the general word will be limited and qualified by the special word".

28. *Id.,* §47:17, at 357–360. This canon is a variant of *noscitur a sociis.*

Presumptions

Introduction. — A presumption is a judge-made rule that sets an automatic, default interpretation on a particular question of the application of a statute. From the viewpoint of a textualist,[29] a presumption may only be overcome by a clear statement to the contrary in the statute. Legislative intent, however gleaned, is of no avail. Consequently, presumptions tilt the interpretive playing field for a limited number of questions and appear arbitrary. On the one hand, they are justified as a way for the courts to protect against easy statutory encroachment certain values underlying the United States Constitution such as separation of powers, due process, and Federalism. On the other hand, they place a burden on the drafter to use "magic language" to overcome the presumption. This language is not always self-evident, and a failure to use it presents a legal pitfall to the unwitting drafter.

There is another potential pitfall where the drafter is unaware of the presumption and instead insists on drafting language to clarify something that requires no clarification. Ignorance is not always bliss; in legislative drafting unnecessary words only get the drafter into trouble. In short, because of presumptions, clarity is sometimes best achieved by silence.

The following paragraphs describe seven of the most frequently encountered presumptions affecting legislation:

Presumption against Implied Repeal

Description. — Perhaps the most frequently encountered and least burdensome presumption is the presumption against one statute impliedly repealing another statute. It is fundamental to the separation of powers doctrine that the judiciary does not show favoritism between congressional enactments but gives effect to each unless a contrary intent of Congress is "clear and manifest".[30] If a repeal is intended, it must be stated.

Clear Statement Example:

SEC.____. REPEAL.

Section ____ of _____ Act is repealed.

Presumption against Retroactivity

Description. — There is a presumption against the retroactive application of a statute affecting substantive rights, which is based generally on principles of fairness

---

29. At least one prominent textualist, Justice Antonin Scalia, questions where the Federal courts get the authority to establish presumptions: "Can we really just decree that we will interpret the laws that Congress passes to mean less or more than what they fairly say?". *Supra*, note 23, at 29.

30. *United States v. Borden Co.*, 308 U.S. 188, 198 (1939).

and on a need to avoid specific prohibitions in the United States Constitution. In terms of general fairness, it has long been considered prudent to avoid upsetting settled expectations and for individuals to have a chance to conform their conduct to the law. In terms of the Constitution, the Ex Post-Facto Clause, the Contracts Clause, the Takings Clause of the Fifth Amendment, the prohibition against bills of attainder, and the Due Process Clause all provide prohibitions against retroactivity that the drafter must observe.

This, however, does leave much room for retroactivity in civil law, and retroactivity may even serve a useful purpose, especially where there is a need to ensure that the statutory scheme is not circumvented between the date of drafting and the date the statute takes effect.

Historically, the presumption against retroactivity was applied in all cases absent a "clear statement" to the contrary. In 1994, however, dicta in a Supreme Court case suggested that the "clear statement" might be satisfied by a finding of "clear congressional intent".[31] The introduction of legislative intent into the calculus of retroactivity, of course, is inconsistent with new textualism. The drafter is best advised to avoid the legal dispute entirely and provide a clear statement on the face of the statute where retroactive application is sought. Where only prospective application is desired, as in the vast majority of enactments, statutory silence is the correct approach.

Clear Statement Example:

SEC.___. EFFECTIVE DATE.

> *This Act is deemed to have become effective on _____.*

Presumption in Favor of Severability

Description.—The various provisions of a statute are presumed to be severable, that is, if one provision is found invalid as having violated the Constitution, then remaining provisions are unaffected and valid if they are capable of independent operation.[32] To establish severability, then, a drafter need only remain silent. In the rare circumstance where *nonseverability* is desired, however, the drafter should so provide by means of a nonseverability section.

Clear Statement Example:

SEC.___. NONSEVERABILITY.

> *If any provision of this Act, or the application of the provision to any person or circumstance, is held to be unconstitutional, the remainder of this Act, and the application of the remaining provisions of the Act to any person or circumstance, shall be invalid and of no force or effect.*

---

31. *See Landgraf v. USI Film Products*, 511 U.S. 244 (1994).
32. *See Buckley v. Valeo*, 424 U.S. 1, 108 (1976); *INS v. Chadha*, 462 U.S. 919, 932 (1983).

Presumption against Federal Preemption

Description.—There is a presumption against Federal preemption of State and local laws in the absence of a clear statement, congressional intent, or a situation warranting an implied preemption.[33] In short, State and local laws are to be given deference. The various loopholes, however, make this one of the weakest presumptions. The weakness of the presumption is rooted in the tension between the Tenth Amendment of the Constitution, reserving to the States all powers not delegated to the Federal Government or prohibited to the States, and the Supremacy Clause, which makes Federal statutes supreme law of the United States. To be safe, the drafter should provide a clear statement wherever the drafter foresees that the Federal statute will need to supersede State action.

Clear Statement Example 1:

SEC.____. PURPOSE.

    The purpose of this Act is to set forth a comprehensive and complete framework to _____. [Blank to be filled in with a description of a national program at odds with State programs.]

Clear Statement Example 2:

SEC.____. EFFECT ON STATE LAW.

    The provisions of this Act supersede any provision of law of any State relating to _____.

Presumption against Abrogation of State Sovereign Immunity

Description.—There is a presumption that a Federal statute does not abrogate the sovereign immunity of the States, without which a State would be amenable to suit in Federal court. The presumption may only be overcome, and sovereign immunity abrogated, if Congress makes "its intention unmistakably clear in the language of the statute".[34] Statutory provisions that authorize in a general way civil actions in Federal courts are not sufficiently unequivocal to overcome the presumption.[35]

---

33. In the absence of a clear statement or evidence of intent, courts will imply Federal preemption where the Federal statutory scheme is so pervasive as to leave the States no room, where the conflict between the Federal statute and a State law is so significant as to make it physically impossible to comply with both, or where the State law stands as an obstacle to the accomplishment of the purposes of the Federal statute. *See, e.g., Arizona v. United States*, 567 U.S. ____ (2012) citing favorably *Gade v. National Solid Wastes Mgmt. Assn.*, 505 U.S. 88, 115 (1992), *Rice v. Santa Fe Elevator Corp.*, 332 U.S. 218, 230 (1947), and *Hines v. Davidowitz*, 312 U.S. 52, 67 (1941).

34. *Atascadero State Hospital v. Scanlon*, 473 U.S. 234, 242 (1985).

35. *Id. at* 246.

The presumption may at first seem unnecessary inasmuch as the Eleventh Amendment of the Constitution establishes the sovereign immunity of the States. Nevertheless, Congress may legislate under its enforcement power of the Fourteenth Amendment to open up States to suit in Federal court. So the presumption does serve a purpose — supporting Federalism.

Clear Statement Example:

SEC.＿＿. ABROGATION OF STATE SOVEREIGN IMMUNITY.

A State may be liable for money damages in any civil action brought in United States district court involving ＿＿＿＿＿＿＿＿＿＿＿. This section is enacted by Congress in exercise of its power to enforce the Fourteenth Amendment of the Constitution.

Presumption against Extraterritoriality

Description. — There is a presumption against the application of a United States statute outside the territorial jurisdiction of the United States that may only be overcome by "the affirmative intention of the Congress clearly expressed".[36] A broadly worded statutory provision does not by itself overcome the presumption.[37] The presumption is necessary to protect against unintended clashes between United States laws and foreign laws. It is assumed that Congress is aware of the presumption when it legislates and phrases its statutes accordingly.

There are a variety of words and phrases that will suffice to overcome the presumption. The term "abroad", "overseas", "outside the United States", "within or without the United States", "person subject to the jurisdiction of the United States", or even "wherever situated" may be used to establish extraterritorial application. Usually, the most precise and explicit reference is the best choice.

Clear Statement Example:

This Act shall apply to any activity relating to ＿＿＿＿, whether carried out within or without the United States.

Presumption against Superseding a Treaty

Description. — A statute is presumed not to supersede a treaty or other international agreement unless Congress clearly evinces an intention to do so.[38] The statutory phrase "notwithstanding any other provision of law" is insufficient to overcome the presumption.[39] The presumption derives from the equal legal status given statutes and treaties under the Supremacy Clause and from the serious consequences atten-

---

36. *EEOC v. Arabian American Oil Co.*, 499 U.S. 244 (1991).

37. *Id.* at 251.

38. "[A]n Act of Congress ought never to be construed to violate the law of nations, if any other possible construction remains". *Murray v. Charming Betsy*, 6 U.S. 64 (1804).

39. *United States v. The Palestine Liberation Organization*, 695 F. Supp. 1456, 1468 (1988).

dant to breaches of international obligations. While the presumption may be overcome by a clear statement, the result is only effective for United States domestic law and does not relieve the United States of its international obligations.

Clear Statement Example:

Notwithstanding section 11 of the United Nations Headquarters Agreement, no office of the Palestinian Authority may be maintained in the United States.

Overuse and Misuse of Statutory Construction Sections

Statutory Construction Sections Defined. — A "statutory construction", "rule of construction", or "statutory interpretation" section is a section that provides explicit guidance on the interpretation of the statute with respect to a particular matter of possible ambiguity or vagueness. To ensure the correct interpretation of the matter, the section usually negates the unintended meaning. Consequently, such a section may appeal to either an intentionalist or a new textualist.

Overuse Common. — The statutory construction section is highly susceptible of overuse. In most cases, the ambiguity or vagueness should have been addressed directly by revising the substantive provision where it arises and not by adding a statutory construction section. This type of section is effectively a band-aid on the legislation. Its principal use occurs near the end of the legislative process when it may be politically unacceptable to re-open and revise key provisions of a bill and yet a dispute on interpretation needs to be resolved.

Misuse to be Avoided. — Statutory construction sections are commonly misused to negate inferences that Congress has no power to negate. Specifically, many statutory construction sections attempt to interpret the United States Constitution by emphasizing that the statute does not alter certain referenced constitutional powers. As such an alteration is beyond the reach of statute anyway, this type of expression is unnecessary, meaningless, and confusing. It is not good legislative drafting.

Also avoid using a statutory construction section as a purely political statement that restates the obvious as a matter of emphasis. In legislative drafting, repetitive language does not solve problems; it creates them.

Examples:

Incorrect:

SEC.___. CONSTRUCTION.

Nothing in this Act may be construed to alter the Commander-in-Chief power of the President under Article II, section 2, clause 1 of the Constitution.

Correct:

SEC.___. STATUTORY CONSTRUCTION.

Nothing in this Act may be construed to require specific statutory autho-
rization for the participation of the United States Armed Forces in the head-
quarters operations of the North Atlantic Treaty Organization. [Interpreting
what is meant by a statutory requirement that the use of the Armed Forces
in hostilities be "specifically authorized".]

Part V: Myths about Legislative Drafting

Introduction

With so many rules and techniques to aid the drafter in writing clearly, the reader
is probably asking "How can the professional legislative drafter defend the current
state of the statute books?" Specifically, how does the drafter answer the following
complaints voiced in the media about legislative writing:

Why Aren't the Laws Written in Plain English?

This leading question is often posed to legislative drafters and what it suggests is
largely not true. The vast majority of the bills, resolutions, and amendments introduced, passed, or enacted into law by Congress are drafted in "plain English". They
are drafted by the professionals of the Senate and House Legislative Counsel Offices
using the same methods of clarity described in this chapter. These drafters have no
use for legalese, political science jargon, or the other mistakes that prevent clear expression. Occasionally the language of a particularly sticky policy is dictated directly
by Members of Congress or their staffs, with mixed results on clarity, but everything
considered Federal legislation is fairly plainly written. Any suggestion that it is not is
what we may call a "bum rap"!

Why Are the Laws So Hard to Read?

A better question than the drafter's choice of English vocabulary is why the laws
are (allegedly) difficult to read. It is certainly true that legislation and statutes are
not recreational, bedtime reading—not even for drafters. Shouldn't reading them
be easier?

To answer this, one needs to understand what impedes readability. While the av-
erage reader craves the interesting and the easily understandable, legislation tends to
be dry and complicated.

The dry, "uninteresting" aspect of legislative writing may be explained simply from two of the drafting rules described in this chapter. First, the need for consistency in the choice of words necessarily results in a rather limited, repetitive lexicon that does not excite the reader. Secondly, legislation, like any other official document, must include formal titles and make precise, formal references that are guaranteed to make the reader yawn. This is largely unavoidable. The drafter who deviates from these principles is likely to pay a price in the interpretation of the writing.

The complicated nature of legislation usually reflects a complicated policy, which in turn reflects our complex, modern society with its frequently intractable socio-economic problems. It also reflects a long history of lawmaking in the United States, so extensive that there is hardly a subject "under the sun" that has not been addressed by statute. More recent Acts tend to carve out exceptions and conditions to earlier Acts and add to the complexity of the statute books. United States statute books sometimes resemble the Grand Canyon, with new layer after older layer of law accumulating, not always fully integrated.

What particularly frustrates Members of Congress and their staffs is the resistance of the drafter to restating the law and instead using "cut and bite" amendments to revise earlier statutes. Amendments that strike, insert, or strike and insert individual words and phrases do make legislation opaque and time consuming to read. However, they avoid gratuitously reopening previously established policy and political wounds, for which Senators and Representatives should be especially thankful. Furthermore, where amendments are being made to the United States Code, they will in any event be seamlessly integrated in the next printing of the Code. So an opaque bill may yet result in a highly transparent law.

So, yes, readability in legislative drafting is sometimes sacrificed to further other objectives.

Why Is Legislation So Long?

Mostly, it is short to medium in length. What makes the occasional bill long is usually (1) the complexity of the policy being expressed, or (2) the number of statutory amendments being made by the bill. The remedies of having simple policy and not amending any existing law are not realistic. Those solutions elevate a momentary transparency at the expense of long-term legal uncertainty and incoherence. Comprehensive governmental reforms tend to require lengthy bills.[40] Get over it!

The only case where the length of a bill should be of concern is with respect to omnibus appropriations bills. At the end of a session of Congress, when time is short and the 12 required appropriations bills have not all been passed, to the shame of

---

40. The classic example is the Patient Protection and Affordable Care Act of 2010 (124 Stat. 119), which runs 905 pages in the Statutes at Large.

Congress, the Appropriations Committee staff will bundle the remaining unpassed bills together into a single bill, without integrating or systematizing the provisions, thereby creating a monster bill that is almost impossible to use because of its duplicative numbering. Instead, the papers should be turned over to a professional legislative drafter for proper preparation like any other bill.

Isn't Legislative Drafting Mind-Numbing?

No. Legislative drafting is a constant challenge to capture someone else's intent precisely. There always seems to be a clearer way to express a matter that is eluding the drafter. Choosing the correct words to capture policy and to achieve economy of language is both intellectually difficult and highly absorbing. It is somewhat akin to doing a crossword puzzle or any other word puzzle. Time often flies while drafting.

Now admittedly there are some extensive periods of tedious work in drafting any long bill or resolution—preparing conforming amendments especially comes to mind—but even here the drafter is likely to have opportunities to demonstrate creativity in organization and presentation of the language.

There is a novelty to drafting each bill and resolution that keeps the process fresh. Each bill and resolution is tailor-made to suit the sponsor and circumstances so that it is rare that two pieces of legislation within the same House of Congress are exactly alike.

Test Your "Clarifying" Skills

Drafting Exercise No. 5

Please "clarify" the following text and format as a section:

> Whenever the Defense Secretary deems that the UN could use, *inter alia*, the back-up of US troops in the Congo, the Secretary shall send a report on the situation on the ground there that requires the use of such troops to Congress. Thereafter, no US military can go to the Congo until 30 days subsequent to the report's review by Congress: *Provided,* That the President may suspend this provision if vital to the national security. If any provision of this section is held invalid, the remainder shall not be affected thereby.

Check your answer in Appendix C.

Postscript

Legislative Drafting and the Rule of Law

It will be of little avail to the people that the laws are made by men of their own choosing, if the laws be ... so incoherent that they cannot be understood ... or undergo such incessant changes that no man who knows what the law is today can guess what it will be tomorrow.[1]

Why Draft Correctly?

Having successfully mastered the five basic steps to drafting legislation, the first-time drafter might reasonably ask "What are the benefits of applying this discipline?" Why be so fussy about how the law is written when judges, especially intentionalist judges, will say what the law is[2] based on their philosophy of statutory interpretation? To put it bluntly, is there any reason to draft correctly?

Not surprisingly, my answer is a resounding YES! It is my deepest conviction that the way we write law reflects the role we envision for law in our society. If we truly want a society that respects the rule of law and democratic principles, we will want our laws to be imbued with the following five values:

Democratic Values to Be Found in Law

(1) **Transparency.** — Statutory law in a democratic society needs to be open and accessible, not obtuse, obscure, and buried. Citizens must be put on notice as to what the law is, and judges, administrators, and private citizens must be able to easily refer

---

1. Alexander Hamilton or James Madison, *The Federalist No. 62* at 2:190 (1788).

2. "It is emphatically the province and duty of the judicial department to say what the law is". Marshall, C.J., writing for the Court in *Marbury v. Madison*, 5 U.S. 137, 177 (1803).

to the law. Law that is open and accessible helps to thwart corruption.[3] For these reasons, every law should be transparent.

(2) **Accountability.**—In addition to being a source of Federal law, Federal statutes are the means by which the people, through their elected representatives in Congress, hold Government officials accountable for their actions. As such, well-crafted statutes facilitate the performance by Congress of its oversight function with respect to the executive branch of Government.

(3) **Predictability.**—A well-written statute is one that produces predictable results. This is achieved by making the law internally consistent and coherent and by setting clear boundaries. Boundaries are important so that Government does not apply statutes unfairly or unequally. Statutes must say what they mean and mean what they say. Otherwise, unintended consequences result. Statutes serve a dual purpose. They not only represent the majority will but also represent where the majority will ends. It is as important to know who is not covered by a statute as to know who is covered. By setting word boundaries so that only the class of persons intended to be covered by a statute is actually covered, minority rights are protected.

(4) **Enforceability.**—For a law to be fully effective it must be enforceable. Otherwise, law degenerates into a political tract or a statement of principles that does not present a rule of decision for the courts. Any situation in which representative government cannot obtain compliance with the laws, or in which a private citizen cannot obtain redress from arbitrary government action outside the law, is inherently anti-democratic.

(5) **Constitutionality.**—A well-written statute is one that stays within the limits that the Constitution imposes on Governmental action. Those limits include the limits associated with due process, equal protection, First Amendment rights, separation of powers, and Federal-State allocation of powers. These are the first principles of our Constitution and are fundamental to maintaining the rule of law. To violate the Constitution knowingly through statutory writing has occasionally been done as a political tactic but is poor legislative drafting and even poorer citizenship.

How the Five-Step Drafting Process Promotes Democratic Values

If the reader is still unconvinced that these values have anything to do with drafting legislation, let us briefly examine each step of legislative drafting to see how it might promote any of the values mentioned.

Achieving the Intended Legal Effect.—Enforceability, accountability, and constitutionality are all goals of "legalizing" legislation. Certainly nothing enhances the

---

3. "Sunlight is said to be the best of disinfectants". Louis D. Brandeis, *Other People's Money* at 92 (1914).

enforceability of a statute like a specific enforcement mechanism. In addition, a drafter's careful choice of subjects and verbs is mainly designed to promote accountability. Ensuring fairness, nondiscrimination, and respect for fundamental rights, the separation of powers, and Federalism all promote the constitutionality of the draft.

Choosing the Right Legislative Vehicle.—"Formalizing" the draft is a matter of ensuring that the legislative format complies with the requirements of the Constitution and the Federal statutes and House and Senate rules made under the Constitution. All legislative vehicles must be specifically provided for, or authorized by, the Constitution, and the use of any such vehicle to by-pass the law-making procedures of the Constitution in order to exercise a legislative veto is invalid.

Relating to Existing Law.—Where legislation amends existing law, the seamless, integrated statutory text that is the end-product promotes transparency by compiling all the law on the same subject in one place. In addition, whether the new legislation relates to existing law by the inclusion of statutory amendments or by overriding existing law, predictability of legal outcomes is promoted because potential conflicts in statutory provisions are being eliminated.

Organizing the Legislative Text.—A well-organized legislative measure, easily usable as a research tool by a judge, administrator, or private citizen, is the embodiment of transparency. Proper organization also establishes the correct relationship of one legislative provision to another and the overall coherence of the statute, which in turn promotes the predictability of its application.

Achieving Clarity of Expression.—At its core, clarifying a draft text is a matter of adjusting word boundaries and necessarily affects the boundaries of the class of persons or objects covered by the legislation. Clearly demarcating this coverage promotes predictability and avoids unintended consequences. Careful word choice and the avoidance of "problem words" have the added advantages of making the text more readable and transparent. Finally, clarity is the eternal enemy of ambiguity, overbreadth, and vagueness, any of which might violate the fundamental fairness guaranteed by the Due Process Clause of the United States Constitution. So, in those situations, clarity promotes the norm of constitutionality.

The Challenge to the Drafter

In the political environment of Congress it is easy to lose sight of these democratic values and to shortchange the basic steps in drafting a well written law. Timelines are short and partisanship is abundant. There are daily pressures on the drafter to turn legislative drafting into political treatise-writing devoid of law. If not vigilant, a drafter may become a mere typist for politicians,[4] an enabler of shoddy legislation. This must be resisted if the integrity of lawmaking is to be maintained.

If you want a Government that is transparent, accountable, and subject to the rule of law, you need to fight for it every day, over and over again, in small ways as well as great. And what better place to wage that battle than around the written word, which may outlive us all?

Conclusion

I hope that, through using this manual, you have come to appreciate three aspects of writing legislation:

First, drafting legislation is about writing law as well as about making policy and playing politics. This may seem obvious but is all too often a novel idea on Capitol Hill.

Secondly, statutes only assume a legal character to the extent that they establish legal relationships and reflect certain enduring legal principles, such as transparency, accountability, predictability, enforceability, and constitutionality. These legal relationships and principles are at the heart of what it means to do professional legislative drafting.

Thirdly, the goal of the legislative drafter is, or ought to be, to ensure that these legal concepts will be woven into the fabric of the statutes through the steps of legalizing, formalizing, integrating, organizing, and clarifying each new prospective law. It is this role that makes the professional legislative drafter indispensable to the legislative process and the rule of law in a democratic society.

> "Let us raise a standard to which the wise and honest can repair …"
>
> *George Washington at the Constitutional Convention, 1787*

---

4. In the political arena, a lawyer must never forget who is the lawyer in the room. "I am not a potted plant", asserted Brendan Sullivan, Esq., while representing Oliver North before the Senate Iran-Contra Investigatory Committee in July 1987.

Appendices

Appendix A

The United States Legislative Process: A Drafter's View

Appendix A contains all that a legislative drafter needs to know about the United States legislative process. While this Appendix focuses on how a Senate-originated bill[1] becomes law, a bill may, of course, originate in the House of Representatives instead of the Senate, in which case the process between the two Houses would be reversed. *See* Appendix B(3) for examples of how the front page of a bill changes during the law-making process.

---

1. The process with respect to bills applies equally to joint, concurrent, and "simple" resolutions, except that concurrent and simple resolution are not presented to the President and "simple" resolutions do not require bicameral passage.

In the Senate

Figure A-1

Senate Legislative Process

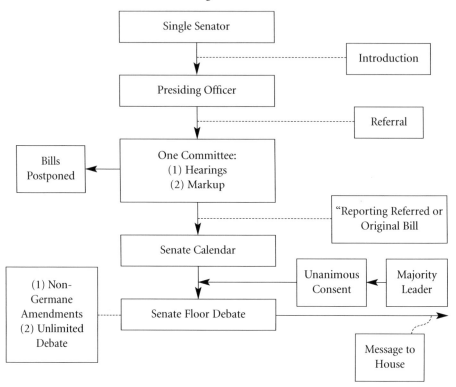

Introduction of a Senate Bill

Alternate Ways to Begin the Process. — The legislative process in the Senate begins either with the introduction of a bill by a Senator or with the "reporting" of an "original" bill by a Senate committee.[2] An original bill is a bill that a committee originates, that is to say, prepares from scratch without the bill having been introduced by a Senator and referred to the committee by the whole Senate.

Designation and Numbering of Bills. — When a bill is introduced in the Senate, or an original bill is reported by a committee to the Senate, the Bill Clerk at the Sen-

---

2. Throughout the legislative process, a Member of Congress or congressional committee may obtain drafting assistance on any bill, resolution, or amendment from the Office of the Legislative Counsel of the Senate or the House of Representatives, as the case may be. *See, e.g.,* section 1303(b) of the Revenue Act of 1918 (2 U.S.C. 275). Each office is under the nonpartisan supervision of the President pro tempore of the Senate or the Speaker of the House of Representatives, as the case may be.

ate desk[3] will give the bill its designation and assign the bill a number, both of which will remain with the bill throughout its entire legislative journey, even if it goes to the House of Representatives!

A designation is simply an abbreviation that identifies the type of legislative measure and the House of Congress originating the measure. In the case of a Senate-originated bill, the designation is simply "S.".[4]

Bills are numbered in the order in which they are introduced during a Congress, without regard to the session of Congress in which the introduction occurs.[5] This means there are many bills from past Congresses bearing the same number,[6] and therefore a bill may only be specifically identified by reference to the numbered Congress in which the bill was introduced. At the end of a Congress, if not enacted, the bill dies[7]. A bill having the same text, of course, may be re-introduced in the subsequent Congress, but the bill will be assigned a new number and will not carry over the congressional action taken on the similar bill in the previous Congress.

Who May Introduce a Bill? — Any Senator may introduce a Senate bill, and it is important to note that the President of the United States may never introduce a bill. This distinguishes the United States legislative system from parliamentary and many other legislative systems. Although the President may recommend legislative measures to Congress,[8] these are only recommendations, and they may not result in the introduction of a bill. As a matter of comity, and perhaps good politics, too, a bill prepared by a department or agency of the executive branch is usually introduced by the chairman of the congressional committee having jurisdiction over the matter "by request", which is always indicated in a parenthetical after the chairman's name on the bill. Such a bill is rarely acted upon by the Senate, although it may serve as the basis for another bill.

---

3. The "Senate desk" is the area in the front of the Senate chamber below the dais occupied by the Presiding Officer. The Bill Clerk is an official under the supervision of the Secretary of the Senate. The Secretary is elected by the whole Senate upon the recommendation of the Majority Leader.

4. Senate-originated joint resolutions, concurrent resolutions, and "simple" resolutions are designated as "**S.J.Res.**", "**S.Con.Res.**", and "**S.Res.**", respectively, and House-originated bills, joint resolutions, concurrent resolutions, and "simple" resolutions are designated as "**H.R.**", "**H.J.Res.**", "**H.Con.Res.**", and "**H.Res.**", respectively.

5. The second section of the Twentieth Amendment of the Constitution requires Congress to convene at noon on January 3rd of each year, unless another date is prescribed by law. By virtue of the two-year terms of Representatives beginning in 1789, a new Congress convenes every odd-numbered year. The first day of a new Senate, for example, is typified by the introduction of a great number of bills, with the first 10 bill numbers reserved for bills favored by the Majority Leader and the next 10 numbers for bills favored by the Minority Leader.

6. There are not as many bills designated "**S.** 1" as there are Congresses only because the first several Congresses did not number their bills.

7. Joint, concurrent, and "simple" resolutions also die at the end of a Congress, although the expiration of a Senate ("simple") resolution would not seem to be required by the Senate's nature as a "continuing body".

8. U.S. Const., art. II, §3, cl. 1. This power and the veto power comprise the totality of the President's legislative powers.

Who Drafts the Introduced Bill? — The usual practice is for the sponsoring Senator to request an attorney-drafter of the Office of the Legislative Counsel to draft the bill for introduction. Although the final product is solely the policy of the sponsoring Senator and may contain some language suggested by the Senator, the Senator's legislative staff, a lobbyist, or even an official of the executive branch, the bulk of the language, including all technical language, is the work of the attorney-drafter.

How Is a Bill Introduced? — A bill may be introduced by a Senator standing on the Senate floor who obtains recognition from the Presiding Officer to do so or, more commonly, by a member of the Senator's staff submitting to the cloakroom staff the bill, signed by the Senator, anytime on a day in which the Senator is attending a Senate session. The cloakroom staff in turn directs the bill to the Bill Clerk for recording as an introduced bill. The Bill Clerk arranges for each introduced bill to be printed by the Government Printing Office.

Sponsors vs. Cosponsors. — The only sponsor of a Senate bill is the Senator who introduces the bill.

Many congressional aides mistakenly believe that cosponsorship gives the cosponsor introduction privileges. There is no such thing as joint sponsorship in Congress. A cosponsor is a Member of Congress who wants to be associated with a bill introduced by another Member of Congress and who obtains the consent of the sponsor at the time of introduction of the bill, or who thereafter obtains the unanimous consent of the whole body, to be listed on the bill as such. Period. Nothing more.

Companion Bills. — Frequently, Senators and Representatives will coordinate to introduce identically worded bills in their respective Houses on the same day or soon thereafter. There is no technical reason for these "companion" bills to be identically worded, however, since only one House's bill may be enacted.[9]

Referral to a Senate Committee

Standard for Referrals. — Upon the introduction of a bill in the Senate, the Presiding Officer of the Senate[10] is required to refer the bill to the committee having jurisdiction over the predominant subject matter of the bill.[11] Rule XXV of the Standing

---

9. A House-passed bill may be considered and not referred to committee if a Senate companion bill has been placed on the Calendar of Business.

10. The Constitution provides that the Presiding Officer of the Senate is the Vice President of the United States or, in his absence, the President pro tempore of the Senate. U.S. Const., art. I, § 3, cls. 4 & 5. In turn, the President pro tempore will ordinarily rotate, for brief periods each, the responsibility of presiding over the Senate among all the Senators of the majority party in the Senate.

11. Rule XVII(1) of the Standing Rules of the Senate.

Rules of the Senate lists the various committee jurisdictions.[12] A referral is customarily made upon the recommendation of the Parliamentarian.[13] A Senator may appeal the decision of the Presiding Officer to the whole Senate.

Where a bill touches upon the jurisdiction of more than one committee, a Senator may request unanimous consent that the bill be referred to multiple committees, a practice called "multiple referral". A multiple referral may be joint or sequential. A joint referral involves the consideration of the same bill by more than one committee at the same time. A sequential referral involves the consideration of the bill by an additional committee only after another committee has reported the bill. A referral in the Senate may not be made of only a part of a bill. Because a single objection will kill a unanimous consent (also known as "UC") request for a multiple referral, such referrals are not common.

Obtaining a Favorable Referral.—The referral of a bill is not an exact science. There are overlapping jurisdictions between committees, and there are subjects that are not listed under any committee's jurisdiction. A Senator will naturally seek to have the Senator's bill referred to a committee on which the Senator sits or which is otherwise friendly to the Senator's views. The temptation to "game" the system is enormous.

A legislative drafter may be drawn into this in three ways. First, the long title and short title of the bill may be drafted to slant the wording toward the subject matter of the committee to which referral is sought. Secondly, where there is a choice of executive branch officials in whom to vest the legal duties and responsibilities under the bill, the drafter may vest those duties and responsibilities in officials whose oversight is conducted by the target committee. Thirdly, a bill may be drafted as an amendment to an Act over which the target committee has jurisdiction even though the bill's subject matter does not neatly fit within that Act. None of these drafting tricks works, however, if the Parliamentarian determines that the predominant subject matter of the bill lies elsewhere.

Circumventing Committee Referral.—Occasionally an introduced bill is not referred to committee. By unanimous consent, the Majority Leader may hold the bill at the Senate desk or place the bill on the Senate Calendar of Business without committee referral.[14]

---

12. The Legislative Reorganization Act of 1946 first established committee jurisdictions in the written rules of each House of Congress.

13. The Parliamentarian is under the supervision of the Secretary of the Senate.

14. Under Senate Rule XIV(4), a House-passed bill will be placed on the Calendar of Business and not referred to committee if objection is made to proceeding to further consideration of the bill. In addition, under Senate Rule XIV(6) (the so-called "over, under the Rule" procedure) a concurrent or simple resolution that has been submitted will be held at the Senate desk when objection is heard to its immediate consideration. The resolution will be laid before the Senate during the Morning Hour of the next legislative day. If the resolution is not then disposed of, the resolution will be placed on the Senate Calendar of Business without committee referral.

Senate Committee Action

Action Not Mandatory.—Committees are the graveyards of most introduced bills. This is so because each committee chairman may choose not to schedule committee consideration of a bill and, as previously noted, the bill will die at the end of the Congress. The discretionary nature of committee action stands in stark contrast to the system in many foreign countries where the legislatures are required to consider every legislative measure. The power of the committee chairman to kill legislation is also an exception to the historical trend toward the diminished power of committee chairmen and the increasing power of minority party members of committees.

Hearings.—Committees consider bills by holding hearings and "markup" sessions.[15] Hearing testimony from the public rarely results in changes to the text of a bill but may play an important role in garnering public support, especially from special interest groups, for the bill. Testimony expressing the support or opposition of the executive branch to a specific bill or amendment, on the other hand, does tend to be influential in shaping the text since opposition by the President implies the threat of a veto.

Markup Sessions.—A "markup" session is a committee meeting in which the committee members consider a specific bill, vote to approve or reject amendments making changes to the text of the bill, and vote on whether or not to place the bill, as amended, on the Senate Calendar of Business.[16] When a committee votes to place a bill on the Calendar the committee is said to have "ordered" the bill "reported".[17] The act of filing with the Senate desk the referred bill, together with any amendments adopted by the committee, or an original bill, for placement on the Calendar of Business is known as "reporting" the bill. When a bill is reported, the Legislative Clerk[18] will assign the bill a calendar number and have the bill reprinted. The calendar number will appear on the face of the reprinted bill and is distinct from the designation number of the bill.

Referred Bills vs. Original Bills.—The target of a markup session may be either a bill that has been referred to the committee or a legislative document prepared by the chairman of the committee, which is frequently known as the "chairman's mark".

---

15. As a reform in the Senate and House rules in the aftermath of the Watergate scandal, all committee hearings and markups and all conference committee sessions are required to be open to the public unless the committee members vote to hold a closed, "executive" session.

16. The markup described is one held at the full committee level. Some committees mark up at the subcommittee level first, with the legislation being reported to the full committee where it undergoes a full committee markup. A subcommittee may mark up only if the subcommittee has legislative jurisdiction over the subject matter of the legislation.

17. A bill may be reported favorably or unfavorably, but since a committee has no obligation to act on a bill a vote to order a bill reported usually indicates a favorable recommendation by the committee.

18. The Legislative Clerk is an official under the supervision of the Secretary of the Senate.

The chairman's mark may be carefully drafted in bill form or may be a loose amalgam of legislative provisions or specifications that will be drafted in bill form after the committee agrees to report the measure. If agreed to, the chairman's mark is reported by the committee to the Senate as an original bill, which is given a designation and number for the first time when it is placed on the Senate Calendar of Business.

Sometimes a markup session will be held on several competing bills on the same subject but shortly on in the session a chairman's mark will be proposed. This is done in order to avoid having to choose among the various referred bills (and among their Senate sponsors) to select a single bill for reporting. The chairman's mark is also a means to assert the power of the chairman and the majority party committee staff.

Markup Amendments: Perfecting vs. Substitute Amendments.—Either a referred bill or a chairman's mark is subject to amendment by any member of the committee. An amendment may be a perfecting or substitute amendment. A perfecting amendment strikes, inserts, or strikes and inserts a word, phrase, or block of text, which is less than the entirety of the underlying text. A substitute amendment strikes the entire text proposed to be inserted by an amendment of another Senator, or the entire text of the bill itself, and inserts replacement language. A substitute amendment to the entire text of a bill is known as an "Amendment In the Nature of a Substitute".

Preparing the Reported Bill.—All amendments agreed to by the committee to a referred bill must be highlighted on the face of the bill when the bill is reprinted in its reported form. This is done by showing deleted text by striking through the text using linetype print and by showing new, inserted text in italic print.[19] These amendments constitute proposals to the entire Senate by the committee and do not become part of the bill until the Senate votes to approve them.

The choice of whether to report a bill with several, individually highlighted perfecting amendments or a single Amendment In the Nature of a Substitute, which buries all the changes in the text, turns on a matter of legislative tactics. Where the changes in text are few and their easy identification is important, the use of perfecting amendments is indicated. Where the changes in text are numerous or are intended to be disguised, or where the overall readability of the reported bill is important, the use of an Amendment In the Nature of a Substitute is indicated. The decision on how to display the amendments is made by the majority staff of the committee, in consultation with the appropriate attorney from the Legislative Counsel's Office, subject to the approval of the chairman.

When an amendment is made to a chairman's mark, on the other hand, there is no way to highlight the amendment by linetype or italic print because the chairman's mark represents the proposal of an original bill that has not yet been printed as a

---

19. In the rare case in the Senate where the bill has been referred to more than one committee, the additional committee or committees will highlight amendments using an alternative typeface style, such as boldface brackets for deletions and boldface italics for insertions, so that each committee's proposed amendments are distinguishable.

Senate legislative measure. No introduced bill is being changed. The amendment is simply included seamlessly in the evolving text of the original bill in regular, Roman typeface. The Senate never votes to approve any change in text that was made by committee in the development of an original bill.

Accompanying Reports. — When a committee orders a bill reported, the committee staff will prepare a report[20] to accompany the bill upon its filing on the Senate Calendar of Business. The report will describe the votes and other actions taken by the committee on the bill and the budgetary and regulatory impact, if any, of the bill and will indicate any changes to existing law that would be made if the bill becomes law. This latter matter is done in compliance with the Senate rule known as the Cordon Rule.[21]

Senate Floor Action

Proceeding to Consideration of the Bill. — Senate floor action on a bill begins as soon as the bill is "called off the Calendar". The Standing Rules of the Senate contain a procedure[22] for calling up bills in the chronological order in which each bill was placed on the Senate Calendar of Business, as indicated by the calendar number of the reported bill. Turning on the happenstance of the actual reporting dates, this process creates an arbitrary agenda for the Senate that does not serve the political needs of the Senate and is rarely followed.

What is more common is that the Majority Leader will ask unanimous consent ("UC") to proceed to the immediate consideration of a particular bill. This is in effect a request for a suspension of the rules. If any Senator objects, the request is not agreed to. Accordingly, such requests are usually negotiated extensively in advance with the leadership of the minority party in order to preclude an objection.

Role of the Majority Leader. — Only the Majority Leader or the Majority Leader's designee offers a UC request to proceed to the consideration of a bill.[23] Although the Majority Leader is nowhere mentioned in the Constitution,[24] the Majority Leader, under the precedents of the Senate, does have the right to be recognized by the Pre-

---

20. Senate concurrent and simple resolutions may be reported without an accompanying report. So "reporting" is sometimes a misleading term!

21. The corresponding rule in the House for the preparation of House reports is known as the Ramseyer Rule.

22. Standing Rules of the Senate, Rule VIII(1).

23. This is a matter of custom and is not a standing rule of the Senate.

24. Consequently, the Majority Leader is not elected by the entire Senate, which is unlike the case of the Speaker of the House who is elected by the entire House of Representatives. Rather, the Majority Leader is elected from among Senators of the same political party in a party caucus held before the start of each Congress.

siding Officer over any other Senator seeking recognition at the same time.[25] This "right of first recognition" is the principal power of the Majority Leader and gives the Majority Leader the opportunity and responsibility to try to establish the legislative agenda of the Senate by fashioning UC requests to proceed to the consideration of bills reported on the Calendar of Business. This right also enables the Majority Leader to lay down amendments ahead of other Senators, which is a significant tactical advantage in the legislative process.

Right to Unlimited Debate. — Floor action in the Senate is shaped largely by two principles that are implicit in the Standing Rules of the Senate. The first principle is that in the Senate there is a right to unlimited debate. Any Senator may speak before the Senate as long as the lungs can last and the Senator can hold the floor. When a Senator holds the floor solely for the purpose of delaying action by the Senate, the Senator is said to be engaged in a filibuster.[26] A filibuster may take place wherever debate is permitted in the Senate, whether the debate is on a bill, floor amendment, or motion, including any motion to proceed to the consideration of a bill. A filibuster may be most effective when the Senate has plans to adjourn or recess.

In recent years, filibusters have taken a different form. Long-winded speeches are no longer necessary to make a filibuster work. A Senator may place a "hold" on a bill by an informal request for a delay in proceeding with a bill. Such a "request" implies a willingness to object to any UC request to proceed to the consideration of the bill. If the bill nevertheless makes it to the Senate floor, a Senator might offer scores of dilatory amendments to the bill or to the amendments of other Senators, which may tie up the Senate for days or weeks. Also, since there is no motion in the Senate for the previous question,[27] a vote on final passage of a bill is not inevitable.[28] Any Senator may block a vote on final passage of a bill simply by objecting to the Majority Leader's unanimous consent request that the Senate proceed to that vote.

Invoking Cloture. — The only check to a filibuster found in the Standing Rules of the Senate is Rule XXII.[29] Rule XXII requires the affirmative vote of three-fifths of all

---

25. Otherwise, the Presiding Officer is required to recognize the first Senator seeking recognition. This contrasts with the House of Representatives where the Speaker or Speaker pro tempore has discretion whether or not to recognize a Member of the House.

26. Senator Strom Thurmond set the record for the longest filibuster by a single Senator on August 28–29, 1957, when he spoke, with minor interruptions, for 24 hours and 18 minutes.

27. The Senate discarded the motion for the previous question in 1806, apparently believing the motion to be unnecessary. Robert C. Byrd, *The Senate: 1789–1989, vol. II*, at 115.

28. The general rule is that the Presiding Officer puts a question to the Senate only after all debate has ceased.

29. The original cloture rule of the Senate was adopted on March 8, 1917, in response to the public outcry over the filibuster on a bill authorizing the President to arm merchant vessels. Public opposition to the filibuster was led by President Woodrow Wilson who condemned the Senate, saying "[a] little group of willful men, representing no opinion but their own, have rendered the great government of the United States helpless and contemptible". Robert C. Byrd, *The Senate: 1789–1989, vol. II*, at 122, 124.

the Senators duly chosen and sworn[30] to bring an end to debate, also known as "invoking cloture". Cloture operates prospectively. Ironically, even when cloture is invoked, 30 more hours of debate is permitted until cloture occurs!

The significance of the cloture rule is how difficult it makes the closing of debate. The requirement of a 60-vote supermajority to invoke cloture[31] is beyond the reach of the majority party in the Senate during most Congresses and forces the Majority Leader to negotiate with the Minority Leader before setting the Senate's legislative agenda.

Nongermane Amendments Permitted. — The second principle governing floor action in the Senate is that, generally speaking, an amendment dealing with any subject matter may be offered to any bill, whether or not the amendment is related to that bill. In other words, there is generally no requirement that a floor amendment be germane or relevant to the target bill or amendment. For example, a Senator may offer an amendment raising the minimum wage as additional text to a bill on immigration reform even though under the Senate rules the Committee on Finance has jurisdiction over the minimum wage but the Committee on the Judiciary has jurisdiction over immigration matters. So the acceptance of nongermane amendments by the Senate is a means of circumventing the committee markup system. Of course, a Senator offering a legislative proposal without the benefit of committee hearings supporting the proposal is usually at a disadvantage when faced with committee opposition.

Exceptions. — There are limited situations where the Senate requires the germaneness of amendments. First, all floor amendments to an appropriations bill must be germane. Secondly, only germane amendments filed before a cloture vote will be in order for consideration after cloture is invoked.[32] In this latter case, germaneness has a more narrow meaning than relevant subject matter. For an amendment to be found germane after cloture is invoked the amendment may only change a date or number, restrict a legal duty or responsibility in the underlying bill, or strike text. Thirdly, a UC agreement may require that amendments be germane and relevant.

Floor Amendments. — As in a committee markup session, on the Senate floor there are two types of amendments: perfecting and substitute amendments. Amendments proposed by the committee reporting the bill must be voted upon before any other amendment is considered. Where a Senator seeks multiple changes in the text of a bill, but only a single vote by the Senate, rather than propose a sub-

---

30. What is sometimes referred to as a "Constitutional three-fifths". Two-thirds of the Senators present and voting are required to invoke cloture with respect to changes in the Senate rules.

31. Furthermore, a cloture vote will not even be taken unless at least 16 Senators petition for the vote.

32. There is usually a mad rush to file germane, first degree amendments by the deadline of 1 p.m. on the day following the filing of the cloture motion.

stitute amendment encompassing all the changes, which may prove long and cumbersome, the Senator may offer a series of amendments in one document, *en bloc*. Another Senator may, however, demand that the amendments be severed and separate votes taken on each amendment.

Amendments Limited to Two Degrees. — Amendments may not be made in more than two degrees. This means that, although an amendment to a bill is permitted and an amendment to that amendment is permitted, it is not in order to propose an amendment to an amendment to an amendment to a bill. This is not a limit on the total number of amendments that may be offered to a bill but a limit on the degree of relationship between amendments. There is an exception to this rule involving Amendments In the Nature of a Substitute, which are most commonly encountered on the bill as reported from committee. Amendments In the Nature of a Substitute are treated as original text for purposes of further amendment.[33] This means an amendment may be made to an amendment to an Amendment In the Nature of a Substitute.

The Amendment Tree. — Substitute amendments are offered before perfecting amendments, but perfecting amendments are voted upon before substitute amendments. As a parliamentary matter, it is possible to have 11 amendments pending at the same time on a bill without having taken a vote. This is known as the "Amendment Tree", and the practice of "filling the tree" is the practice of a single Senator, usually the Majority Leader,[34] arranging for all 11 amendments to be proposed so that the next vote on an amendment will be a vote on an amendment of the Senator's liking. This is an attempt to set the Senate's legislative agenda, but its weakness is that there is no guarantee in the Senate that there will be a vote on any amendment and, if there is one, there is no guarantee that the amendment will pass. As soon as an amendment on the "Tree" is voted upon, another amendment may take its place. The advantage of the "Tree", on the other hand, is that it blocks action on any matter not to the liking of the Senator setting up the "Tree". Nevertheless, the use of the "Amendment Tree" tactic is rare.

Unanimous Consent Agreements

Senate floor action may be regulated by a UC agreement, usually requested by the Majority Leader, that certain procedures will govern debate on a specific bill or resolution. A UC agreement is typically sought on the overall time for debate, a limit on the number of amendments to a specific list of first degree amendments, a requirement that all second degree amendments be germane and relevant, and a limit on

---

33. To limit the number of floor amendments that may be offered to its reported bill, a committee may choose to report only perfecting amendments.

34. *See, for example,* the efforts of Majority Leader Trent Lott to fill the Amendment Tree on an immigration bill. *Cong. Rec.* S9028 (Sept. 22, 2000) (daily ed.).

the time for debate for each specific amendment. When the time for debate is controlled in the Senate, it is usually equally divided between the Members of the majority party and the Members of the minority party under the "regular order". Time divided in this fashion is controlled by the chairman and ranking minority member of the committee of jurisdiction over the bill, who collectively are referred to as the "managers" of the bill.[35] Because the objection of any Senator will block agreement to a UC request, these requests are usually extensively negotiated between the two parties before they are made. It is not unusual for unregulated debate to continue for days until a UC agreement is reached.

Senate Passage

Engrossment. — In the event that the Senate votes final passage of the bill, the bill and all the amendments that were adopted by the Senate will go to the Enrolling Clerk of the Senate.[36] The Enrolling Clerk has the responsibility for "executing" the instructions in each amendment adopted by the Senate.[37] Unlike committee amendments, floor amendments adopted by the Senate are not highlighted in the text of the bill. Rather, the Enrolling Clerk integrates each amendment seamlessly into the text of the bill, producing an entirely new document, which the Government Printing Office will reprint. The work of the Enrolling Clerk in executing amendments adopted by the Senate to a bill is referred to as the "engrossment" of the bill.

Authority of the Enrolling Clerk. — The Enrolling Clerk may not make drafting changes in the text of a bill but may make minor "technical and clerical corrections" in the text.[38] The authority for even these very limited changes to a bill has to be granted by the Senate, and the Senate does so at the beginning of a Congress by agreeing to a unanimous consent request conferring the authority on the Secretary of the Senate for the duration of the Congress, what is known as a "standing order".

When the Enrolling Clerk has finished the work of producing a new bill document, the Secretary of the Senate will attest that the text is true by signing the document and affixing the seal of the Senate. This is the official, engrossed copy of the bill.

---

35. After the Majority and Minority Leaders, managers are entitled to preferential recognition by the Presiding Officer.

36. The Enrolling Clerk is under the supervision of the Secretary of the Senate.

37. For example, if an amendment directs that a block of text of the bill is to be stricken, the Enrolling Clerk will delete that block of text from the bill.

38. "Technical corrections" made by the Enrolling Clerk are mainly redesignations of legislative provisions and cross-references that are necessitated by amendments adopted during floor consideration of the bill.

Messaging to the House of Representatives

Once the bill has been engrossed, the Enrolling Clerk and an assistant will formally present the bill to the House of Representatives through a short ceremony that is right out of the Middle Ages. The two Senate officials will carry the bill to the door of the House chamber and request permission to enter. The House will suspend its pending activities, and the House Member wielding the gavel will announce that a message has come from the Senate and grant the Senate officials leave to approach the dais and lay the "message" before the House. The Senate officials will make a short bow and march together to the dais to perform their task. The bill is now before the House!

In the House of Representatives

Figure A-2

House Legislative Process

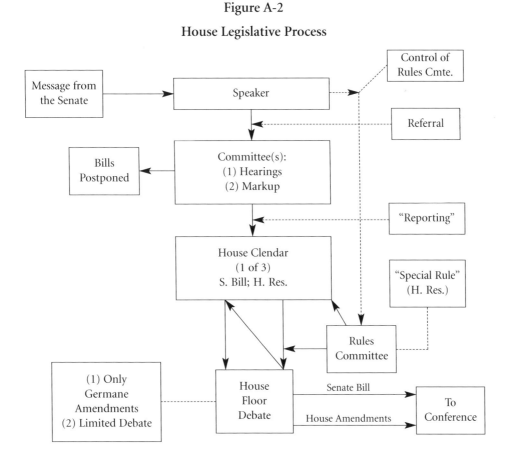

Initial House Action

No Introduction of a Bill from the Other House. — There is no such thing as the "introduction" of a Senate-passed bill in the House of Representatives. This is so because the Senate-passed bill has legislative status in the House without the need for sponsorship by a Member of the House. Instead of introduction, the Senate-passed bill will either be referred by the Speaker to a House committee or held at the Speaker's table in the House chamber. If there is already a House companion bill on the calendar,[39] it is unlikely that the Senate-passed bill will be referred to committee because committee action in the House has already been concluded.

The House, of course, may introduce its own bills in much the same manner as the Senate introduces bills.

House Reprint of the Bill. — After the Senate-passed bill is received by the House, it is reprinted as a new version of the bill, retaining its original Senate designation and number but labeling the bill as "**In the House of Representatives**" and referring to the bill not as a "**Bill**" but as "**An Act**". The reference to "**An Act**" is misleading. Having passed only one House of Congress, the bill is not an Act of Congress. Rather, the reference seems to indicate that enactment is now possible since the second House's approval will necessarily send the bill to the President's desk.

Blue Slip Rule. — The Constitution requires that all revenue-raising legislation, which is primarily tax and tariff legislation, shall originate with the House of Representatives.[40] If the House receives a Senate-originated bill having this subject matter, the House may vote to return the bill, with a blue slip[41] attached to the official copy of the bill, to the Senate as a violation of the Constitution. The risk that a bill will be "blue slipped" is a significant deterrent to the Senate passage of this type of legislation but does not preclude the Senate from considering tax or tariff matters. Rather, the Senate will await passage of a House-originated bill and will amend that bill to reflect the Senate's tax or tariff policies.

The House maintains that the same Constitutional requirement governing revenue-raising legislation also covers appropriations bills. The Senate disagrees and takes the sensible view that a spending bill is different from a tax or tariff bill. Accordingly, the Senate will occasionally introduce and consider a Senate-originated appropriations bill.

---

39. In the event that the House companion bill is on a legislative calendar other than the Calendar of the Committee of the Whole House on the state of the Union, the Senate-passed bill may be considered by the House and agreed to by a privileged motion.

40. U.S. Const., Art. I, §7, cl. 1.

41. The blue slip is actually the House resolution ordering the return of the Senate-passed bill, which resolution is engrossed on blue colored paper like any other engrossed legislation of the House.

Historically, however, the Senate has not prevailed in its interpretation of the Constitution and does not send Senate-originated appropriations bills to the House. Instead, if the Senate has first considered a Senate appropriations bill, before going to final passage on that bill, the Senate will await receipt of a House-originated appropriations bill and will convert the text of the Senate bill into an Amendment In the Nature of a Substitute to the House bill.

Referral to a House Committee

No Bar to Consideration of Senate Bills. — The Senate-passed bill may be referred to one or more House committees. This is merely an extension of the principle that a House of Congress is not required to generate its own legislation on a subject but instead may act on the other House's legislation on that subject. Institutional pride, however, usually causes the House committee to consider a House bill, if any, on the same subject rather than the Senate-passed bill. In the case of consideration of a House bill, a committee may act on either a referred bill (or portion thereof) or a committee "original" bill.[42]

Standard for Referrals. — A different standard applies in the House to determine committee referrals than in the Senate. The Speaker of the House is required to refer a bill (or portion thereof) "to the maximum extent feasible" to each House committee having jurisdiction of any provision of the bill under Rule X(1) of the House Rules.[43] A referral is customarily made after consultation with the Parliamentarian, who is under the supervision of the Clerk of the House.[44]

The House standard for committee referrals encourages multiple referrals and, unlike the role of the Presiding Officer in the Senate, a multiple referral in the House is done at the initiation and in the discretion of the Speaker.[45] Multiple referrals may be joint, sequential, or "split". A split referral involves the referral of only a portion of the bill to the additional committee.

---

42. House original bills are less common than Senate original bills. *See* note 45, *infra*.

43. Rule XII(2) of the Rules of the House of Representatives. In making a committee referral, the Speaker is required to designate a single committee as the committee of primary jurisdiction and may impose time limits on the action of any additional committee if and when the primary committee reports the bill.

44. The legislative jurisdiction of House committees is listed in Rule X(1) of the Rules of the House of Representatives.

45. The greater likelihood in the House of a multiple referral of a bill than in the Senate means that there is a corresponding decreased likelihood of a House committee generating an "original" bill than is the case in the Senate. Instead, the chairman of a House committee intending to mark up a bill that implicates the legislative jurisdiction of another committee will first introduce the bill so that the Speaker may make a multiple referral.

House Committee Action

Hearings and Markups. — A House committee may hold hearings and a markup session on a referred Senate-passed bill just as it does on any House-originated bill. Markup sessions in a House committee are very similar to markup sessions in a Senate committee, except that the larger membership of House committees usually means that each Member of the House will be allowed only a limited amount of time to address the committee. Markup amendments are considered and displayed in reported legislation in the same manner as are markup amendments in a Senate committee.

House Calendars. — House procedures for reporting legislation are more complicated than in the Senate. Unlike the Senate, which has only one legislative calendar, the House may place a reported bill on one of three principal legislative calendars, as follows: (1) the Calendar of the Committee of the Whole House on the state of the Union, also known as the "Union Calendar"; (2) the House Calendar, or (3) the Private Calendar. In addition, the Speaker of the House may direct that a bill placed on one of these calendars also be placed on the Corrections Calendar,[46] where appropriate, and this placement will expedite its consideration.

A bill or resolution is referred to one of the principal legislative calendars based on its subject matter.

Union Calendar. — All bills and resolutions "raising revenue, involving a tax or charge on the people, directly or indirectly making appropriations of money or property or requiring such appropriations to be made, authorizing payments out of appropriations already made, releasing any liability to the United States for money or property, or referring a claim to the Court of Claims"[47] are reported to the Union Calendar. The House interprets the scope of this calendar to include any public legislation that directly or indirectly relates to a cost to the government.[48]

House Calendar. — All other public bills and resolutions are reported to the House Calendar,[49] including resolutions requesting the transmittal of information from the executive branch to Congress and some "sense of Congress" resolutions.

Private Calendar. — Each bill or resolution of a private character, which affects only an individual or entity, and not a population group, is reported to the Private Calendar.[50] The Speaker calls for the consideration of legislation on the Private Cal-

---

46. Rule XIII(b) of the Rules of the House of Representatives.

47. Rule XIII(1)(a)(1) of the Rules of the House of Representatives.

48. The test is whether a bill sets "in motion a train of circumstances destined ultimately to involve certain expenditures". However, resolutions appropriating funds from the contingent fund of the House are reported to the House Calendar not the Union Calendar. Note to Rule XIII(3) of the Rules of the House of Representatives.

49. Rule XIII(1)(a)(2) of the Rules of the House of Representatives.

50. Rule XIII(1)(a)(3) of the Rules of the House of Representatives.

endar on the first Tuesday of a month, but if objection is made the legislation is recommitted to the reporting committee.

House Publication of Calendars. — Whenever the House is in session, the House publishes on a daily basis a document entitled "Calendars of the United States House of Representatives and History of Legislation" that is an especially useful research tool because it contains the listing of all legislation under each House calendar as well as the history of all House and Senate legislation that has been reported from any committee in either House or considered by either House of Congress.

Rules Committee Action

Role of the House Rules Committee. — A key difference between the House and the Senate is the contrasting role played by the Rules Committee of each body. The House Rules Committee has jurisdiction to regulate the order of legislative business of the House, a power not possessed by the Senate Committee on Rules and Administration or by any Senator or other Senate committee. The House Rules Committee is effectively a legislative traffic cop.

Special Rules. — The House Rules Committee reports to the House Calendar a simple resolution, designated "**H.Res.**", that, when adopted, makes a specific bill or resolution on the Union Calendar or the House Calendar the pending business of the House and regulates the debate on that legislation. This permits the House to consider a bill out of the regular order[51] in which the bill would otherwise be called off a House calendar or even to discharge a committee from further consideration of a bill that has been referred to the committee and has not yet been reported to a House calendar. Such a resolution is commonly referred to as a "special rule".

What makes these resolutions especially powerful is that they are privileged under the House rules, which is to say, they have priority in interrupting the current business of the House, and they may be called up by any member of the Rules Committee.[52] No dilatory motion (other than a single motion to adjourn) may be entertained to frustrate a vote on a special rule.[53]

A special rule typically waives points of order against the consideration of the bill, limits the time for debate, and specifies whether floor amendments will be in order. If no amendments are permitted, the special rule is referred to as a "closed rule". If amendments are permitted, the special rule is referred to as an "open rule". If specified amendments are permitted, but all others prohibited, the rule is said to be a

---

51. In fact, the resolution is referred to as "prescribing a special order of business".

52. Rule XIII(5) of the Rules of the House of Representatives.

53. Rule XIII(6) of the Rules of the House of Representatives. Special rules are ordinarily in order for a vote beginning the next legislative day after the Rules Committee reports the rule.

"modified closed rule". The special rule may even make an amendment or amendments to the bill, which become part of the bill when the special rule is adopted.

A special rule also specifies whether the bill is to be considered under the Committee of the Whole House procedure described below or whether the bill is to be considered "in the House".[54] Special rules are themselves considered by the House acting "in the House" and not in the Committee of the Whole House.

Majority Party Control of the Rules Committee. — The House Rules Committee acts to report a special rule ordinarily upon the request of a House committee chairman. It is easy for the Rules Committee to act quickly. At the beginning of each Congress,[55] the House establishes the party ratio of membership on the Rules Committee to favor disproportionately the majority party. In addition, the Speaker of the House determines the membership of the Committee. The result is that the Rules Committee and the special rules reported from the Committee reflect the policy preferences of the majority party, especially those of the Speaker.

Committee of the Whole House

In General. — Bills and resolutions referred to the Union Calendar are required by the regular rules of the House to be considered first in the Committee of the Whole House on the state of the Union (commonly known as the "Committee of the Whole procedure").[56] When the House resolves itself into the Committee of the Whole, frequently ordered by special rule,[57] the Speaker will step down from the dais and become the chairman of the fictional committee consisting of the whole membership of the House.[58]

Advantages. — The advantages of the Committee of the Whole procedure are several. First, the Speaker is permitted to engage actively in debate, and this permits the Speaker to assume a direct party leadership role on the floor of the House. Secondly, because the quorum required for action in the Committee of the Whole is only 100 Members, not the usual 218 Members when acting as "in the House", legislative ac-

---

54. There is a presumption that bills reported to the Union Calendar will be subject to the Committee of the Whole House procedure, but a special rule may waive this procedure in favor of treatment "in the House".

55. Unlike the Senate, which is a "continuing body", the House must adopt its rules anew for each Congress.

56. Rule XVIII(3) of the Rules of the House of Representatives. Occasionally, legislation not on the Union Calendar receives consideration in the Committee of the Whole by special order.

57. In the absence of a special rule, a motion may be made to resolve the House into the Committee of the Whole, but unlike the case of the special rule, the motion necessitates a vote of the full House. Rule XVIII(2) of the Rules of the House of Representatives.

58. The Committee of the Whole House procedure originated in the English House of Commons where the device was first used to permit test votes to confront the monarch without constituting a final vote of the Commons.

tivity is more easily sustained in the Committee of the Whole. Thirdly, strict time limits apply to the consideration of amendments in the Committee of the Whole that would not otherwise apply. This enables numerous amendments to be considered despite the unwieldy size of the House membership.

Five-Minute Rule.—Specifically, the Committee of the Whole procedure involves the application of the so-called "five-minute rule".[59] This rule limits the proponent of an amendment and one opponent only five minutes each to speak on the amendment. Additional five-minute increments to speak may be obtained by offering a second degree amendment to the amendment or by the "pro forma amendment" to "strike the last word".[60] Nevertheless, the overall effect of the five-minute rule is to limit debate severely and to foreclose anything resembling the filibuster practice of the Senate.

Points of Order and Motions.—The Committee of the Whole proceeds by considering the bill section-by-section.[61] This means that, after disposition of a section, no further amendment to the section may be made. The House possesses a rule that greatly restricts the number of floor amendments. In contrast to the Senate, the House requires that amendments be germane to the subject matter of the bill. In addition, there is a nondebatable motion[62] that a Member may make in the Committee of the Whole to close or limit debate on a portion of the bill or a pending amendment, but adoption of the motion does not force a vote on that amendment or bar further amendments.

The Committee Rises.—After the Committee of the Whole concludes its deliberations on a bill, the Committee "rises" and reports the bill and any adopted amendments to the House, which of course has the same membership as the Committee of the Whole. This technically requires holding additional votes to approve the amendments and final passage of the bill. To expedite matters, the amendments may be approved as a group, *en bloc*.

Ordering the Previous Question.—In addition, a motion for the previous question[63] is available to the Members when acting "in the House" but not in the Committee of the Whole.[64] This is the motion having deep roots in English parliamentary practice that permits a simple majority to close debate and bring a matter to a direct vote. It is, of course, a motion not available in the Senate. The previous question may be specifically ordered in advance by the special rule governing procedures on the bill.

---

59. Rule XVIII(5)(a) of the Rules of the House of Representatives.

60. The amendment is customarily withdrawn before being voted upon but after the proponent has extended the debate.

61. In the case of a revenue bill, general appropriations bill, lighthouse bill, or river and harbor bill, the bill is considered paragraph-by-paragraph.

62. Rule XVIII(8) of the Rules of the House of Representatives. A vote to close debate on a portion of a bill does not bar the offering of any amendment that had been reprinted in the Congressional Record at least one day earlier.

63. Rule XIX(1)(a) of the Rules of the House of Representatives.

64. Section XII of Jefferson's Manual of Parliamentary Practice. Jefferson's Manual governs the rules of the House of Representatives to the extent not inconsistent with other House rules.

Motion to Commit or Recommit. — One motion to commit or recommit the bill to a standing or select committee of the House is always available to opponents of the bill after the previous question has been ordered or is pending, and the motion may not be waived. This is sometimes the only chance the minority party has to derail the majority party's legislative railroad in the House. The motion to commit or recommit may contain instructions to further amend the bill, which the minority party may use to reflect its policy differences. When accompanied by instructions, the motion is entitled to 10 minutes of debate, equally divided between proponents and opponents of the motion.

Other Floor Procedures

Hour Rule. — In the regular procedures of the House, a Member of the House may not consume more than one hour in debate on a question before the House.[65] At the end of the hour, a motion for the previous question is ordinarily offered. The combination of the hour rule and a motion for the previous question is used to speed the passage of special rules and conference reports. Typically, an hour allotment is divided between both majority and minority party members.

Suspension of the Rules. — In the case of a relatively noncontroversial bill,[66] on specified days of the congressional session, a majority party member of the committee having primary jurisdiction over the bill may make a motion to suspend the rules and pass the bill. Forty minutes for debate on the motion is permitted, equally divided between proponents and opponents of the motion, and no amendments are in order, except that the motion itself may propose an amendment or amendments. Two-thirds of the Members of the House present and voting, a quorum being present, must approve the motion and the bill in a single vote for the bill to pass under the suspension of the rules procedure.

Corrections Calendar. — If the bill is called up from the Corrections Calendar, only one hour of debate and one amendment are permitted. Final passage of the bill requires a three-fifths vote of the Members voting, a quorum being present. If the bill is rejected, the bill remains on the calendar to which it was originally referred.

Calendar of Motions to Discharge Committees. — A simple majority of the Members of the House may discharge a committee from further consideration of a bill by approving a motion to this effect. These motions are placed on a separate Calendar of Motions to Discharge Committees[67] and must be called up for a vote. If the motion is adopted and immediate consideration of the bill is ordered, the bill will be

---

65. Rule XVII(2) of the Rules of the House of Representatives.

66. In addition, many "sense of Congress" resolutions are considered under the suspension of the rules procedure.

67. Rule XIII(c) of the Rules of the House of Representatives.

considered under the general rules of the House. The Senate has no comparable motion and may only discharge a committee upon unanimous consent.

Calendar Wednesday. — There is also a rarely used procedure called Calendar Wednesday whereby on Wednesday of each week a standing committee, called in alphabetical order, will be permitted to call up from the Union or House calendar one bill reported by the committee for which the Rules Committee has not reported a special rule. A simple majority only is required for passage of a bill under this procedure. The Calendar Wednesday procedure may be dispensed with by unanimous consent or a three-fifths vote.

House Passage

Replacing the Senate Text with a House Substitute Amendment. — If the House considers its own bill instead of the Senate-passed bill, immediately before going to final passage of the House bill, the House will call up the Senate-passed bill and propose a motion that the text of the House bill, as amended, be substituted for the text of the Senate-passed bill. In doing so, the House text will be reprinted in italics as an Amendment in the Nature of a Substitute to the Senate-passed bill.

Alternatively, Direct Action on the Senate Bill. — On the other hand, if the House considers only the Senate-passed bill, then any perfecting amendment adopted by the House to strike, insert, or strike and insert a word, phrase, or block of text would appear in italics, individually numbered in the order in which each amendment occurs in the Senate-passed bill. In the event that the House, during its floor action, rewrote the entire text of the Senate-passed bill by means of a single Amendment in the Nature of a Substitute, the entire text of the Senate-passed bill would be line-typed and at the end would appear the House amendment in italics.

Engrossment. — In either situation, the Enrolling Clerk of the House, who is under the supervision of the Clerk of the House, has the responsibility to prepare a new document that either lists the numbered House perfecting amendments or, in the case of an Amendment In the Nature of a Substitute, integrates into the substitute any amendment made to that substitute. This process is referred to as the "engrossment" of the House amendment or amendments. The House Enrolling Clerk operates in the same manner as the Senate Enrolling Clerk. As in the Senate, the engrossed document requires the attestation of the chief administrative official of the body, in this case the Clerk of the House. The engrossed House amendment or amendments to the Senate bill will be reprinted on blue paper while the engrossed Senate bill will remain on white paper.[68]

---

68. In the case of a conference consisting of a House-originated bill with Senate engrossed amendments, the House bill will be reprinted on blue paper and the Senate amendments on white.

What Constitutes Official Papers. — The final action of the House of Representatives, in the case of receipt of a Senate-passed bill, is passage of the Senate bill, together with the engrossed amendment or amendments of the House to that bill. The two engrossed pieces of legislation, with the original attestations, constitute the "official papers".

Resolution of Differences

Figure A-3

Resolution of Differences

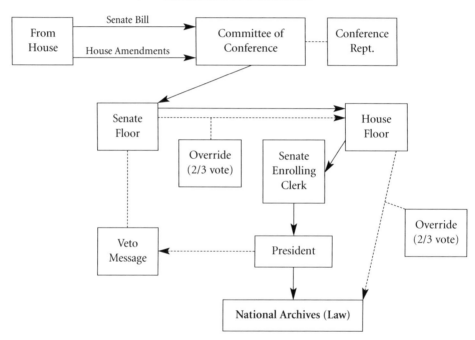

Conference Committee

Only a Single Bill in a Conference Committee. — If the Senate-passed bill and the House amendment or amendments are controversial, they are likely to go to a committee of conference to resolve the differences between the two Houses. It is important to note that, contrary to common parlance, there are never two bills in conference, one from each House. Rather, what goes to conference is a bill from one House and the amendment or amendments to that bill from the other House.

Requesting and Agreeing to Conference. — Upon passage of the Senate bill with a House amendment or amendments, the House has a choice to make, which is made on tactical, political grounds. The House may insist on its amendments and request a conference with the Senate before messaging the official papers to the Senate, or the House may message the papers to the Senate without requesting a conference, permitting the Senate the opportunity to accept the House amendment or to make the request for the conference itself.

As a general rule, the House requesting the conference will act last on the conference report. This is so because the House requesting the conference brings the official papers to conference and turns them over to the House agreeing to the conference. In order to act on the conference report, a House of Congress must be in possession of the official papers.

The sequence in taking up the conference report becomes important if one House is more likely to approve a conference report than the other House. If the first House to act fails to agree to the conference report, the conference report may be recommitted to the conference committee, which would resume its deliberations and might modify the conference report to make it more acceptable. If, on the other hand, the first House to act agrees to the conference report but the second House defeats the conference report, then the conference committee cannot resume. This is so because the conferees are deemed discharged upon the approval of the conference report by the first House to act on the report.

Appointment of Conferees. — The House or the Senate may appoint conferees[69] when requesting or agreeing to a conference with the other body or on a later date. Appointments are made by the Presiding Officer of the respective House, and the appointees are almost always drawn from the committee or committees having jurisdiction over the Senate bill and House amendments, including the chairman and ranking minority member of each principal committee involved. The larger membership of the House means that a greater number of conferees will be appointed by the House than by the Senate.

Conference Report vs. Statement of Managers. — When a committee of conference is successful in resolving the differences between the two Houses, the committee will produce a document, usually reprinted as a report of the House of Representatives, consisting of two parts: (1) the Conference Report, and (2) the Joint Explanatory Statement of the Committee of Conference, also known as the "Statement of Managers".

Contents of Conference Reports. — The term "conference report" is a misnomer. It is not a report at all but rather the compromise legislative text that the conference committee recommends for approval by the two Houses. The statement of managers, on the other hand, is an actual report explaining how the conference committee resolved the differences between the two Houses on the legislation. The statement of managers may be a useful reference tool for establishing the legislative intent behind the legislation because it is made available to all Members of Congress before a vote is taken to approve the conference report.

---

69. Also known as "managers". Conference managers usually include the floor managers of the legislation.

Most conference reports represent a complete rewrite of the bill in conference. This is done by preparing an Amendment In the Nature of a Substitute, the text of which will appear entirely in italic print, to the bill. In the case of a House amendment to a Senate-passed bill, the text of the substitute amendment will be preceded by a motion that the Senate recede from its disagreement to the House amendment and agree to the amendment with a further amendment (in the nature of a substitute), and the House agree to the same. If the House also wishes to change the long title of the Senate bill to reflect the change in the text made by the House, the House must prepare a separate amendment, usually in the form of a substitute title, as it is not in order to amend both the title and text with a single substitute amendment. Nor may the preamble of a resolution be amended with the same amendment that amends the text of the resolution.

In the rare case where the House sends to conference a numbered list of engrossed perfecting amendments to the Senate-passed bill, rather than an engrossed Amendment In the Nature of a Substitute, the conference report will consist of a series of instructions for the disposition of each numbered amendment.

Reaching Agreement in Conference. — Many of the lesser differences to be resolved by the two Houses in the conference report are decided by congressional staff, subject to the approval of the conferees. The conferees will, however, meet to offer and discuss amendments to the more controversial provisions.[70] Ordinarily, each issue to be resolved is tracked in a document called a "comparative print", which presents a section-by-section comparison of the Senate-passed bill with the House engrossed amendment or amendments.

On each matter in controversy, there are three possible motions to dispose of the matter. First, the amending House may recede from its position. Secondly, the House originating the bill may recede from its disagreement to, in other words, accept, the amendment of the other House. Thirdly, the House originating the bill may recede from its disagreement to the amendment of the other House, with a further amendment representing a compromise between the two Houses.

Conference Reports Not Amendable; Amendments in Technical Disagreement. — The power of the conference report lies in the rules of the House and the Senate that prohibit the amendment of any conference report. Each House must either accept or reject the compromise legislative text proposed by the conferees. This ensures that an identical text is adopted by both Houses. In the rare case where a conference report consists of the resolution of a series of numbered amendments, if the conference committee cannot agree to resolve differences on a specific numbered amendment, the conference committee may choose to report the amendment in "technical disagreement" to the two Houses for a separate vote on the matter at the time that the

---

70. Sometimes when the legislation is noncontroversial the conferees will rely completely on staff to prepare the conference report and the statement of managers and will meet only to sign the documents. This is referred to as a "paper conference".

rest of the conference report is being considered. This permits the amendment in technical disagreement to be rejected without killing the entire conference report.

Scope of Conference. — A conference report must be drafted to avoid any point of order, the principal one being that the text of the conference report has exceeded the permissible scope of the conference. What is beyond the scope of conference is sometimes difficult to determine. In the case of several perfecting amendments, the scope of the conference report provision is narrowly construed to lie strictly between the parameters of each amendment and the bill.[71] In addition, the conference report is not permitted to address language in the bill that was not amended by the other House. That language is in effect "locked in". In the case of a single substitute amendment to the entire Senate text, however, all of the legislative text sent to conference by both Houses is in play and, consequently, there is wider latitude to alter language, even where the language is close to being identical in both the Senate bill and the House amendment.

Voting on Conference Reports. — Before submitting a conference report to the two Houses, a majority of the conferees of each House must sign both the conference report and the statement of managers. Then the conference committee will provide the official papers, together with the conference report, to the House that will act first. If that House votes to approve the conference report, then the official papers will be transmitted to the second House, to be bundled with the already deposited, duplicate original copy of the conference report. A conference report is treated as privileged in each House of Congress and is given an expedited vote.

Amendments Between the Houses

The differences between the Senate-passed bill and the House amendment do not have to be resolved by a conference committee. The official papers may be messaged back and forth between the Houses, much like a game of ping pong, with each House having the opportunity to amend the last amendment made by the other House, until a House of Congress concurs in the last amendment made by the other House. At this point the two Houses have agreed to an identical text, and the bill is now ready for enrollment.

The practice of passing amendments between the Houses is most helpful near the end of a session of Congress when it may be difficult to convene a conference or at anytime when the two Houses believe that the differences between the two Houses on the bill are relatively minor or technical.

---

71. So, for example, if the Senate bill contains a reference to "$100,000,000" and the House amendment strikes that dollar amount and inserts "$200,000,000", the scope of the possible conference report language lies in the range of not less than $100,000,000 or more than $200,000,000.

Enrollment

After the conference report on the Senate-passed bill is agreed to, or amendments between the Houses on the Senate-passed bill reach an identical text, the legislative documents are sent to the Senate Enrolling Clerk for enrollment.[72]

In the case of a conference report, enrollment consists of converting the italic text to Roman text and transferring the text to the form of an Act of Congress. In the rare case of the conference report consisting of numbered amendments, or in the case of amendments between the Houses, the Enrolling Clerk will need to "execute" the amendments, that is to say, to integrate the amendments seamlessly into the underlying text.

When the Enrolling Clerk completes the enrollment, the Government Printing Office will reprint the enrolled bill on parchment paper. The enrolled bill will then be signed by the Vice President of the United States or the President pro tempore of the Senate and by the Speaker of the House of Representatives. The enrolled bill is now ready for presentation to the President.

In most cases the presentation of the enrolled bill to the President, known under the Constitution as "presentment", will occur within a few days of the last vote in Congress on the conference report. There is, however, no deadline for presentation. The Majority Leader, to whom the Enrolling Clerk is ultimately responsible, does occasionally delay the presentation in order to force the President's approval or rejection of the bill to occur at a time that will be most helpful or harmful, politically, to the President, as the Majority Leader may desire.

Presidential Action

The Constitution allows the President 10 days (excluding Sundays) to approve the enrolled Senate bill by signing the bill or to disapprove the enrolled bill by not signing the bill and returning the bill to the Senate, together with the President's objections, commonly referred to as a "veto message". If the President returns the bill without his signature, the President has vetoed the bill, and the bill may not become law unless Congress overrides the veto. If the President does not sign and does not return the bill within the 10-day period, the bill does become law, unless the Congress by its adjournment prevented the return, in which case the bill may not become law, having been "pocket vetoed".[73]

---

72. Where the two Houses have acted on a House-passed bill, the enrollment is made by the House Enrolling Clerk.

73. Because the Constitution does not define "adjournment", Congress attempts to ensure that

It is important to note that the President may not make any change to the enrolled bill no matter how clerical or technical. Congress bears full responsibility for how the law reads.

Veto Overrides

In the event of a Presidential veto of the Senate enrolled bill, upon the receipt of the veto message by the Senate, the Senate is required to reconsider the vote on the bill and, if two-thirds of a quorum of Senators votes to re-approve the bill, notwithstanding the President's veto, the bill will be messaged to the House of Representatives for the same procedure. If two-thirds of a quorum of the House re-approves the bill as well, the bill shall become law as of the date of the House vote.

Official Custody of the Law

The new law in the form of the official, parchment paper document of the approved bill is held by the National Archives and Records Administration.[74]

---

intrasession and end of session recesses do not constitute an adjournment that would permit a pocket veto to occur. It does this in intrasession situations by bringing the House of Congress that originates the bill into a pro forma session every three days and at the end of session by authorizing the Clerk of the House or the Secretary of the Senate to receive veto messages on behalf of the respective House of Congress.

74. The custody of statutes is prescribed by law. The first custodian of United States statutes was the Secretary of State.

Appendix B

House and Senate Legislative Forms

1 — Legislation Originating in the House of Representatives

_____ CONGRESS
_____ Session

H. R. _____

_____

IN THE HOUSE OF REPRESENTATIVES

(Insert month/day/year)

Mr. [Ms.] _____

_____ introduced the following bill; which was read twice and referred to the Committee on _____

_____

A BILL

(Insert title of bill here)

Be it enacted by the Senate and House of Representatives of the United States of America in Congress assembled,

_____ CONGRESS
_____ SESSION

H. J. RES. _____

———————

IN THE HOUSE OF REPRESENTATIVES

———————

(Insert month/day/year)

Mr. [Ms.] _____
_____
_____
_____ introduced the following joint resolution; which was read twice
and referred to the Committee on_____

———————

JOINT RESOLUTION

(Insert title of joint resolution here)

Resolved by the Senate and House of Representatives of the United States of America in Congress assembled,

_____ CONGRESS
_____ Session   **H. CON. RES.** _____

_____

IN THE HOUSE OF REPRESENTATIVES

_____

(Insert month/day/year)

Mr. **[Ms.]** _____
_____
_____

submitted the following concurrent resolution; which was _____
_____

_____

CONCURRENT RESOLUTION

(Insert title of concurrent resolution here)

Resolved by the House of Representatives (the Senate concurring),

_____ CONGRESS
_____ Session   **H. RES.** _____

IN THE HOUSE OF REPRESENTATIVES

(Insert month/day/year)

Mr. [Ms.] _____
_____
_____

submitted the following resolution; which was _____
_____

RESOLUTION

(Insert title of resolution here)

Resolved,

AMENDMENT NO. _____ Calendar No. _____

Purpose: _____
_____
_____

IN THE HOUSE OF REPRESENTATIVES _____ Cong. _____ Sess.

   H.R. _____

   S. _____

(title) _____
_____
_____
_____

                         _____

          ( ) Referred to the Committee on _____
               and ordered to be printed.
          ( ) Ordered to lie on the table and to be printed

Intended to be proposed by _____

Viz:

1

2

3

4

5

6

7

8

2 — Legislation Originating in the Senate

_____ CONGRESS
_____ Session   **S.** _____

_____

IN THE SENATE OF THE UNITED STATES

_____

(Insert month/day/year)

Mr. **[Ms.]** _____
_____
_____
_____ introduced the following bill; which was read twice and referred
to the Committee on _____

_____

A BILL

(Insert title of bill here)

Be it enacted by the Senate and House of Representatives of the United States of America in Congress assembled,

_____ CONGRESS
_____ SESSION

S. J. RES. _____

_____

IN THE SENATE OF THE UNITED STATES

_____

(Insert month/day/year)

Mr. **[Ms.]** _____
_____
_____
_____ introduced the following joint resolution; which was read twice
and referred to the Committee on _____

_____

JOINT RESOLUTION

(Insert title of joint resolution here)

Resolved by the Senate and House of Representatives of the United States of America
in Congress assembled,

_____ CONGRESS

_____ Session   **S. CON. RES.** _____

—————————

IN THE SENATE OF THE UNITED STATES

—————————

(Insert month/day/year)

Mr. [Ms.] _____

_____

submitted the following concurrent resolution; which was _____

_____

—————————

CONCURRENT RESOLUTION

(Insert title of concurrent resolution here)

Resolved by the Senate (the House of Representatives concurring),

_____ CONGRESS

_____ Session   **S. RES.** _____

———————

IN THE SENATE OF THE UNITED STATES

———————

(Insert month/day/year)

Mr. [Ms.] _____

_____

_____

submitted the following resolution; which was _____

_____

———————

RESOLUTION

(Insert title of resolution here)

Resolved,

AMENDMENT NO. _____ Ex. _____ Calendar No. _____

Purpose: _____

IN THE SENATE OF THE UNITED STATES _____ Cong. _____ Sess.

    S. _____ (or Treaty _____)

    H.R. _____

(title) _____

———————

        ( ) Referred to the Committee on _____
             and ordered to be printed.
        ( ) Ordered to lie on the table and to be printed

Intended to be proposed by _____

Viz:

1

2

3

4

5

6

7

8

3 — Legislative Stages of the Same Bill

A. Bill As Introduced

101st CONGRESS
1st Session

S. 358

To amend the Immigration and Nationality Act to change the level, and preference system for admission, of immigrants to the United States, and to provide for administrative naturalization, and for other purposes.

IN THE SENATE OF THE UNITED STATES

February 7 (legislative day, January 3), 1989

Mr. Kennedy (for himself and **Mr. Simpson**) introduced the following bill; which was read twice and referred to the Committee on the Judiciary

---

A BILL

To amend the Immigration and Nationality Act to change the level, and preference system for admission, of immigrants to the United States, and to provide for administrative naturalization, and for other purposes.

Be it enacted by the Senate and House of Representatives of the United States of America in Congress assembled,

TITLE I — IMMIGRATION ACT OF 1989

SECTION 101. SHORT TITLE; REFERENCES IN TITLE.

(a) Short Title. — This title may be cited as the "Immigration Act of 1989".

[Remainder of Text Omitted]

B. Bill As Reported

101st CONGRESS
1st Session

S. 358

Calendar No. 130

[**Report No. 101-55**]

To amend the Immigration and Nationality Act to change the level, and preference system for admission, of immigrants to the United States, and to provide for administrative naturalization, and for other purposes.

IN THE SENATE OF THE UNITED STATES

February 7 (legislative day, January 3), 1989

Mr. Kennedy (for himself, **Mr. Simpson, Mr. Moynihan, Mr. D'Amato,** and **Mr. Dodd**) introduced the following bill; which was read twice and referred to the Committee on the Judiciary

June 19 (legislative day, January 3), 1989

Reported by **Mr. Biden**, with an amendment

[Strike out all after the enacting clause and insert the part printed in italic]

A BILL

To amend the Immigration and Nationality Act to change the level, and preference system for admission, of immigrants to the United States, and to provide for administrative naturalization, and for other purposes.

Be it enacted by the Senate and House of Representatives of the United States of America in Congress assembled,

[**Original Text in Linetype Followed by Substitute Text in Italic**]

C. Bill As Passed the Senate and Referred in the House

101st CONGRESS
1st Session   **S. 358**

To amend the Immigration and Nationality Act to change the level, and preference
system for admission, of immigrants to the United States, and to provide for administrative naturalization, and for other purposes.

———————

IN THE HOUSE OF REPRESENTATIVES

July 25 (legislative day, January 3), 1989

Referred to the Committee on the Judiciary

———————

AN ACT

To amend the Immigration and Nationality Act to change the level, and preference
system for admission, of immigrants to the United States, and to provide for administrative naturalization, and for other purposes.

*Be it enacted by the Senate and House of Representatives of the United States of Amer-
ica in Congress assembled,*

TITLE I — IMMIGRATION ACT OF 1989

SECTION 101. SHORT TITLE; REFERENCES IN TITLE.

(a) Short Title. — This title may be cited as the "Immigration Act of 1989".

[Remainder of Text, As Passed by the Senate, Omitted]

D. House-passed Substitute to Senate Text.

In the House of Representatives, U.S.,

October 3, 1990.

Resolved, That the bill from the Senate (S. 358) entitled
"An Act to amend the Immigration and Nationality Act to change the level, and preference system for admission, of immigrants to the United States, and to provide for
administrative naturalization, and for other purposes", do pass with the following:

AMENDMENTS:

Strike out all after the enacting clause, and insert:

SECTION 1. SHORT TITLE; TABLE OF CONTENTS.

(a) Short Title.—This Act may be cited as the "Family Unity and Employment
Opportunity Immigration Act of 1990".
(b) Table of Contents.—The table of contents of this Act is as follows:

[Remainder of Table of Contents and Text Omitted]

E. Conference Report, Reconciling Senate and House Texts

101st Congress		Report
2d Session	**HOUSE OF REPRESENTATIVES**	101-955

===

IMMIGRATION ACT OF 1990

_____

October 26, 1990.—Ordered to be printed

_____

Mr. Brooks, from the committee of conference, submitted the following

CONFERENCE REPORT

[To accompany S. 358]

The committee of conference on the disagreeing votes of the two Houses on the amendments of the House to the bill (S. 358) to amend the Immigration and Nationality Act to change the level, and preference system for admission, of immigrants to the United States, and to provide for administrative naturalization, and for other purposes, having met, after full and free conference, have agreed to recommend and do recommend to their respective Houses as follows:

That the Senate recede from its disagreement to the amendment of the House to the text of the bill and agree to the same with an amendment as follows:

In lieu of the matter proposed to be inserted by the House amendment insert the following:

SECTION 1. SHORT TITLE; REFERENCES IN ACT; TABLE OF CONTENTS.

(a) Short Title.—This Act may be cited as the "Immigration Act of 1990".

(b) References in Act.—Except as specifically provided in this Act, whenever in this Act an amendment or repeal is expressed as an amendment or repeal of a provision, the reference shall be deemed to be made to the Immigration and Nationality Act.

(c) Table of Contents.—The table of contents of this Act is as follows:

[Remainder of Table of Contents and Text, in Italic, Omitted]

F. Act of Congress, As in Statutes at Large

104 STAT. 4978   PUBLIC LAW 101-649—NOV. 29, 1990

Public Law 101-649
101st Congress

An Act

To amend the Immigration and Nationality Act to change the level, and preference
    system for admission, of immigrants to the United States, and to provide ad-
    ministrative naturalization, and for other purposes.

*Be it enacted by the Senate and House of Representatives of the United States of Amer-
ica in Congress assembled,*

SECTION 1. SHORT TITLE; REFERENCES IN ACT; TABLE OF CONTENTS.

(a) Short Title.—This Act may be cited as the "Immigration Act of 1990".

(b) References in Act.—Except as specifically provided in this Act, whenever in this
Act an amendment or repeal is expressed as an amendment or repeal of a provision,
the reference shall be deemed to be made to the Immigration and Nationality Act.

(c)Table of Contents.—The table of contents of this Act is as follows:

[Remainder of Public Law Omitted]

Appendix C

Drafting Exercises: The Answers

Drafting Exercise No. 1

Answer:

The Secretary of State may provide counternarcotics assistance to West African countries through which illegal drugs are trafficked. In addition, it is the sense of Congress that other foreign countries should provide similar assistance to West Africa. The Secretary of State shall submit to Congress periodically a report describing the results of the United States assistance. If Congress enacts a joint resolution disapproving a report, no funds may be made available to provide the assistance. In this Act, the term "counternarcotics assistance" means the donation of equipment for interdiction and the training of law enforcement officials.

Explanation:

Neither the Assistant Secretary of State, a subordinate, nor the Department of State, a Government bureaucracy, were appropriate subjects of sentences and were replaced with the "Secretary of State", the department head. Verbs were changed to conform to standard usage. Note especially that the second sentence must be written using hortatory language as directing foreign countries lies outside the powers of Congress. The sentence in which Congress triggered a funding cut-off by agreeing to a concurrent resolution is an unconstitutional legislative veto and is replaced by the "enacts a joint resolution" language. Expedited procedures should be added and linked to that sentence for the sentence to be fully effective.

Drafting Exercise No. 2-A

Legislative Proposal No. 1: *A Senate joint resolution, designated S. J. Res. ___, should be used because the legislative language is intended to be binding, narrowing the choice to a bill or joint resolution, and joint resolutions are customarily used on matters relating to war or armed conflicts.*

Legislative Proposal No. 2: *A Senate simple resolution, designated S. Res. ___, should be used because the creation of a committee within one House of Congress may be done by a simple resolution, and the involvement of the other House of Congress and the President is unnecessary and undesirable. The use of binding, self-executing language does not require a bill or joint resolution, as is ordinarily the case, because the subject matter is entirely internal to the Senate.*

Legislative Proposal No. 3: *A House concurrent resolution, designated H. Con. Res. ___, should be used because "sense" language is nonbinding, narrowing the choice to a concurrent or simple resolution, and the sentiment being expressed is that of "Congress", requiring bicameral action.*

Legislative Proposal No. 4: *A House bill, designated H.R. ___, should be used because Government reorganization requires binding, self-executing language, which narrows the choice to a bill or joint resolution, and this subject matter is not one of the extraordinary and emergency kind customarily handled by joint resolutions.*

Drafting Exercise No. 2-B

Answer:

_____ CONGRESS
_____ Session   **S. CON. RES.** _____

_____

IN THE SENATE OF THE UNITED STATES

_____

_____20__

Mr. Softy submitted the following concurrent resolution; which was _____

_____

CONCURRENT RESOLUTION

Expressing the sense of Congress regarding additional aid for Haiti.

Whereas the devastating 7.0 magnitude Haitian earthquake of January 12, 2010, resulted in more than 230,000 deaths and left more than 1,000,000 Haitians homeless;

Whereas Haiti desperately needs both short-term humanitarian aid and long-term development aid; and

Whereas aid to Haiti from the international community has fallen far short of Haiti's needs: Now, therefore, be it

Resolved by the Senate (the House of Representatives concurring),

SECTION 1. It is the sense of Congress that the President should seek to obtain more aid for Haiti from the international community.

SEC. 2. The Secretary of the Senate shall transmit a copy of this concurrent resolution to the President.

Drafting Exercise No. 2-C

Answer:

AMENDMENT NO. [TBD] _____ Ex. _____ Calendar No. 1

Purpose: To substitute a humanitarian assistance program for Haiti and to increase the duration and level of funding.

IN THE SENATE OF THE UNITED STATES   115th Cong. 1st Sess.

S. 5079

H.R. _____

To authorize the provision of humanitarian assistance for Afghanistan, and for other purposes.

_____

( ) **Referred to the Committee on** _____
     and ordered to be printed.
( ) **Ordered to lie on the table and to be printed**

Amendments intended to be proposed by Mr. Flats

Viz:

1 On page 1, line 4, strike "Afghanistan" and insert "Haiti".

2 On page 1, lines 6 and 7, strike "food" and insert "food, medicines,".

3 On page 1, line 9, strike "Afghanistan" and insert "Haiti".

4 On page 1, lines 11 and 12, strike "$100,000,000 for each of the fiscal years 2018 and 2019" and insert "$200,000,000 for each of the fiscal years 2018, 2019, and 2020".

NOTE: In the event of an adoption of the perfecting amendments proposed by Mr. Flats, an additional amendment will need to be prepared to amend the long title, as follows:

Amend the title to read as follows: "A bill to authorize the provision of humanitarian assistance for Haiti, and for other purposes.".

Drafting Exercise No. 3-A

Answers:

Legislative Proposal No. 1: *The Year 2 Proposed Legislation will be construed to su-persede the Year 1 Law, without any action required by the drafter, by application of the rules of statutory construction that the specific prevails over the general and the later-in-time prevails over the earlier-in-time.*

Legislative Proposal No. 2: *The Year 2 Proposed Legislation requires an override provision since the rules of statutory construction are in conflict and amending the Year 1 Law would be inappropriate because of its limited subject matter. The Year 2 Legisla-tion should read as follows: "Notwithstanding any other provision of law, humanitarian assistance may be provided to victims of ethnic violence in Africa.".*

Legislative Proposal No. 3: *The Year 2 Proposed Legislation proposes a change in a rule of general and permanent application, and so the change should be integrated with that rule by making a statutory amendment, as follows:*

The Year 1 Law is amended by inserting "or ethnic strife" after "natural disaster".

Drafting Exercise No. 3-B

Answer:

SEC.___. AMENDMENTS OF THE NATIONAL EMERGENCIES ACT.

Section 101(a) of the National Emergencies Act (50 U.S.C. 1601(a)) is amended—

(1) in paragraph (1), by adding "or" at the end;

(2) in paragraph (2), by striking "; or" and inserting a period; and

(3) by striking paragraph (3).

Explanation:

Review of the list contained in section 204 of title 1 of the United States Code indicates that title 50 of the Code has not been reenacted as positive law and, thus, may not be directly amended. The source note immediately below the statutory text indicates that the text is derived from section 101 of Public Law 94-412 the short title of which is the "National Emergencies Act". This is the "true" law and the proper target of any further amendments. The title 50 citation may be used within parentheticals as a secondary cite.

The only step remaining is to strike the offending paragraph (3) and to "clean up" by making conforming changes to punctuation and connectors.

Drafting Exercise No. 4-A

Answer:

_____ CONGRESS
_____ Session   **S. _____**

_____

IN THE SENATE OF THE UNITED STATES

Mr. [Ms.] _____
_____ introduced the following bill; which was read twice and referred to the Committee on _____

_____

A BILL

To establish the Office of Regulatory Drafting within the Office of Personnel Management, and for other purposes.

Be it enacted by the Senate and House of Representatives of the United States of America in Congress assembled,

SECTION 1. SHORT TITLE.

This Act may be cited as the "Plain English Regulatory Drafting Act of 20__".

SEC. 2. PURPOSE.

The purpose of this Act is to promote transparency in Government.

SEC. 3. DEFINITION.

In this Act, the term "Executive agency" has the same meaning given the term in section 105 of title 5, United States Code.

SEC. 4. OFFICE OF REGULATION DRAFTING.

(a) Establishment.—There is established within the Office of Personnel Management the Office of Regulatory Drafting.

(b) Head of Office.—The Office shall be headed by a Regulatory Counsel, who shall be appointed by the President, by and with the advice and consent of the Senate.

(c) Duties.—To carry out the purpose of this Act, the Regulatory Counsel may assist any Executive agency seeking to write regulations in plain English.

SEC. 5. REPORT.

Not later than one year after the effective date of this Act, the Director of the Office of Personnel Management shall submit to Congress a report on the activities of the Office.

SEC. 6. AUTHORIZATION OF APPROPRIATIONS.

(a) In General.—There is authorized to be appropriated to the Office of Personnel Management $10,000,000 for the fiscal year 2031 to carry out the provisions of this Act.

(b) Availability of Funds.—Amounts appropriated under subsection (a) are authorized to remain available until expended.

SEC. 7. EFFECTIVE DATE.

This Act takes effect on October 1, 2030.

Drafting Exercise No. 4-B

The correct cross-references for the four blanks in sections 107 and 108 are as follows:

Blank No. 1:

Correct: *subsection (a)*

Reason: *Refer to the fewest units of organization necessary to make clear the cross-reference.*

Blank No. 2:

Correct: *paragraph (1)*

Reason: *Never refer to the unit of organization while writing within the unit.*

Blank No. 3:

Correct: *subsection (b)(2)(B)*

Reason: *Cite the highest unit first even though the target language is contained in the lowest unit.*

Blank No. 4:

Correct: *section 107(b)(2)(B)*

Reason: *Make each cross-reference as specific as possible. Spell out the name of the unit designation, and never capitalize the "s" in section except at the beginning of a sentence.*

Drafting Exercise No. 5

Answer:

SEC.___. USE OF THE UNITED STATES ARMED FORCES IN THE DEMOCRA-
TIC REPUBLIC OF THE CONGO.

(a) Report.—Whenever the Secretary of Defense determines that the United Nations may use the support of United States Armed Forces in the Democratic Republic of the Congo, the Secretary shall submit to Congress a report describing the
situation in that country requiring the use of those forces.

(b) Prohibition.—

(1) In General.—Subject to paragraph (2), no member of the United States
Armed Forces may be deployed to the Democratic Republic of the Congo until 30
days after submission of the report described in subsection (a).

(2) Waiver.—The President may waive the application of the 30-day period in
paragraph (1) if the President determines that the waiver is vital to the national security of the United States.

NOTE: The inclusion of the sentence on severability is unnecessary as the Federal
courts will presume severability.

Acknowledgments

I would especially like to thank William Mays, Director of Publications of the International Law Institute of Washington, D.C., (ILI) and Production Editors Tim Colton, Jessica Newman, Joellen Craft, and Kasia Krzysztoforska of the Carolina Academic Press of Durham, North Carolina (CAP) for their hard work in bringing about the publication of this book. Also, the support of Chairman Don Wallace, Jr., and Executive Director Kim Phan of ILI and Publisher Keith Sipe and Acquisitions Editor Jefferson Moors of CAP was much appreciated throughout the process. The front cover was expertly designed by Kate McCall of ILI and Tim Colton of CAP from an original photograph by the author. I would also like to thank Francis L. Burk, Jr., for reviewing parts of the manuscript and Donald A. Ritchie and Susan Mangiero for their good counsel. Finally, the book would not have been possible without the loving patience of my dear wife, Mary Linda Rynearson.

Table of Cases

Index